Guidance, Selection, and Training

Guidance, Selection, and Training

Ideas and Applications

PETER C. MOREA

Department of Business Studies,
Enfield College of Technology

Routledge & Kegan Paul
London and Boston

First published 1972
by Routledge & Kegan Paul Ltd
Broadway House, 68–74 Carter Lane
London EC4V 5EL and
9 Park Street
Boston, Mass. 02108, U.S.A.
Printed in Great Britain by
Ebenezer Baylis and Son Limited
The Trinity Press, Worcester, and London

ISBN 0 7100 7236 8

To Sally and to my parents

CONTENTS

A*

supervisory problems. Job description and task analysis. Specification of knowledge and skill requirements. Determining the capabilities of trainees. Statement of training requirements. Development of appropriate training methods. Training course evaluation.

FIGURES

TABLES

Preface

More and more people are faced with the task of giving careers guidance to school-leavers and adults, of selecting employees, and of training or retraining young, mature, and older workers. This book attempts an introduction to these three areas of guidance, selection, and training. It is primarily written for students of business studies and undergraduates interested in the applications of social science; for certain specialized groups, such as personnel officers, careers masters, and professionals in youth employment; and for line and general managers with responsibility in these areas.

The rationale of the book is specific: in guidance, selection, and training, the methods we adopt should be based on sound theory. Theory provides the practitioner with a framework within which to consider data. An awareness of the theoretical framework also enables the practitioner to know what assumptions are made, and how they affect the relevance of his data. Guidance, selection, and training employ certain techniques, such as tests, interviews, and interest inventories. To use a technique effectively the practitioner needs to understand the ideas and concepts which it embodies. An applicant for an engineering apprenticeship scores high on a test of intelligence but low on mechanical aptitude; would he be suitable? To use a technique with no awareness of its underlying theory seems at best pointless, but at worst it is harmful and likely to give the wrong answers. The book, therefore, adopts the rationale of the Enfield Business Studies degree, on which I have taught for a number of years, that competent business and professional practice can only originate from sound, well-formulated theoretical explanation. Were a sub-title required, it would be 'Pragmatism Abandoned'.

In the following chapters I outline a number of ideas, concepts, theories, useful in the employment situation, and in particular those providing a basis for techniques and procedures of guidance, selection, and training. I then examine several of these techniques and procedures, and observe how they may be used in practice.

In the debate on student unrest it is sometimes asserted that 'students are there only to learn, and have nothing to teach the lecturer'. This has not been my experience, and in writing the book I am indebted to many undergraduates at Enfield who have given me new ideas and insights in this area. I have benefited particularly from students' knowledge of a number of subjects, obtained through the multi-disciplinary teaching of a Business Studies degree. The book similarly attempts not to be constrained within one academic discipline. Guidance, selection, and training have primarily developed as applied areas of individual psychology, which is where their concepts have mainly originated. But social psychology, sociology, and the study of organizations, now have much to say which is relevant to these areas. The book in a limited way adopts a multi-disciplinary approach.

My acknowledgments go to my colleagues teaching different specialisms in Business Studies at Enfield, who have considerably influenced my thinking, and particularly the Departmental Head, Alan Hale. Thanks are due also to other colleagues and friends who have read and commented on chapters: Ray Aldridge-Morris, Gerald Mars, Stephen Poppleton, Alexander Romiszowski, David Sladen, Peter Sneddon, and Colin Wilson. Finally, most people in the United Kingdom writing in this area have some indebtedness to Professor Alec Rodger of Birkbeck College, University of London. I have a considerable debt, which I gladly acknowledge.

PART I

Background

CHAPTER 1

Work

'I like work: it fascinates me. I can sit and look at it for hours'
(Jerome K. Jerome, *Three Men in a Boat*).

Overview

In the Introduction we consider what is meant by work, and
examine some of the functions work fulfils for the individual and
society. A review of the meaning and significance of work over the
ages is introduced as an attempt to place our ideas in some
perspective. We turn next to a more specific consideration, how
jobs are studied and analysed, since this provides a basis for
procedures in guidance, selection, and training. The chapter ends
with a brief introduction to the element of change.

INTRODUCTION

Towards a Definition

'When *I* use a word', Humpty Dumpty said, in a rather scornful
tone, 'it means just what I choose it to mean—neither more nor less'
(Lewis Carroll, *Through the Looking-Glass*).

Social scientists have observed that an individual's work has many
repercussions for him. His length of life, his health, wealth, status
and prestige in society, choice of wife, all are affected by the nature
of his occupation. The sort of job he does may influence his
attitudes and values, and modify the way he sees himself. His
work largely determines his style of life. Such findings need to
be incorporated into any view of work we might adopt in guidance,
selection, or training. If we cannot derive one satisfactory, all-
purpose definition of work, we should at least become aware of
its many aspects.

Physicists are not really interested in the concept, but at an
elementary level refer to work as 'energy used to achieve a given

3

purpose'; immediately, with the idea of 'purpose', they introduce a non-physical property. Such a definition is obviously inadequate for any discussion of social behaviour, since it includes areas of behaviour we would not normally classify as work, like leisure activities. Dancing, playing a game, and attending a concert are normally not regarded as work, but they use up energy and we do them for a purpose. It immediately seems useful to limit our discussion to paid employment. In the following from the Glacier Papers (1965), Brown refers explicitly to those activities done under a contract of employment:

> Employment work is the application of knowledge and the exercise of discretion within the limits prescribed by the immediate manager and by higher policies towards an objective set by the immediate manager; the whole being carried out within an employment contract.

In the following chapters it is employment work we are concerned with.

Central to many definitions is this economic aspect of work, its means to command money, goods, or services. For an economic or even sociological analysis of work behaviour, Cotgrove's definition (1967) would seem adequate: 'any activity which is directed towards the production of goods and services which typically have a value in exchange and which are carried out for a valuable consideration.' But according to this description housewives do not work, which is a view many would not accept, particularly many housewives. The artist also fails to fit neatly into an economic concept of work, since any painter who daubs so badly or so far in advance of his time that his canvases do not sell, would apparently not be working.

But for the individual, work is not just a way of making money. Studies of unemployment have in particular made it evident that work has other important functions for the individual (Israeli, 1935; Eisenberg and Lazarsfeld, 1938; Komarovsky, 1940). The unemployed feel they are respected less by other people and experience a loss of status; their jobs had given them a place and an identity in their society. A man seems to derive the sense of his personal worth and of meaning in his life largely from his work. Unemployed, he feels purposeless and struggles to maintain a belief in his own value. Work has a social function, integrating the individual in society and enriching him through social relationships.

4

A lecturer, burdened with routine administrative duties, may see his 'real work' as teaching and research. Shimmin (1966) points out that 'sculptors and artists also frequently distinguish between their "real work" and what they do for a living'. This brings us to another view of work, one in terms of the individual's perception. Such a view would traditionally be regarded as psychological, though it cannot be divorced from more social factors, since how an individual sees his job, evaluates its significance and worth, even how he sees himself, are influenced by the society around him. Shimmin's definition of work (1966) introduces an emphasis on the individual's perception: 'employment within the social and economic system which is perceived by the individual as his main occupation, by the title of which he is known and from which he derives his role in society.' Shimmin's definition embraces the activities of the missionary, the housewife, the artist and lecturer on their 'real work', with those of more ordinary employees, but proves rather vague on the financial rewards of employment work.

Such a view gives insufficient emphasis to the economic system. The doctor's wife and the baker's are both housewives, at home tending children. They differ in their social status, in how they perceive themselves, and in their whole style of life. For the time being, and until the feminist reformers have their way, the husband's work within the economic system remains very relevant for a housewife.

As we shall see, any analysis of work which emphasizes the way in which the individual perceives the job is useful in occupational guidance and counselling. But generally we might consider work within certain broad dimensions. First, in employment the individual uses energy for a number of purposes, a usual and particularly important purpose being the economic one. Men normally work for payment. Secondly, work is done in society, and has social and psychological repercussions for the individual. Thirdly, people perceive meaning in their work in different ways.

Personality and Employment Role
In considering work it is useful to make the distinction between role and personality. We observe, for example, that most doctors have much in common with each other. Their dress is conventional; their manner at the bedside and in the surgery is friendly, supportive but not intimate; they tend to maintain a

certain reserve and detachment with their patients. Similarly the members of many other occupational groups have certain common characteristic patterns of behaviour. This typical behaviour of doctors, civil engineers, lawyers, can be partially explained in terms of their occupational roles. The differences within the groups, why Dr Smith differs from Dr Jones, usually in professionally unimportant areas, may be explained in terms of personality.

'Doctor' is in social psychological terms a 'position', 'a category of persons occupying a place in a social relation' (Secord and Backman, 1964); specifically 'doctor' is an employment position. 'Role' is the dynamic aspect of this employment position; according to Linton (1945) 'what the individual has to do in order to validate his occupation of the status'. Linton uses the term 'status' here for what we have referred to as 'position'. So by the doctor's role we mean what he has to do as a doctor, putting into effect those duties, rights, and activities that are ascribed to him professionally.

No attempt will be made here to define personality since a separate chapter is devoted to the concept, other than to say that in using the term we refer to properties of individuals, such as aggressiveness or introversion.

As Linton points out (1945), occupational positions with their related roles exist in most societies, prescribing appropriate behaviour for the people who hold the positions. This role prescription stipulates the duties and activities of the role occupant generally; it indicates what behaviour is appropriate to other role occupants in society—how the doctor should behave with patients, colleagues, nurses; it indicates also how these other role occupants should in return behave with regard to this role. The role prescription may suggest the nature and extent of the role occupant's participation in the wider society, as, for example, in some communities a senior businessman is expected to become involved in local welfare.

Though the role and its prescription may account in part for these characteristics being common to members of a certain occupational group, they do not explain why some characteristics exist and not others, why the doctor's dress is sober and his bedside manner friendly but reserved. To explain the origins and existence of certain occupational characteristics we need to see what functions they fulfil.

Functions of Work

We can study an element of culture such as a work activity, or the marriage ceremony, in terms of what it does for society, a social group, or for one individual in that society. This is part of the structural-functionalist approach adopted by many sociologists and anthropologists. Radcliffe-Brown (1935), for example, says that 'the function of a recurrent activity . . . is the part it plays in the social life as a whole and therefore the contribution it makes to the maintenance of the structural continuity'. The definitions we have examined were attempting to answer the question, 'what is work?' But we are now asking what function and purpose work has in society, and what individual and group needs it is satisfying.

Merton (1957) distinguishes between two types of functions, latent and manifest, which we can illustrate with employment work. If we asked a manual worker why he worked he might simply say 'to earn a living', and if pressed further would possibly add, 'I'm a skilled man and my job gives me some satisfaction.' However, if we observed the same man unemployed for an extended period, or even read some of the unemployment studies, we might think the reasons he gave for working were inadequate. The studies suggest that his relationship with his wife and children might deteriorate; that he would avoid his men friends, though previously their company had meant much to him; that he might drink and smoke more heavily, quite irrationally since his income was now down. We would have to conclude his work had fulfilled needs other than the two he was conscious of, economic and personal satisfaction, and that his job in some way contributed to his psychological and social well-being. Here the worker had not been fully aware of what his job meant to him. Some of its functions were latent or hidden from him, though they were real enough in terms of his experience and of their effect on his personal well-being.

So with work, or with any cultural activity or institution, there is a distinction between those functions of which the individual, the group, or the society is unaware, and those of which they are conscious. The distinction in Merton's terms is between latent and manifest functions. It is obviously analogous to Freud's concept of latent and manifest dream content.

The distinction is not rigid, since people, especially in a sophisticated culture, become increasingly aware of the functions cultural elements have for them. Nowadays working men will often give reasons for working which show considerable insight and an awareness of work functions which years ago only a social analyst might have appreciated. They will say, 'Work gives you a feeling of self-respect', or 'I'd go crazy if I didn't work'. However, where latent functions still exist, a survey in which people are asked why they work may miss as much as it reveals, since it is concerned only with manifest functions.

The existence of latent functions means we are unaware of their satisfying certain needs in society. In a certain culture, work, unknown to the individual, may serve to maintain his sense of social worth and to integrate him in society, but these consequences of working are unintended and unrecognized. When changes occur in work and work practices, at the level of the firm or society, they may alter both the latent and manifest functions. But the consequences of any such changes in manifest functions are at least foreseeable, and may be planned for. Latent functions are by definition unrecognized by those involved, and so work changes may have unforeseen and unintended effects.

The account from Trist and Bamforth (1951) of the repercussions of technological changes in British coal mines illustrates the point. It was not foreseen that the introduction of the new Longwall method would severely disrupt the total social system of work which had centred around the old production technology. Miners now worked in large instead of small groups; their jobs became highly differentiated which affected the pattern of status hierarchy among them; workers were now widely distributed underground which made effective supervision difficult. The men no longer had the emotional support they had previously obtained through working in small groups, and which was necessary in such dangerous work. Morale dropped; productivity was low; absenteeism and sickness increased. In the situation prior to change, the organization of work around the original technology had specific functions, fulfilling certain individual and group needs. In redesigning work procedures to accommodate the new production methods, no account had been taken of the latent functions served by the original work practices.

Friedmann and Havinghurst (1954) suggest employment work has certain functions common throughout our society: 'The five functions [of work]—income, regulating of life-activity, identification, association, and meaningful life-experience—are . . . found in any situation defined by society as a "job"'. But though these functions are normally found in Western society each will differ in its importance from one social group to another, from one individual to another. Other work functions may vary even more. Different people give different reasons for working. Studies reveal other variations within a society where work may fulfil certain needs with one occupational group such as professional men, and not with manual workers. This variety in the functions of work is significant for guidance and selection. Selection and particularly guidance should centre upon the needs a job can satisfy in an individual. The functions work has for him, for his social group, for the society of which he is a member, largely determine the satisfactions the individual obtains from his job, and the extent to which he is motivated by it.

WORK DOWN THE CENTURIES: AN HISTORICAL ANALYSIS

This brief history primarily surveys the changing functions of work through the ages. It is essentially an account of how these functions have been perceived and analysed either by an educated, contemporary elite, such as the medieval theologians, or by the social observers of a later time, as is the case with the Protestant ethic. The common people may have been unaware of many of these functions—the latent functions. But those that were manifest, though more clearly observed by an educated elite, were communicated to the ordinary people through the normal processes of culture. For example, it is not the peasants' account of work in the Middle Ages we hear, but that of Aquinas and the Scholastics who might have expressed it in this way: 'The peasant says he works only to earn subsistence for himself and his family; but work is also redemptive and provides the basis for the structuring of society.' Some of the following survey derives from Tilgher (1930), *Work: What it has meant to Men through the Ages.*

The Greeks
The Greeks had a word for it; work is πόνος, a burden, a heavy troublesome task. For the Greeks work was an undesirable necessity, not intrinsically satisfying, and not an end in itself. It

9

was a means to an end, that of avoiding hunger and attaining a degree of possessions and wealth which enabled a man to be independent and to lead the 'good life', free and not subject to the mighty. Of course most work at the time was heavy and grinding, physical labour. Slavery as a social institution seems related in part to such a view of work.

The Hebrews

For them too work was a drudgery, but drudgery at least with a purpose other than earning the necessities of existence. For the Hebrews work was harsh and painful, but did expiate before God man's original sin in the Garden and all his subsequent sins against the Creator. Work now had a deep value. The expiation was for a purpose, to restore the former harmony in life and to lead to a better state, the Kingdom of God on earth.

The Early Christians

Like the Hebrews, the early Christians accepted work as expiation, but added to this a further concept. Work creates wealth, and wealth can be used for fulfilling the greatest Christian precept, charity. The wealth gained by work can be given to the poor. But the functions work fulfils are still regarded as extrinsic to its nature. Work is not itself satisfying or valuable, but is valued for what it may achieve. Tilgher points out that through the early Christians the status of manual work and sheer physical labour is raised. Such activity was despised by the Greeks, regarded as servile and left to the slaves. But the Christian monks freely embraced manual labour in the monastic system. Work and prayer provided the basis for life in the monasteries, and with their increase, manual work assumed a modest dignity. Even in the monastic system, however, where men either became choir monks or lay brothers, it was still the choir monks who were thought of as doing the work of real and intrinsic value, making manuscripts, reading the Word of God, and singing the Holy Office.

The Christians of the Middle Ages

Work remains a burden; for the majority of men and women its nature has scarcely changed. But there is a development on the thinking of the early Christians, since to the two functions of work they proposed, expiation and the creation of wealth for charity, the medieval view adds a third, more social and explicitly of this world. The medieval philosophers saw that work provided an essential basis for their society, having an explicit (and latent) function in structuring society into a unified and cohering system. The individual's job places and integrates him in society. He has, therefore, as a human being a right to that employment which gives to him and his family a meaningful position in that social system. It is within this context that Thomas Aquinas's concept of the 'just price' emerges. Payment for work must be determined not only by the value of the job done but also by what income is sufficient to support the worker and his family.

But employment remains an optional extra, a right but not a duty. A man only need work if no other way exists of supporting himself and his family. The Protestant ethic parted company here.

The Protestant Ethic

You must work, said Calvin, because to work is to do the Will of God. For Calvin, casual and occasional work, probably quite common among medieval artisans, was not enough. For his followers, planned, methodical, continual work was the order of the day. To work is to do the will of God, and so success in the form of money and property is a sign of God's favour and pleasure. The money might be given to the poor, though there are difficulties here. But its significance and importance is primarily as a token of God's approval, a sign of predestined election to God's chosen and saved. And the opposite is also true; not to succeed at work and be poor must show God is not pleased, that one is not of the elect. Poverty in this world is a sign almost of moral bankruptcy. But there arises a dilemma. Making a profit is good, but to enjoy that profit in soft living, luxury, and showy possessions is wrong. It is this final *coup de grâce* of the Protestant ethic which, as Weber perceived, contributed to the rise of capitalism.

On the one hand existed a need for economic success, since this was a tangible sign of election. But there must also be thrift and austerity, with no wasteful spending of accumulated wealth. To give to the poor was a dubious solution since the poor were visibly not of God's chosen. There was a simple alternative—use the profit to finance new work, to buy more land, to re-invest in one's own or other people's economic developments. Capitalism begins here.

These men saw themselves as working to serve God, and this was the manifest function of work for them. But in the new culture a further function for employment work had emerged, latent, with unintended and unrecognized consequences. The moral authority of the Catholic Church and its concept of the 'just price' had been rejected, and economic activity was free to go its own ways and make its own laws. Money and property accumulated in the hands of a few men. A new structuring of society had emerged, capitalism, a function in part of this Protestant view of employment work.

Karl Marx and Alienation

The industrial revolution of eighteenth- and early-nineteenth-century Europe changed work and the conditions of life for many. Among the commentators and analysts of these changes was Marx.

He regarded work as all-important for man, and outlined his view in his early writings (his *Economic and Philosophic Manuscripts of 1844*). Man creates himself and his history through labour. In work he obtains a personal and social identity, and achieves his human nature. Providing this level of fulfilment, work is necessarily a free and existential activity for man, not a mere economic chore. The value and importance of man's work is embodied in the product of his labour and the act of production.

Marx looked at work in his contemporary industrial society and did not find it good. He saw labour as forced, unfulfilling in itself, become merely an economic activity, a means only to food, shelter, etc. Man now fully existed only when he did not work, as in his family and social life. The work of most men was uncongenial, physically and intellectually damaging. Even the products of a man's labour belonged not to him but to some other man. Marx saw that the consequences of all this were damaging. Man's work, important to him at many levels, was now reduced so low as to deprive him even of his self. Man became alienated by his labour.

He is alienated from his own self, since his labour is now uncongenial, alien, coerced, and its products belong to another. He is estranged from his nature, since it was essentially in his work that man proved his nature. 'This production', says Marx, 'is his active species life.' He is estranged from his fellow men since after all he now sees them to be like himself, also alienated from their true nature and 'species being'.

Scientific Management

For Marx labour was not a mere economic activity; for the scientific management pioneers, at the beginning of the twentieth century, this is just exactly what it was. Men, they thought, work primarily for money. So when men take payment from an employer they must wholly accept his authority for the contracted hours of work. The employer can and should use his legal authority to exercise close control over employees, motivating them through financial rewards and punishments. The contract of employment becomes important, and the employer contracts with the individual employee, not with a group of workers. Implicit in this view of work is the concept of economic man, which we will briefly consider in the next chapter.

By 1900 the mechanization of the industrial revolution was well established, and now man was seen as another machine, specifically as a highly adjustable extension to the metal machines of the engineers. To maximize the efficiency of this machine-extension, man, managers simplified working procedures through time and motion study, then standardized the new procedures. They introduced rest pauses, provided good lighting, heating, ventilation, etc., in order to minimize wear and tear, and to reduce the fatigue of this piece of human machinery. Scientific management adopted the physicist's account of work, and saw human labour as simply an output of energy for a financial purpose.

The Hawthorne View

In 1927 studies of production were begun at the Hawthorne Plant of the Western Electric Company. Out of them emerged a new view of the function of work in industrial society, proposed by Elton Mayo and later others, subsequently referred to as the Human Relations School. The scholastics had looked at the medieval peasant and said that through his labour he redeemed himself before God. The early human relations writers said the industrial operative thinks he works only for pay, but he works also because his employment integrates him satisfyingly into a social group. Employment work, it is suggested, has become an essential element in the individual's life, since it binds him to society and gives him a position in that society which he experiences as meaningful. 'Man's desire to be continuously associated in work with his fellows is a strong, if not the strongest human characteristic,' says Mayo (1945).

The Hawthorne view of work was then broadly on the following lines. In modern urban society a man will normally like work, since it is mainly through his job that he obtains the esteem, and the sense of belonging and of personal worth that are so important to him, and which are only experienced through close association with other people. Where a man does not like his job it is usually because it fails to integrate him socially. The significant latent function of work in modern industrial civilization is social, to give men meaningful and satisfying personal relationships.

The implications for industry and commerce of such a human-relations analysis are well known. Management should develop and maintain at the work-place social systems capable of providing these essential personal relationships. This is to be done through developing cohesive working groups which give the individual a sense of belonging and security; through fostering superior-subordinate ties which are supportive and satisfying; through ensuring good communications, consultation, involvement, and participation in decision-making. The value of such a programme depends primarily on the soundness of this view of work and the individual on which it is based.

The Contemporary Scene

'That free men should be willing to work day after day, even after their vital needs are satisfied, and that work should be seen as a mark of uprightness and manly worth, is not only unparalleled in history but remains more or less incomprehensible to many people outside the Occident' (Eric Hoffer, *The Ordeal of Change*).

We are examining analyses of the contemporary functions of work and the employment role, in terms of individual needs. We are concerned with their function in satisfying the personality needs of the worker, rather than to what extent they are functional for the social system as a whole. A statement from Jaques (1961) may be seen in these terms:

Working for a living is one of the basic activities in a man's life. By forcing him to come to grips with his environment, with his livelihood at stake, it confronts him with the actuality of his personal capacity—to exercise judgment, to carry responsibility, to achieve concrete and specific results. It gives him a continuous account of the correspondence between outside reality and his inner perception of that reality, as well as an account of the accuracy of his appraisal and evaluation of himself (even though he may not always desire to observe the account). And more, in the quality of the enthusiasm or apathy which he brings to his work, he is faced with the state of balance between the forces of life and the forces of death within him. In short, a man's work does not satisfy his material needs alone. In a very deep sense, it give him a measure of his sanity.

Is such a function of employment work perennial or merely contemporary, universal or, as the quote from Hoffer might suggest, found only in Western society? Jaques's analysis accords with the accounts referred to earlier of extended unemployment in the industrial West. It seems primarily a latent function of work since the majority do not explicitly perceive their job in these terms. But since employment forces us to face reality and to deal in some way with our phantasies and illusions about ourselves it may function not only, as Jaques suggests, to measure our sanity, but in part to maintain it.

What other manifest functions does the employment role have for the contemporary worker? The accompanying study of Morse and Weiss (1955), in Table 1.1, asks people who say they would work even in the absence of financial need, why they would do so. It studies manifest functions and indicates what work consciously means to the worker. Occupational and class differences become immediately apparent. Sub-cultures exist within the total culture.

The study suggests (this breakdown of data is not given in Table 1.1) that men in working-class jobs are less likely to wish to keep on working than those in middle-class occupations, though the difference in numbers is very slight. But significantly, with one working-class group, unskilled workers, only half would want to.

Though the overall difference between working and middle-class groups in the numbers that would keep working is slight, the reasons they give for wanting to do so vary more significantly. Working-class groups speak of needing activity, of being bored and restless without a job; whereas middle-class men talk of interest, accomplishment, satisfaction, of incentives which, as we shall see, accord with Maslow's concept of self-actualization. Related to this is the finding that far more of the middle-class group would want

TABLE I.I *Reasons for working*

Morse, N. C., and Weiss, R. S. 'The function and meaning of work and the job', *American Sociological Review*, April 1955.

'If by some chance you inherited enough money to live comfortably without working, do you think that you would work anyway or not?' 80 per cent of the employed men answered that they would want to keep on working. This 80 per cent was then asked: 'Why do you feel that you would work?' One reason only from each man is given.

Positive reasons :	*Number*	*Per cent*
Enjoy the kind of work	27	9
To be associated with people	4	1
To keep occupied (interested)	93	32
Justifies my existence	14	5
Gives feeling of self-respect	13	5
Keeps individual healthy, good for a person	30	10
Other	4	1
Total positive reasons	185	63

Negative reasons ; without work would :		
Feel lost, go crazy	42	14
Feel useless	5	2
Feel bored	11	4
Not know what to do with my time, can't be idle	29	10
Habit, inertia	17	6
To keep out of trouble	3	1
Other	2	0
Total negative reasons	109	37
		100

Total responding	294
Not ascertained	20
Total would work	314
Total would not work	79
Not ascertained	8
Total sample	401

to stay in the job they have. Working-class men who want to keep working would change their actual job. This follows from the previous point since middle-class reasons for working tend to be intrinsic to certain jobs, whereas with the working-class group they were primarily intrinsic merely to being in employment.

Though there is this variation in the extent of satisfaction with one's present job, most men in this study expressed some satisfaction with it. But again the reasons given for being satisfied vary considerably. Service workers stress the social satisfactions of their work; unskilled workers mention money, as do managers; professional men and craftsmen stress the content of their jobs. The individual wants satisfaction and some sort of return from his work, which is after all the main activity of his life, but in an imperfect world he experiences the realities of a job which is not ideal. He experiences this discrepancy between his own personal needs and the demands of the job as uncomfortable. In social-psychological terms, he experiences dissonance (Festinger, 1957). So typically he adopts views, attitudes, opinions about the job that reduce the dissonance—'Well, at least the money is good', 'They don't pay much, but personally it's very satisfying'.

At another level Hoffer (1964) says: 'No one will claim that the majority of people in the Western World, be they workers or managers, find fulfilment in their work. But they do find in it a justification of their existence.' More cynically it might be suggested, they do not find a justification for existence in their work, they put it there. But will this last? Is it still true of all levels of Western society? A recent study (Goldthorpe *et al.*, 1968) found that a number of manual workers had abandoned their quest for satisfaction at work. Work had become instrumental for them, a means to the economic end, money. They found their satisfactions in activities away from their employment, in family life, and as a consumer. Some of the younger generation are rejecting the attitudes to work of their middle-class parents. The hippies and beats are on the move.

Conclusion

Much in this historical outline of work is wholly applicable only to the mass of ordinary people. Work was presumably no heavy, troublesome task for the Greek mathematicians. Nor in the Middle Ages was work so burdensome for the philosopher as for the peasant, though it may have functioned to integrate both in society.

In approaching employment problems we need to know what functions and meaning work has for a particular individual or group. Only in the section on contemporary society have we made any such division, and there only by class.

In guidance, selection, and training we study and analyse jobs and occupations. We will now clarify certain terms used in this area, and list some uses of job analysis. We will then consider methods.

It is important to relate these methods and techniques of job analysis to our previous discussion. We have considered definitions which express different views of work, and stress different aspects such as pay or the individual's perception of the job. We have seen that employment serves many functions, both manifest and latent, changing from age to age, culture to culture, and even within a society serving different functions for different groups and individuals. Some such view or theory of work and what it is, and what functions it serves, is implicit in any technique and method of job analysis.

Any scheme of job analysis, in its choice of categories, largely determines for us how we will think about work. By what it stipulates as the relevant dimensions for considering the job, the scheme of analysis has implicitly evaluated what are the relevant functions of work for the individual.

In implementing any approach to a problem we adopt a viewpoint. This is reasonable and the very stuff of technology, since we must adopt views and make assumptions if we are to operate at all. The real error is in not realizing we are doing just this. We need to be aware of the theoretical position implicit in the job analysis we are adopting, of the basic assumptions of the theory, in what situation it holds, and what are its limitations. We should know what data support the theory. Only when we are operating with this knowledge are we being truly scientific in our approach to guidance, selection, and training, and only then, and this is the real point, will our decisions as practitioners be most effective.

We can take this a step further. Implicit in a view of work is normally some idea about human behaviour. When we speak of employment work our terms will suggest we tend also to think of personality and behaviour in a certain way. For example, a human-relations approach to work problems rests largely upon a view of man as powerfully motivated by social needs as the quotation from Mayo suggests. So a job analysis implies a view of work and of human behaviour. In a scheme of analysis for guidance, selection, or training this view of behaviour is usually concerned with the nature of personality and of human learning. The theory may be crude or sophisticated, but what remains important is an awareness of the theory implicit in the job analysis scheme.

A Clarification of Terms

A number of different terms are used in the study of work roles, with some variation in the meanings ascribed to them. The usage to be adopted here is as follows.

Job Description. This is primarily a role prescription for the occupational position, but includes also the conditions of work. A job description refers normally to the activities, duties, and responsibilities of a job, to the physical and social work environment, and to its rewards. The dimensions adopted necessarily express a view of what are the relevant considerations; they embody a conception of work and personality.

Job Specification. This is a job description, together with a specification of the necessary physical and personality characteristics of the job occupant. It is useful to see such a statement of job requirements as relative to the purpose of the specification. A job specification for personnel selection may differ slightly from one of the same job for training or guidance.

Job Grading or Evaluation. This is a job specification for the purpose of providing a comparative evaluation of a job against other jobs. The comparison and evaluation are usually in order to determine the job's worth in money terms.

Job Analysis. We are adopting this as a blanket concept to embrace all of the above three terms, that is, to refer to any kind of study of a job. It is used to refer also to the actual process of examining a job for any of the above purposes.

The Purposes of Job Analysis

After an extensive review of the literature, Zerga (1943) lists twenty different purposes of job analysis:

1. Classifying and grading jobs.
2. Determining pay levels.
3. Specification of selection requirements.
4. Clarification of job roles, and their activities, duties, and responsibilities.
5. Establishing of transfers.
6. Adjustment of grievances.
7. Facilitating of communication and understanding between management and men.
8. Establishment of promotion hierarchies for career progression purposes.
9. Investigating accidents.
10. Revealing unsatisfactory working procedures.
11. Determining operating and maintenance procedures on machinery.
12. Work measurement.
13. Specifying of authority invested in work position.
14. Appraisal of individual merit.
15. Determining causes of individual failure.
16. Education and training.
17. Facilitating job placement.
18. Studying health and fatigue at work.
19. Vocational guidance.
20. Determining jobs suitable for disabled and convalescing workers.

Alternatively we can categorize the purposes of job analysis under five headings which embrace most of those listed by Zerga:

1. *For guidance and selection.* A job analysis serves many functions here such as providing information for job advertisements and handouts, which we will examine later. It is essentially concerned with establishing criteria for decisions, by determining the factors relevant to success and satisfaction in a job, and indicating the predictors of these.

2. *For training.* At its simplest we might see the purpose of job analysis in this area as an attempt to stipulate what the trainee needs to know, and how most usefully he might be taught it.

3. *For job design.* Here the purpose of the analysis is primarily as a basis for 'the organization of a job to satisfy both the technological and organizational requirements of the work to be

accomplished in an organization and the personal requirements of the individual performing the work' (Davis and Valfer, 1965).

4. *For job grading and evaluation.* The purpose of the job analysis is here to specify on what dimensions the different jobs should be compared and to evaluate them along these dimensions. This provides the basis for a rational salary structure and for the development of promotion hierarchies.

5. *For performance appraisal.* The form of an analysis for employee appraisal is often similar to one for training. Its purpose is to establish a list of the essential requirements of a job, and in this way to provide a superior with relevant criteria on which to assess the performance of a subordinate.

Methods of Job Analysis

There are many different schemes of job analysis, and here we will give just two. The first is one developed by the National Institute of Industrial Psychology (Reeves, Wilson, and Stringfellow, 1951) for purposes of guidance and selection. We have incorporated into their plan two items proposed by Alec Rodger. In articles (Rodger, 1955; Rodger and Cavanagh, 1962) and in his lectures at London University he has argued for the need to base analysis of jobs and occupations on the study and comparison of people who have proved suitable or unsuitable in them. This suitability or unsuitability should be seen not only as difficulty experienced with the work, but in terms also of liking or disliking it. Table 1.2 constitutes categories proposed for a job description.

The N.I.I.P. Paper revives an earlier division for the classification under type of work, into 'mainly office, mainly practical, mainly social'. Such a division may well be useful but there are alternatives. In Chapter 4 we list different classifications of interests which might provide alternative categories for type of work.

Under working conditions the headings, 'physical, social, and economic' seem non-controversial, but there remain other possible formulations. Some social scientists might argue for the inclusion of 'supervision' as a separate heading rather than embracing it under 'social'. Since the classic experiment of Lewin, Lippitt, and White (1939) much evidence has accumulated, particularly from the Ohio State Leadership Studies, to support a view of supervision as a key factor in employee productivity and satisfaction.

TABLE 1.2 *Job description card, adapted from the National Institute of Industrial Psychology Paper No. 2,* Studying Work

	Job Card
Job Title	Type of Work

Department	Number employed
Outline of work done duties and responsibilities	

duties and responsibilities most often found difficult by job occupants

Training	*Working conditions* physical
	social
	economic
Prospects	what do people like about the job?
	what do people dislike about the job?

The importance of working conditions partly remains a matter for further research. In a study of accountants and engineers, Herzberg, Mausner, and Snyderman (1959) found that working conditions were a source of dissatisfaction, and employees tended to complain not of the job itself but of conditions surrounding the job, such as supervision, personal relationships, the physical working conditions, salary, company policy, administrative practices, benefits, and job security. But these factors were never given as a cause of satisfaction. Herzberg likens these working conditions to hygiene factors. They must attain a certain minimum level, or employees will be dissatisfied, but these factors do not in themselves motivate or satisfy the individual.

What then are the factors that do positively motivate employees? Herzberg's accountants and engineers gave as sources of work satisfaction such matters as the tasks of the job, any indications that they were doing their work successfully, and opportunities for personal growth in their work. These satisfying and motivating factors refer to the job itself. It is as part of an attempt to assess a job in these terms that the job description asks, 'what do people like about the job?'

In some organizations the work role is clearly defined, explicit, and static. There are no doubts about what the individual has to do; this is made clear to him; and it does not change much. In other organizations the reverse is true. These two extremes, typified in the distinction between 'mechanistic' and 'organismic' organizational structures (Burns and Stalker, 1961), will make differences in two apparently similar jobs. It would be possible to capture this difference under outline of work done. Alternatively one might view such organizational factors of sufficient importance to warrant a separate heading under working conditions.

The N.I.I.P. add to this job description a categorization of the job requirements, the well-known Seven-Point Plan. Together they constitute a job specification. We will subsequently examine the Seven-Point Plan, analysing its theoretical basis. In general terms we may say it adopts essentially a trait approach to personality, which we examine in Chapter 3, and also makes the time-honoured distinction between abilities and interests. This last we will also return to.

For this or any other job analysis the best sources of information are normally the job occupants, and their supervisors and managers. The work study or industrial engineering departments may also provide useful data. The information is usually obtained by asking questions, and the job analysis plan suggests what are the relevant questions.

Gathering information by asking the right questions, of oneself or of other people, may be aided by a specific approach. This is the contrasting of the successful and unsuccessful job occupants proposed by Rodger (1955, 1962), already referred to. By this we attempt to pinpoint determinants of success and failure in a job or occupation. In completing the job description we might attempt to analyse work done, training, prospects, working conditions, by contrasting successes and failures among past and present job occupants. Three sub-headings, 'duties and responsibilities most often found difficult by job occupants', 'what do people like about the job?', 'what do people dislike about the job?', are aimed specifically at this contrasting of successes and failures.

A second scheme for job analysis is that of Munro Fraser (1962, 1966), and is one primarily for selection. His scheme is attractively simple, having five headings only, which serve as a framework both for a complete job specification, including a description, and also as a plan for assessing the individual. By this approach the job is described under the headings of a specification. We examine the job and describe it in terms of what it requires of the individual, under these five headings:

1. *First Impression and Physical Make-Up*. Here we are concerned with what the job demands in terms of appearance, manner and speech, as well as health.

2. *Qualification*. What level of general education and specific training is required by the job?

3. *Brains and Abilities*. What appropriate levels are required for the job?

4. *Motivation*. What kinds of satisfactions and incentives does this position offer the individual? What demands and level of personal drive does it need from the job occupant?

5. *Adjustment*. What are the nature and extent of the pressures this job will place on the occupant?

By adopting motivation and adjustment as headings in his job specification Munro Fraser assumes it is useful to assess the relationship between the individual and the job in such broad terms. For example, an alternative approach is to conceive of motivation in terms of specific interests. However, motivation seems a more dynamic concept than interests, and gives greater emphasis to the relevance of individual drive in work performance and satisfaction. Similarly the concept of adjustment implies here that success at employment work requires a process of accommodation and adjustment.

Glacier Concepts

We have already given the Glacier definition of employment work (p. 4). It is useful to see the individual employment role as consisting of many tasks, a task being defined by Jaques (1964) as 'a discrete unit of work with target completion time and quality standards, either given by a manager to a subordinate explicitly or implicitly, or generated by a general responsibility'.

We might view a job description as an analysis of an employment role into its constituent tasks. Such tasks will normally have a prescribed and a discretionary content, and the distinction is important. The prescribed element of a task is covered by rules, regulations, policies, procedures, controls, signals, visual displays. These specify clearly what has to be done. The role occupant merely has to follow the instructions and do it. The train driver simply obeys signals. The laboratory technician executes the series of stipulated processes and tests the sample. In the complete bureaucracy all work, other than at a top policy-making level, would be of this nature. But at present the tasks of most employment roles contain a discretionary element. Discretionary content refers to 'those aspects of a task about which a subordinate must exercise his own discretion in order to fulfil his manager's instruction to him' (Jaques, 1964). The centre lathe turner is handed the drawing and told to produce the component. He decides how he will approach the task, what speeds to operate at, the type of cutting tool to use, and cutting angles to adopt. He exercises discretion. The manager, having seen the sales figures and the market research data, gives a decision on the advertising campaign. Here, to fulfil company policy, he must use his judgment.

It is often this discretionary content of the task which is the real work, which we experience as effort and may produce strain. It is primarily this exercise of judgment and discretion which, as the quote from Jaques suggests, gives the individual at work a measure of his sanity. Through his concept of the 'time-span of discretion' Jaques proposes it as the true measure of the value of a job, and as a basis for payment. It may prove useful also in guidance selection, and training, to see the discretionary elements of tasks as the important and critical aspects of jobs and occupations.

WORK, JOB ANALYSIS, AND CHANGE

Any study of work and its functions, and any analysis of occupations and of specific jobs, is made usually in a changing situation. The account contained in a specification is of the job at the time of study, though likely developments in the job may be indicated. It would be misleading to pretend that the social, organizational, and economic environment is normally static, and to ignore the likelihood of a job changing in a changing environment. Some organizations are more subject to change than others. It is suggested in the chapter on management training that senior positions in an organization tend to be more dynamic and changing than those lower in the hierarchy. The information contained in a job analysis may be valid only for a short time.

The general functions of work also change and vary from time to time, culture to culture, and social group to social group. In terms of the individual this means that the need-satisfactions sought in a job vary in different times, in different societies, in different classes and sections of society, and even from one individual to another. The form of the job analysis affects how we see the job, and suggests what are its important and significant features. But what ultimately is relevant is relative to the perception of the job occupant. There are dangers in such a phenomenalist view, but it serves to stress that only the functions an employment role might have for a typical occupant, not those it has for the job analyst, are relevant.

REFERENCES

Brown, W., in Brown, W. and Jaques, E. (1965), *Glacier Project Papers* (p. 55), Heinemann.

Burns, T. and Stalker, G. M. (1961), *The Management of Innovation*, Tavistock.

Cotgrove, S. (1967), *The Science of Society*, Allen & Unwin.

Davis, L. E. and Valfer, E. S. (1965), 'Intervening responses to changes in supervisor job designs', *Occup. Psychol.*, 39, 3, 171.

Eisenberg, P. and Lazarsfeld, P. F. (1938), 'The psychological effects of unemployment', *Psychol. Bull.*, 35, 358–90.

Festinger, L. (1957), *A Theory of Cognitive Dissonance*, Harper & Row.

Friedmann, E. A. and Havinghurst, R. J. (1954), *The Meaning of Work and Retirement*, University of Chicago Press.

Goldthorpe, J. *et al.* (1968), *The Affluent Worker : Industrial Attitudes and Behaviour*, Cambridge University Press.

Herzberg, F., Mausner, B. and Snyderman, B. (1959), *The Motivation to Work*, Wiley.

Hoffer, E. (1964), *The Ordeal of Change*, Sidgwick & Jackson.

Israeli, N. (1935), 'Distress in the outlook of Lancashire and Scottish unemployed,' *J. appl. Psychol.*, 19, 67–9.

Jaques, E. (1961), *Equitable Payment*, Heinemann.

Jaques, E. (1964), *Time-Span Handbook*, Heinemann.

Komarovsky, M. (1940), *The Unemployed Man and his Family*, Dryden Press.

Lewin, K., Lippitt, R. and White, R. K. (1939), 'Patterns of aggressive behaviour in experimentally created social climates', *J. soc. Psychol.*, 10, 271–99.

Linton, R. (1945), *The Cultural Background of Personality*, Appleton-Century-Crofts.

Marx, K., *Economic and Philosophic Manuscripts of 1844*, Foreign Languages Publishing House, Moscow, 1961.

Mayo, E. (1945), *The Social Problems of an Industrial Civilization*, Harvard Business School.

Merton, R. K. (1957), *Social Theory and Social Structure*, Free Press.

Morse, N. C. and Weiss, R. S. (1955), 'The function and meaning of work and the job', *American Sociological Review*, April.

Munro Fraser, J. (1962), *Industrial Psychology*, Pergamon.

Munro Fraser, J. (1966), *Employment Interviewing*, Macdonald & Evans.

Radcliffe-Brown, A. R. (1935), 'On the concept of function in social science', *American Anthropologist*, 37.

Reeves, J. W., Wilson, V. W. and Stringfellow, C. D. (1951), *Studying Work*, National Institute of Industrial Psychology Paper No. 2.

Rodger, A. (1955), 'The effective use of manpower', British Association Address, September; printed in *Advancement of Science*, No. 46, Sept.

Rodger, A. and Cavanagh, P. (1962), 'Personnel Selection and Vocational Guidance', in *Society: Problems and Methods of Study*, ed. A. T. Welford, Routledge & Kegan Paul.

Secord, P. F. and Backman, C. W. (1964), *Social Psychology*, (p. 456) McGraw-Hill.

Shimmin, S. (1966), 'Concepts of Work', *Occup. Psychol.*, 40, 4.

Tilgher, A. (1930), *Work: What it has meant to Men through the Ages*, Harcourt Brace.

Trist, E. L. and Bamforth, K. W. (1951), 'Some social and psychological consequences of the longwall method of coal-getting', *Human Relations*, 4, 1–38.

Zerga, J. E. (1943), 'Job analysis, a résumé and bibliography', *J. appl. Psychol.*, 27, 249–67.

PART II

Guidance and Selection

CHAPTER 2

Personality

Overview

We have examined work and jobs. We now need to consider ideas and theories about people, before reviewing ways of placing them in satisfactory employment. Three informal views of man are introduced first. We then discuss the nature of explicit, formal theories of personality, and specifically consider those of Maslow, Allport, and Cattell. The chapter ends by reviewing the concept of traits and two types of validity in guidance and selection.

INTRODUCTION

'There is nothing so practical as a good theory' (K. Lewin).

After an employment interview a manager might remark of an applicant: 'He seems well suited for the vacancy; he has the ability and the experience. But if we offered him the job I don't think he would stay long. He's never stayed in any job very long.' The statement implies a certain view of people and what causes their actions, suggesting that someone's past behaviour is necessarily a good guide to what he will do in the future. It specifically suggests that staying in jobs for only a short time is a permanent tendency some people may have, possibly as a trait of instability. Clearly the idea can be challenged. An alternative, environmental view would suggest that how long a person stays in a job is more a function of the nature and circumstances of the job itself than of the individual's personal idiosyncracies. For such a view the length of an applicant's stay in previous employment gives no real clue as to how long he might stay in any future job. There is some evidence to support such an idea (Wickert, 1951).

The manager's statement implies only a generalization, that there are some people who never stay long in jobs and that the applicant is one of them. A theory attempts to explain why. But both generalization and theory affect the manager's evaluation of the applicant and his decision on whether to employ him.

We generalize and theorize about people all the time, so in guidance and selection we should only adopt generalizations and theories which are useful. There may be weaknesses in those of our own we have unconsciously developed from childhood, and someone else may have a more helpful view of personality to offer. Secondly, if we are more aware of the view of personality we adopt, our own or someone else's, we will know when it applies, its limitations and assumptions, and when it is no longer relevant. We shall argue that theory, here personality theory, normally provides a better basis for decision-making than do mere generalizations. We need to base our guidance and selection on an explanation of relationships between people and work, rather than just on the knowledge that relationships exist.

Subsequently we will examine some techniques of guidance and selection, such as tests and assessment schemes. These techniques embody a theoretical explanation of personality or an explanatory concept, like 'intelligence'. To use a technique correctly we need to understand its theoretical basis. Without this understanding we are likely to make unwarranted generalizations and predictions, so selecting an unsuitable applicant or giving bad guidance.

INFORMAL AND GENERAL THEORIES

Certain views of the individual have developed which are in a sense popular in origin, and not the work of a particular theorist. We will examine just three of these, centred round the concepts of economic man, social man, and self-actualizing man. Such views are often highly general and inexplicit, but have been adopted by managers and by social scientists and have provided the basis for much of their work.

Economic Man

Originally, and in its narrower sense, the concept of man as an economic animal interprets his behaviour as primarily rational, in that he attempts always to maximize his economic and material gain. The pioneers of scientific management had such a view, and it is found in their writings, such as those of F. W. Taylor, at the beginning of this century. It was, as the term might suggest, the concept of the individual originally adopted by most economic theorists, and remains so still though in a more sophisticated form. Feelings are treated as essentially irrational and needs other than economic regarded as of little importance. So if a piece-worker reduces his income by restricting his output to please his workmates and to be accepted by them, he is behaving irrationally.

What McGregor (1960) describes as Theory X is an elaboration and development of this concept. He suggests managers have made certain assumptions about human behaviour, and adopted them as generalizations providing a basis for action. Among them are the following:

> 'The average human being has an inherent dislike of work and will avoid it if he can.'
> 'Because of this human characteristic of dislike of work, most people must be coerced, controlled, directed, threatened with punishment to get them to put forth adequate effort toward the achievement of organizational objectives.'
> 'The average human being prefers to be directed, wishes to avoid responsibility, has relatively little ambition, wants security above all.'

Whatever the evidence for Theory X, with this rational, economic creature as its basic concept, many managers formally or implicitly operate in terms of it. A characteristic spuervisory and management strategy emerges. Money is the real incentive, so output should be tied to pay by means of piece-work and bonus schemes. As workers are so uninterested and irresponsible, jobs should be simplified, routine work procedures introduced, and the men's physical condition kept at its best by rest pauses, good heating and lighting, etc. These factors, together with the worker's laziness, make it necessary for the manager to maintain close supervision.

Social Man

A second view of personality has emerged from an awareness of man's social needs at work, where the individual is seen as highly motivated by a search for social satisfactions. These are obtained at the work-place through warm, face-to-face association with his peers and involvement in the small, primary group, and also by a relationship with his supervisor which is experienced as supportive and which enhances his feeling of personal worth. As we indicated in Chapter 1, social man arrived with the Hawthorne Studies.

In our discussion of the human relations school we indicated the managerial strategy that has emerged from such a view of personality. Likewise it is such a view of man which contemporarily provides part of the foundations for a Participative Group Management System advocated by Likert (1961, 1967) and others.

Self-Actualizing Man

A third set of generalizations about the individual stresses his need to find fulfilment in work. Maslow (1954) refers to a need for self-actualization, a need 'to become everything one is capable of becoming'. Such a concept is central to the assumptions McGregor (1960) suggests are an alternative to the model of man in theory X. It is contended that many very successful managers already function in terms of such a view of personality, which McGregor labels theory Y. Among its basic assertions are the following:

> 'The expenditure of physical and mental effort in work is as natural as play or rest.'
> 'Man will exercise self-direction and self-control in the service of objectives to which he is committed.'
> 'Commitment to objectives is a function of the rewards associated with their achievement. The most significant of such rewards, e.g. the satisfaction of ego and self-actualization needs, can be direct products of effort directed towards organized objectives.'
> 'The average human being learns, under proper conditions, not only to accept but to seek responsibility.'
> 'The capacity to exercise a relatively high degree of imagination, ingenuity, and creativity in the solution of organizational problems is widely, not narrowly, distributed in the population'.

If managers see personality in this way they will normally adopt certain styles and strategies. Usually a view of man as a social animal is also incorporated into such an approach. The emphasis is placed on giving a man work that provides intrinsic satisfactions, satisfactions that arise from using his abilities, and from allowing him to be what he wishes to be. The job must be made challenging, meaningful, significant, in the nature of its job tasks, and through an organizational structure which involves the individual in the process of decision-making.

FORMAL THEORIES OF PERSONALITY

The Concept of Personality

As with work, we can give no general definition of personality. There is little agreement on the use of the term, which reflects in part the inadequacy of barely a hundred years' scientific study of the concept, but primarily results from the variety of functions it serves in a variety of fields, educational, clinical, occupational, and others. We have to define personality in terms of a given theory.

We can say what is not meant by the term. Personality does not refer to what the publicity man means (if indeed he means anything) when he writes of 'a great personality of stage and screen', referring perhaps to a social stimulus value or a capacity to influence people. Such usage implies that some people have personality and others do not, or at least that the more fortunate have more of it than others. In normal scientific use, all people have personality. The man who 'has no personality' is usually shy, dull, retiring; in fact, the adjectives describe just what sort of a personality he has.

But it is to be distinguished, as Allport (1961) points out, from the term 'character', which implies a moral estimate of an individual. Character is personality measured against some moral code or other standard. As has been said, we must define personality with reference to a specific theory.

Characteristics of Personality Theories

There are many theories of personality, but Hall and Lindzey (1957), contrasting them with other types of psychological theory, suggest a number of generalizations that may be made about them. These authors point out that modern personality theory owes its beginning mainly to medical practitioners, such as Freud and Jung. By and large it has remained the field of practitioners, of people dealing with real life problems, in education, psychotherapy, psychiatry, and in the social, vocational, and industrial fields. Because of this, most personality theorists have been preoccupied with practical applications and use. 'Can we produce a theory that will explain these neurotic symptoms, and suggest what their origins and cure may be?' 'Can we explain why some bright children do badly at school?' 'Why are so many people full

of prejudice against minority groups such as immigrants or Jews?'
'Why do some men make good supervisors and others don't? Is
it something to do with their personality?'

The first characteristic of such theories, therefore, is an emphasis
on explanations which help with problems of real life, not laboratory ones—an emphasis on practical applications. Freud's theories,
intended in part to provide an understanding of abnormal behaviour, illustrate the point, though here we are primarily interested in theories of relevance to the employment situation,
and relevant particularly to guidance and selection.

A second characteristic has been their emphasis on the study of
motivation. Some explanation of drives, needs, or whatever
motivates and causes human behaviour is essential and central to
any understanding of human personality. Personality theories
attempt to throw light on this problem of motivation.

Thirdly, the integration of psychological knowledge about
human behaviour has been regarded as an important function of
personality theories. Experimental laboratory psychologists have
tended to examine and explain only segments of behaviour, such
as reaction time, remembering, visual perception, whereas the
personality theorists attempt to fit the segments together. Though
integration into a total view of the person seems a Utopian
objective in the present state of knowledge, for the purpose of
practical applications to work problems it presents too limited an
objective. We will develop this consideration in the final chapter,
suggesting that human behaviour in the work situation should be
seen not only in terms of total individual personality, but in terms
also of the physical, social, and organizational environment within
which the personality acts.

The most popularly known account of personality, Freud's
psychoanalytic theory, illustrates these generalizations. Aimed
originally at a specific problem area it was primarily concerned
with the treatment of mental illness, and, developed and modified
over the years, has proved continually useful in the clinical field.
His theory analyses the development of human behaviour and
seeks to identify the important stages of psychosexual development, suggesting that failures in development at certain stages of
infancy and childhood are the main factors in adult neurosis.
How that one *idea*, now part of common culture, has revolu-
tionized clinical *practice*!

Psychoanalytic theory is concerned also with consciousness, with the structural organization of personality, and with the way in which instinctual energy is transformed. And it is probably because of its comprehensive and integrative character, and its essential concern with motivation and the primary drives of humanity, that Freudian theory has so influenced the thought and culture of the twentieth century. From the novels of D. H. Lawrence, through shades of meaning in words like 'repression' and 'sublimation', to the television commercial and the advertiser's prose, Freud's ghost moves, perhaps a little startled at the practical uses to which his ideas are now put.

Holistic and Trait Theories

Before examining the accounts of personality proposed by Maslow, Allport, and Cattell, it is useful to consider a division of such theories into holistic and trait types. The trait approach analyses personality into bundles of bits, qualities, elements, however they may be termed. It assumes one may usefully study isolated and separate elements of an organism, such as aggression or mechanical aptitude, and compare one individual with another in terms of these elements. Any factor-analytic approach such as that of Cattell necessarily makes this assumption, though statistical techniques make it possible to compare individual with individual on several factors at the same time. The trait theorists of human ability, like Burt and Thurstone, whose work we will study in the next chapter, also partly adopt this view in concepts such as intelligence and perceptual fluency. Allport is unsympathetic to such a view, but concedes that an analysis and comparison of people in terms of these elements has a limited usefulness. Allport's 'common trait' solves, for him, the dilemma of uniqueness versus generality in personality. In its extreme form the trait approach adopts the basic assumption of reductionism, that the total organism is merely the sum of its parts and no more.

Since Freud certain theories of personality have developed which are termed organismic or holistic. Holistic means 'whole' or 'entire', and derives from the word 'holy' which originally meant complete, referring to man's religious aspiration for completeness. Personality is a whole, and has the characteristics of an organism in being unified, distinct from its environment, and having interrelated parts. A holistic approach is concerned primarily with the study of a total personality, examining its internal structure and dynamics. The essential idea of holism is the Gestalt dictum that 'the whole is more than the sum of its parts'. If this is so, then analysing the individual into parts and comparing individuals in terms of such elements is of doubtful validity.

This emphasis on wholeness is part possibly of a general contemporary reaction against centuries of a more fragmented and limited approach to life, at least in the civilization of the West. T. S. Eliot coined the phrase 'dissociation of sensibility' to describe what he thought to be one of the effects of the Reformation in Europe whereby the emphasis on individual judgment led to a division between reason and sensibility which persisted for three hundred years. Eliot and others have attempted in literature to restore this association of thought with feeling.

The development of psychosomatic medicine is another example of a renewed emphasis on the whole. Certainly holistic theories contrast with the deliberately limited studies of the experimental psychologists in, say, motor skills or perception. Gestalt psychology with its emphasis on meaningful wholes in all forms of perception contributed much to the development of holistic theories.

A Holistic Theory of Personality : A. H. Maslow

Maslow's model of man emphasizes the wholeness and total structure of personality, and stresses also motivation, which we have already suggested normally plays an important part in personality theory. Since Maslow is particularly interested in motivation, we may find his theory useful in the employment situation for analysing the motives and incentives to work.

In a collection of essays Maslow (1954) makes three basic assertions:

> First of all and most important of all is the strong belief that man has an essential nature of his own, some skeleton of psychological structure that may be treated and discussed analogously with his physical structure, that he has needs, capacities, and tendencies that are genetically based, some of which are characteristic of the whole species, cutting across all cultural lines, and some of which are unique to the whole individual.

His second assertion is

that full health and normal and desirable development consist in actualizing this nature, in fulfilling these potentialities, and in developing into maturity along the lines that this hidden, covert, dimly seen essential nature dictates, growing from within rather than being shaped from without.

And lastly,

psychopathology in general results from the denial or frustration or the twisting of man's essential nature.

This account of man stresses the innate and genetic aspects of human personality. Environment, learning, experience remain important, but primarily to the extent that they help or hinder the development of personality according to its genetic blueprint.

Maslow's statement that man 'has needs . . . that are genetically based' relates to that part of his theory by which it is best known, the hierarchy of prepotency of needs. We see that men have different wants and drives and motives. How might we usefully classify them? Maslow proposes a hierarchy based on the principle of relative potency; which is that some needs are normally stronger, more demanding and fundamental than others. His hierarchy, in its order of potency and with the more basic needs first, is as follows:

Physiological needs
> Hunger, thirst, sexual gratification, etc.

Safety needs
> The need to avoid danger, have security, etc. The terrified reaction of babies to a loud noise or to a loss of support in the mother's arms, and the adult's concern for a secure job or provision for retirement, are examples of these.

Belongingness and love needs
> We could loosely identify these as social needs, and they include our wanting to give and receive love and affection, and to belong to and identify with a social group.

Esteem needs
> These embrace our need for that appreciation and recognition which give a feeling of worth and value.

Need for self-actualization
> A need, says Maslow, 'to become everything one is capable of becoming'. Since this need can never be completely satisfied, it is an almost limitless source of motivation.

Maslow lists other possible needs, such as desires to know and understand, and aesthetic needs, but the above five are his basic categories of the source of human motivation.

In an earlier article (1943) Maslow says of the hierarchy of prepotency: 'The most prepotent goal will monopolize the consciousness and will tend of itself to organize the recruitment of the various capacities of the organism.' So an individual who lacks food, security, and affection, would normally want food before anything else. At any given moment, if a number of needs are unsatisfied, the one most likely to determine a person's behaviour is the need highest in the hierarchy. In such a situation, Maslow continues, 'the less prepotent needs are minimized, even forgotten or denied'. Religious missionaries have long since learnt that the full stomach precedes the willing ear.

'But when a need is fairly well satisfied, the next prepotent (higher) need emerges, in turn to dominate the conscious life and to serve as the centre of the organization of behaviour, since gratified needs are not active motivators.' This last point, that a satisfied need has little effect on immediate behaviour, is important. A man who is economically and emotionally secure may behave with complete disregard for security.

Maslow points out that there is an overlap in the emergence and satisfaction of needs adjacent in the hierarchy. For example, we would expect a person whose safety needs are not yet satisfied completely to begin to experience a need also for love and belonging.

Since the motivation of employees is a basic problem of industry, Maslow's theory may be of use here. What makes men work? Can the real motivators of human behaviour be found in the workplace? If they can, are they universal? Or do they vary from place to place, from social class to social class, and individual to individual? There is still much disagreement about the importance of money as an incentive to work. The hierarchy of prepotency suggests that the importance of money as an incentive varies with the extent to which the two most fundamental needs, the physiological and safety needs, are satisfied. This in turn is affected by cultural expectations as regards, say, food and security. The further complication exists of the power of money to symbolize, say, love, and to obtain esteem in certain societies. It has become apparent that by discussing the individual motivated in employment we are considering again the functions of work from a different viewpoint.

Centers (1948) analysed data on the attitudes to work of a cross-section of Americans. Professional and business men wanted 'self-expression' in their jobs more than did workers lower in the occupational scale. The former also expressed far less need for security than workers in the lower groups. Using Maslow's theory, we could interpret this in terms of the higher group being satisfied already on the first two needs in the hierarchy, which would then no longer be active motivators, whereas the lower occupational group would still be stuck on the safety needs level. From this, and following the theory, we could now suggest what might be the best motivators for the two groups; presumably they would be different in each case. Other studies, such as that of Porter (1961), have also found this relationship between position on the occupational scale and the Maslow need hierarchy.

Maslow's formulation has interesting possibilities as the basis for such studies of employment incentives. Heller and Porter (1966) used his classification of needs as the basis for a questionnaire on satisfaction at work, and found little difference between groups of British and American managers in their evaluation of their own work satisfactions.

G. W. Allport: A Theory of Personal Dispositions and Common Traits

We have made the distinction between a trait analysis of personality and the holistic view. In a discussion of Allport it is necessary as well to distinguish between a nomothetic and an idiographic approach to the study of the individual. A music critic reviewing a new symphony may care to analyse it in terms of its structure, cohesion, or internal dynamics, that is, in terms of itself. Or his starting-point may essentially be a comparison of this symphony and its sections with other similar works. The first approach is primarily idiographic in that characteristically it attempts to understand one particular work, event, or individual. As we shall see, Allport's concept of 'personal dispositions' is in this sense idiographic. But the critic comparing a number of different symphonies may be attempting, like Aristotle in his study of Greek tragedies, to formulate general statements about the symphony. Even if his interest is the analysis of one composition,

X's second symphony, but his approach is to compare it with other works, he is assuming the validity of such a comparison and implying the existence of general laws that may be derived from such a comparison, against which he may evaluate X's second symphony. This approach, designed for discovering general laws, or assuming that such general laws are possible, is termed nomothetic. Allport is unsympathetic to the nomothetic analysis of the human personality, but proposes the concept of the 'common trait' for what he sees as its limited usefulness.

The Units of Personality. If for the study of personality we intend to 'break it down' into bits, then the choice of what elements or units to use becomes important. One approach to what Allport calls this 'search for elements' was proposed by faculty psychology, popular during the last century. Its elements were the 'faculties'. Basically faculty psychology said that human personality consisted of a number of faculties, such as those of memory, artistic aptitude, aggressiveness, and docility. These faculties functioned in a general and comprehensive way, so that X's aggressiveness developed in a certain sort of situation, such as his home, would manifest itself in most other situations too. Memory trained in a specific discipline would quickly adapt itself to another field. But this generality of function is at variance with common experience. The boy who goes to school on a Monday morning with most of the football scores in his head may still have difficulty in remembering Shakespeare or historical dates. The man with the 'aggressive faculty' may be pathetically timid in some situations. Faculty psychology failed to account for these variations and apparent inconsistencies in human behaviour, and was replaced by another kind of explanation, using different units or elements.

Behaviour was now understood in terms of established connections between specific stimuli and specific responses. Popularly the approach is associated with Pavlov and his dogs. According to such an analysis, personality may be regarded as made up of specific links, habits, connections, which are established by experience, training, and education. The basic unit of analysis is the s-r (stimulus-response) link. Such an approach, much refined and developed, remains dominant in many areas of modern psychology.

We will illustrate this approach. A youth cleans his teeth

because he was taught to do so by his parents. He changes his dirty clothes, again parental training. But though he changes his clothes, cleans his teeth, tidies his room, washes regularly, etc., there is no nucleus of behaviour that could be called 'cleanliness'. What is there is simply a series of learnt habits, not a faculty of cleanliness. This is proved by the youth's untidiness at work and his invariably dirty shoes. Faculty psychology failed to explain this apparent inconsistency, whereas this theory of identical elements simply suggests that we respond to a specific stimulus in a specific way, like Pavlov's dogs. So the youth faced with his untidy room, tidies it, because his mother used to praise him when a child if he did this, and smacked him if he failed to. But that is as far as it goes, and when he sees his untidy bench at work he feels no inclination to tidy it. He responds only to specific things, his dirty teeth, his dirty clothes, his room in a mess, or to something similar or identical to one of them.

Allport (1961) gives another example. My mother trains me to wipe my feet at the door of our house. Eventually I come to wipe my feet at the doors of most other houses because of the similarity or identicalness of the elements in these other situations; there has been a generalization of the stimulus, door, doormat, entering a house, etc. Similarly I learn to take off my hat when the door opens, to 'say good morning nicely', and to wipe my feet if asked into the house. They are all separate and different responses but are made proximately and so become associated in a chain of response. To the observer this series of behaviours that I carry out at most people's doors might suggest the presence of an underlying faculty of courtesy. But an identical-elements theorist would regard this as an illusion; we have here simply a series of separate habits that have become associated in time and which occur in response to a specific kind of stimulus.

The usefulness of this stimulus-response sort of explanation in certain areas of behaviour, such as learning, is well established. In later chapters we will study such explanations in more detail when we examine theories of learning and their possible use in training. But the s-r model is possibly less useful for analysing behaviour at the more complex level of personality.

At the level of personality we are concerned with two complimentary aspects of human behaviour, its variability and its consistency. We see the variability when the same or apparently same stimulus, such as the doormat, produces different reactions from an individual on different occasions. When Mr X is frightened he usually turns and runs, but once, terrified in the presence of his wife, he stood firm. Outside work Mr Y has many opportunities to steal but never does so; at work he pilfers frequently. If personality is a bundle of stimulus-response connections, and behaviour is a response to identical elements, why do these variations in behaviour occur in apparently similar situations? The obvious answer is that the situations were not really identical. The problem then becomes one of determining which situations are the same, which are different, and in what way they differ. Outside the laboratory, situations are so complex that this becomes an almost impossible task. So the value of seeing personality in terms of s-r connections is limited.

The consistency of behaviour presents a similar position. A rude comment, the door slammed in my face, a book dropped on my toe, frequent interruptions when I am speaking, all seem rather different, but all make me react aggressively. The problem becomes that of finding identical elements or stimuli in apparently different situations, since they all cause me to behave similarly. We can suggest there has been a generalization of stimulus from one situation to another, but the difficulty of specifying outside the laboratory what has really happened leads us to reflect that other explanations of behaviour may be more convenient and useful. One such explanation suggests that we carry around from situation to situation general tendencies to behave in certain ways. We might almost be back with faculty psychology again, but not quite.

Personal Dispositions. Racial prejudice is an example of such a 'general tendency'. We see that an individual is hostile to a variety of people who have one element in common, that they are not of the individual's own cultural group. In many different situations he is aggressive with them. Our approach is now to assume the existence of an underlying hostile tendency to 'foreigners'. We cannot see or touch this tendency as an entity; we assume it is there from certain actions of the individual that we have observed, and on the basis of its assumed existence we predict how the individual will behave with outsiders in the future. In other words, this hostile tendency to foreigners which we are putting forward as an explanation is a hypothetical construct.

Social psychologists have adopted as a key concept for their analysis of behaviour a hypothetical construct of the 'general tendency' sort, that of the 'attitude'. But attitudes have objects tied to them. One has an attitude towards public schools, a political party, or censorship. Allport, wanting for the analysis of personality a unit similar to that of attitude, but more general in not being tied to an object, adopted the hypothetical construct of a 'trait'.

Allport's theory of personality makes possible both an idiographic and nomothetic analysis. When he is concerned with the first, with understanding one particular, unique individual, he refers to the trait as a 'personal disposition'. When he is nomothetic in his approach, and compares one individual with another, he uses the term of the 'common trait'. We will examine the nature of this idiographic analysis first.

For Allport traits are essentially unique and so cannot be compared. Dr Jones and Mr Smith are both highly aggressive, and we can regard their aggressiveness as a trait. But the aggressiveness of Dr Jones is uniquely his own. To understand him we need to appreciate the individual quality of his aggressiveness, and to know how it relates to his interests, values, and other traits, and its function in his total personality system. It is traits in this sense that Allport labels personal dispositions.

He defines them as follows: 'A personal disposition is a generalized neuropsychic structure (peculiar to the individual), *with the capacity to render many stimuli functionally equivalent*, and to initiate and guide consistent (equivalent) forms of adaptive and stylistic behaviour.' The clause I have italicized makes the point that many different stimuli are similarly categorized and reacted to in terms of the disposition. They effectively become one sort of stimulus for the individual, such as aggression-provoking, and produce the same, aggressive response. Personal dispositions or traits account for the consistency in behaviour, providing an alternative to an S-R explanation in terms of stimulus generalization.

The last part of Allport's definition, 'to initiate and guide consistent . . . forms of adaptive and stylistic behaviour', emphasizes that personal dispositions and traits are the source of behaviour; they are motivating. 'Ambition' is a trait which motivates the individual. Other traits such as 'timidity' are more stylistic and expressive of personality, and determine rather the

45

manner of performance. Whatever X does he does in a timid way. But such traits may be motivating too, as when because of his timidity he avoids playing games. Similarly Y's ambition, besides being a motivating force, has an expressive quality and a style of his own, which tells us something about him.

While the existence of dispositions explains the consistency in our actions, it is the way they are organized that accounts for the variability of behaviour. It seems useful to see this organization as a hierarchy of personal dispositions within an individual personality, as in the following sequence:

RADICALISM

AGGRESSIVENESS		SELFISHNESS
impulsiveness		untidiness

At the top of the hierarchy is the disposition dominant in the make-up of the individual. On the next, lower level are the aggressiveness and selfishness which are central to his personality but of less importance and influence than his radicalism. Lowest on the hierarchy are his impulsiveness and untidiness, which though of less importance than those dispositions on higher levels, do sufficiently influence his behaviour to justify their being classified as traits.

A brief observation of this person's behaviour shows that he tends to be selfish. Further observation confirms this, his selfishness showing itself as an unwillingness to do anything for anyone else in ordinary, everyday circumstances. One might be surprised, therefore, to find that he is a local councillor, self-sacrificing and unsparing of his time in effecting social improvements, doing welfare work, etc. Here his radicalism is in conflict with his selfishness, but being higher in his hierarchy of traits determines his behaviour in this situation.

The same man is untidy at work, drops litter in the street, and leaves the bathroom in a mess. But he keeps his own room clean and tidy; here his selfishness, more important than untidiness in his trait hierarchy, directs what he does.

Allport suggests three levels of personal dispositions, cardinal, central, and secondary. The categorizations are simply positions in a continuum, but are convenient and useful divisions. A cardinal disposition is an absolutely dominant trait, and probably not everybody has one. Examples are Volpone's greed or a desperate ambition to achieve financial security sometimes found in people who have experienced real poverty.

Central dispositions are those highly characteristic of the individual. Mrs X is characteristically motherly or good-natured. Aggressive behaviour is somehow always typical of Y. Secondary traits are far less central to an individual's personality, less crucial to any description of him—one might not bother to mention them in a reference. They tend to be focalized, and may approximate more to an attitude. Frequent untidiness might be such a secondary disposition.

The Proprium or Self Concept. Rather than categorizing personal dispositions as cardinal, central, or secondary, we might have described their centrality and importance in terms of whether they were more or less 'propriate'. The proprium is Allport's term for the self, a concept which has passed in and out of psychological fashion over the years.

The individual not only experiences entities outside himself, he experiences himself. Through his superior intelligence and his capacity for speech, man may become an object to himself. He comes to perceive, consider, and experience, (1) his body, (2) his identity, (3) his feelings for himself, (4) what things outside himself he identifies with, (5) his ideals, (6) himself as a rational being, (7) his life intentions (Allport, 1961, chapter 6). Man seems not to be born with this sense of self, and psychologists have traced the stages of infancy, childhood, and adolescence, through which it develops.

Allport (1961) says of these seven aspects of selfhood: 'They are all states of self-relevance that we *feel*. Each in its way is an intimate region of personality involved in matters of importance to the organized emotional life of the individual. Together they compose the me as felt and known.' The proprium is the amalgam of these aspects of the self. The proprium is, therefore, core and central to the individual personality, since the individual experiences it as such. And we may evaluate personal dispositions in terms of how propriate they are, that is, in terms of how close they are experienced as being to this personality core, the proprium. Is my kindness or assertiveness, for example, merely peripheral to my personality, or highly propriate, very much part of what I regard as the 'real me'?

The proprium, since it embraces such important aspects of the self as life intentions, ideals, objects of identification, may be seen as a most important source of motivation in such a model of personality. Allport also suggests that once established it 'becomes the principal source of subsequent learning'.

The proprium is a holistic type of concept, and like personal dispositions provides primarily for an idiographic analysis of personality. An approach to personality with these terms provides a basis for the vocational-counselling style of careers guidance. This we will examine in Chapter 6. In vocational counselling the proprium or self concept functions frequently as a key concept.

We shall see in Chapter 6 that the appraisal style of guidance, like traditional personnel selection, adopts a nomothetic analysis. Allport's theoretical framework also makes possible such a nomothetic analysis, through the concept of the 'common trait'.

Common Traits. Allport sees an individual's personality and its constituent elements as unique. X's assertiveness is peculiarly his own and like no one else's. But there are situations, such as in selection, where it would seem to be useful to compare people; has such a comparison any real meaning? Is a nomothetic analysis of personality of any value? Allport's answer is that it has a value, though limited.

He argues we are able profitably to compare the personal dispositions of different people along certain dimensions because after all (Allport, 1961), 'Normal people in a given culture-area necessarily tend to develop somewhat roughly comparable modes of adjustment'. Within a culture common socialization processes will occur by which we learn behaviour in line with many of the expectations of that society. So the personality traits of different people will usually have common areas where they may usefully be compared. We may, therefore, construct a test of honesty or verbal facility that meaningfully compares different individuals and enables us to make certain predictions about their behaviour. When we do this we are comparing people not on their real, unique personal dispositions, but merely on what these dispositions have in common, on their common traits. Mr X's common trait of honesty which we measure against Mr Y's has now been made something of an artifact by forcing it into the strait-jacket of our categories, definitions, and dimensions. We had to do this in order to compare them at all. Allport defines common traits as 'those aspects of personality in respect to which most people within a given culture can be profitably compared'.

A Definition of Personality. Allport's definition is as follows: 'Personality is the dynamic organization within the individual of those psychophysical systems that determine his characteristic behaviour and thought.' The phrase 'psychophysical systems' refer to habits, interests, attitudes, values, and above all to personal dispositions (or traits) and to the proprium.

Trait Theory, Factor Analysis, and R. B. Cattell
A number of trait theories, such as those of Cattell and Eysenck, derive from the statistical techniques of factor analysis. The origins of these theories in factor analysis means they are essentially nomothetic in their approach.

Correlation is a basic concept of factor analysis, and we will examine them both in the next chapter. For the purposes of this chapter we can simply say that the traits or factors of these theorists derive from empirical findings that certain behaviours tend to be found together in an individual; in other words that certain performances such as answers to a questionnaire, test scores, and real-life actions evaluated in some way, may often correlate with one another. For example, a factor analyst might find by comparing different people that someone who is aggressive is usually also a suspicious sort, tends to be rigid and precise in work and other activities, avoids compromise and likes doing things by himself. If such elements of behaviour consistently come together and cluster in an individual they may usefully be thought of in trait terms, and called traits or factors.

Cattell's definition of a trait (1965) emphasizes its correlational basis: 'A unitary configuration in behaviour such that when one part is present in a certain degree, we can infer that a person will show the other parts in a certain degree.' The phrase 'unitary configuration' suggests the trait is not a mere artifact which only seems to be there because of a statistical correlation, rather that the statistical correlation indicates the presence of a real, separate trait.

The approach is nomothetic because in its practice and in its derivation it compares one individual with another. For example, we might factor-analyse all the answers to a questionnaire where items such as the following appear: 'If you were standing in a bus queue, and someone walked from the back of the queue and stood in front of you, would you (a) say nothing but feel angry, or (b) be unconcerned, or (c) tell him to get to the back of the queue?' If two individuals tick, say, (c), the assumption in factor analysis is that they have responded identically. Whereas the more idiographic view of Allport and others would suggest a difference in the meaning of the same response, this meaning relating to other traits, to the internal personality dynamics and its total functioning. But essentially the very texture of the behaviour responses is seen as different, for the assertiveness the answer of one individual indicates is qualitatively different from the next individual's assertiveness—X's assertiveness is uniquely his own.

We have earlier contrasted theories which emphasize the wholeness of personality with a trait approach which reduces personality into separate elements. The distinction remains valid since trait theory rejects the contention that 'the whole is more than the sum of its parts'. However, the ability of factor analysis to investigate many correlations simultaneously may possibly reduce the original force of the distinction. Factor analysis is multivariate in that it can analyse many variables, such as elements of behaviour, at the same time. Cattell (1965) makes the point:

> Where total organisms have to be studied, the theoretical possibility must be faced that one can sometimes hope to find a law only if *the total organism* is included in the observations and experiences—not just a bit of its behaviour. In this respect, the emphasis on 'wholeness' in the multivariate method is actually the same as in the clinical method, but it is quantitative and follows explicit calculations of laws and general conclusions.

Cattell's Source Traits and Surface Traits. Cattell suggests that the number of factors or personality traits that influence behaviour is about twenty-six, though in fact much of behaviour may be accounted for by about sixteen of these. These two dozen or so factors Cattell terms source traits. Such a trait 'operates as an underlying source of observed behaviour' and 'it will be evident that a source trait as discovered by factor analysis is some kind of unitary influence in personality which affects a whole structure of responses' (Cattell, 1965).

Source traits are the real traits, and Cattell distinguishes them from surface traits, which are not really personality traits at all. Behaviours that are frequently observed clustering together may do so not on account of one underlying trait, but because of cultural and social influences, because certain types of experience are common, and because certain environments cause two or more traits to interact together in a specific way. Cattell instances neuroticism as a surface trait. Vague anxieties, phobias, phantasies, tensions, and indecision, tend to cluster and go together in the same individual, but are not the result of one underlying source trait, 'neuroticism'. Rather, they are acceptable ways of expressing one's inability to cope, which may be caused by a variety of circumstances, environmental, physical, as well as by an interaction of a number of personality traits.

Source traits, then, are the real, underlying personality structures, evidenced by clusterings of behaviours. But, as the idea of a surface trait suggests, behaviour is influenced by passing moods, as when an individual may be under considerable stress, and is affected also by the nature of the situation in which it occurs. From this concept of permanent, basic personality structures, source traits, determining behaviour through changing moods and circumstances, emerges Cattell's concept of personality (1965). He defines it thus: 'Personality is what determines behaviour in a defined situation and a defined mood.'

The Sixteen Personality Factors Questionnaire. Cattell and his associates have developed a test to measure the sixteen most important of these source traits; it is usually referred to as the 16 P.F. test. A full account of the test is given in Cattell (1965), and in the 16 P.F. *Handbook.* Here we will briefly examine the first four factors to illustrate the nature of Cattell's account of personality. These sixteen source traits may be seen in terms of continuums or dimensions along which individuals vary. An individual possesses a trait to a greater or lesser degree, and the descriptions Cattell adopts apply most meaningfully at the extremes. Most people, for example, are around average intelligence, and intelligence test scores are normally distributed about this average. So descriptions such as 'able to perceive remote and complex logical relationships' versus 'has great difficulty in following any simple discussion' apply to people on the extremes of this continuum of intelligence. Cattell describes the sixteen factors in these bipolar terms, and the following tables are from the *Handbook* (1970 edition).

TABLE 2.1 *Source trait factor A*
(reprinted from Cattell and Eber, *Sixteen Personality Factor Handbook*)

low score		high score
SIZOTHYMIA	*v.*	AFFECTOTHYMIA
(*reserved, detached, critical, aloof, stiff*)		(*warmhearted, outgoing, easygoing, participating*)
critical	*v.*	good natured, easygoing
stands by his own ideas	*v.*	ready to co-operate, likes to participate
cool, aloof	*v.*	attentive to people
precise, objective	*v.*	softhearted, casual
distrustful, sceptical	*v.*	trustful
rigid	*v.*	adaptable, careless, 'goes along'
cold	*v.*	warmhearted
prone to sulk	*v.*	laughs readily

Cattell's first source trait, factor A, is a continuum labelled at the one end, sizothymia, and at the other, affectothymia. In Table 2.1, and the following two tables, other more popular terms for similar behaviours are given, those at the top being more characteristic than those at the bottom.*

TABLE 2.2 *Source trait factor C*
(reprinted from Cattell and Eber, *Sixteen Personality Factor Handbook*)

low score		high score
EMOTIONAL INSTABILITY OR EGO WEAKNESS	*v.*	HIGHER EGO STRENGTH
(*affected by feelings, emotionally less stable, easily upset, changeable*)		(*emotionally stable, mature, faces reality, calm*)
gets emotional when frustrated	*v.*	emotionally mature
changeable in attitudes and interests	*v.*	stable, constant in interests
easily perturbed	*v.*	calm
evasive of responsibilities, tending to give up	*v.*	does not let emotional needs obscure realities of a situation, adjusts to facts
worrying	*v.*	unruffled
gets into fights and problem situations	*v.*	shows restraint in avoiding difficulties

* Factors A, C, and E, in Tables 2.1–2.3, are from the 16 P.F. *Handbook*. Reproduced by permission of the copyright owner, the Institute for Personality and Ability Testing, 1602 Coronado Drive, Champaign, Illinois, U.S.A.

Cattell's factor B is that of general intelligence, and we will examine this in the next chapter. Factor C is a continuum with emotional instability or ego weakness descriptive of one end and higher ego strength descriptive of the other.

Cattell's source trait next in importance is factor E, a continuum with submissiveness describing one extreme, and with the other extreme termed dominance or ascendance. Cattell lists the sixteen factors in the order of importance established by his research. This means these first few factors account for many of the differences in individual behaviour.

TABLE 2.3 *Source trait factor E*
(reprinted from Cattell and Eber, *Sixteen Personality Factor Handbook*)

low score		high score
SUBMISSIVENESS	*v.*	DOMINANCE OR ASCENDANCE
(*obedient, mild, easily led, docile, accommodating*)		(*assertive, aggressive, competitive, stubborn*)

submissive	*v.*	assertive
dependent	*v.*	independent-minded
considerate, diplomatic	*v.*	stern, hostile
expressive	*v.*	solemn
conventional, conforming	*v.*	unconventional, rebellious
easily upset by authority	*v.*	headstrong
humble	*v.*	admiration demanding

Cattell divides source traits into three modalities or categories; they are abilities, dynamic traits, and temperament or general personality traits. Intelligence falls into the ability category. A dynamic trait is essentially motivational, and provides the drive, push and direction of behaviour. Any interest, such as in music or business, is a dynamic trait. 'Ambition', 'radicalism', 'motherliness' are potentially dynamic traits, since they are all sources of behaviour and action. The temperament or general personality trait is expressive and stylistic, determining the manner and form of what the individual does. In fact, we have already made this last distinction in our discussion of Allport.

Types of Traits
The division of traits into those that determine what we can do, such as intelligence, and those that are motivational and determine what we wish to do, such as an interest in music, is an old one. It

has been with psychology many years. Rodger and Cavanagh (1962) point out that other ways of making this distinction have been as talents and temperament, abilities and interests, aptitudes and preferences, and skills and attitudes. They label the same categories as capacities and inclinations.

In the Job Description Card proposed above (p. 22) the same division is made, but from a different viewpoint. The 'duties and responsibilities most often found difficult by job occupants' are concerned with job difficulties which we might usefully see, for the time being, as primarily a function of the individual's ability or capacity type traits. Similarly 'what do people like about the job' and 'what do people dislike about the job' may usefully be viewed as primarily related to the individual's interest, inclination, and motivational type traits. Rodger and Cavanagh (1962) suggest that the individual's capacities (ability traits) and the job's difficulties determine the individual's satisfactoriness to his employer. It is his inclination (motivational traits) and the job likes and dislikes that determine the individual's personal satisfaction. These ideas are expressed in Table 2.4.

TABLE 2.4 *Model of Relationship between Traits and Work*
(see Rodger and Cavanagh, 1962)

Types of traits	*Headings in job analysis*	*Work behaviour*
ability ——	difficulties ——	satisfactoriness to employer
motivational ——	likes and dislikes ——	satisfaction to employee

The model is simple and has proved very useful. We will subsequently indicate what appear to be its limitations. It clearly illustrates that implicit in the headings and categories of a job-analysis scheme are views or theories of both work and personality.

The Trait Approach in Guidance and Selection
Rodger and Cavanagh have stressed the usefulness of a trait type of analysis in occupational guidance and personnel selection. This conceptualizing of the individual as a 'bundle of qualities' inter-acting with each other provides the personnel selector and occupational guider with a framework for the data, observations, ideas and insights that are gathered by tests, interview, questionnaire, and the other assessment techniques. The distinction between capacities and inclinations, between, that is, Cattell's ability and dynamic source traits, adds to the usefulness of the trait analysis.

What then are its limitations in guidance and selection? First, the concept of personality as a bundle of qualities leads to our viewing it as a rather static and fixed entity. Seeing personality this way we might underestimate the effect of the immediate environment on behaviour. Adopting a trait approach we may underestimate the relevance to behaviour of the individual's roles.

Perhaps a more significant limitation is the reduced emphasis a trait analysis gives to motivation, which normally is so central to any explanation of behaviour. Two people of similar ability are placed in identical jobs. One works purposefully and makes a success of the job; the other hardly applies himself and is quite inadequate. Obviously an analysis of their different motivations is likely to provide a useful explanation. A trait analysis could cope, giving an account in terms of differences in interests, one person being high, the other low on the interest relevant to the job. Alternatively we might suggest they differ in a general trait of ambition. Both are adequate explanations, and both are probably capable of measurement and prediction. But by expressing in such a static term, that of trait, something so dynamic and all-pervasive in behaviour as motivation, they tend to underplay its importance. A Maslow approach, with need hierarchy as the basic dimension, gives greater emphasis to the force of motivation.

Thirdly, the capacities and inclinations type of division may have its dangers. To see adequate performance of job x as related to y level of ability, or even to y level of ability plus interest z, is to think in additive or mechanistic terms. Performance results from a more dynamic and interactional process. With high levels of motivation an individual may compensate for an apparent lack of ability. The possession of certain abilities can cause the individual to acquire related interests. The limits which ability places on performance may be very broad—as good training has often shown.

Finally, and related to this point on training, a trait approach may fail to recognize the modifiability of behaviour, in the adult as well as the adolescent and infant. It needs to take account of learning. In fact developments in trait theory and research are occurring along these lines.

Predictive and Construct Validity
Do personality theories predict? For example, using tests and interview, and adopting a trait or any other theoretical model,

would it be possible to forecast the suitability or unsuitability of this school-leaver for scientific work? In subsequent chapters we will provide evidence that such predictions are possible within limits.

At the commencement of this chapter we suggested that knowing why relationships exist, for example between job record and personal stability, is better than mere knowledge that the relationship does exist. Another way of expressing the same idea is that construct validity should prove more useful than predictive validity.

Predictive validity, sometimes unkindly referred to as crude empiricism, exists where we simply know that one set of data is predictive of other data. For example, using statistical correlational techniques we might find that the speed at which a man puts fifty matches into a matchbox correlates with his subsequent success as a riveter. His speed with the matches is predictive, therefore. If he is fast with the matches he is likely to make a good riveter. If he is slow with them, he will be a poor riveter. Predictive validity is most useful, and many tests and techniques operate on this basis. But unless we know why the correlation exists we cannot extrapolate and generalize further. We cannot say under what other similar or rather different circumstances the relationship will continue to exist, and when it will cease to hold. Would the matchbox test be predictive with older men, or with women, or with immigrants? Would it still prove useful with a slightly different type of riveting, or even with drilling? We cannot attempt to improve the predictive usefulness of the test, because we do not know why it predicts and, therefore, do not know in what way it should be changed.

We are able to extrapolate, extend our generalizations, improve on our original predictions, only if we have an explanation for the relationships. Construct or concept validity is validated prediction, where the data are interpreted and explained in terms of a theory or concept such as intelligence or introversion. Adopting this theory of personality, we might make specific predictions on the basis of test scores that school-leavers with such-and-such a score will be successful in this type of occupation. Employing construct validity in this way, the process becomes essentially that of deriving predictions or hypotheses from the underlying theory or concept, and then testing them. Testing the predictions and hypotheses against the data we gather is, in fact, a validating or rejecting of the underlying theory and construct. The process of construct validity, theoretical explanation → hypotheses and predictions → empirical data, is the process of scientific method.

REFERENCES

Allport, G. W. (1961), *Pattern and Growth in Personality*, Holt, Rinehart & Winston.

Cattell, R. B. (1965), *The Scientific Analysis of Personality*, Penguin.

Cattell, R. B. and Eber, H. W., *Handbook for the Sixteen Personality Factor Questionnaire*, Institute for Personality and Ability Testing.

Cattell, R. B., Eber, H. W. and Tatsuoka, M. M. (1970 edition), *Handbook for the Personality Factor Questionnaire in Clinical, Educational, Industrial and Research Psychology*, for use with all forms of the test.

Centers, R. (1948), 'Motivational aspects of occupational stratification', *J. soc. Psychol.*, 28, 187–217.

Hall, C. S. and Lindzey, G. (1957), *Theories of Personality*, Wiley.

Heller, F. A., and Porter, L. W. (1966), 'Perception of managerial needs and skills in two national samples', *Occup. Psychol.*, 40, 1–14.

Likert, R. (1961), *New Patterns of Management*, McGraw-Hill.

Likert, R. (1967), *The Human Organization*, McGraw-Hill.

Maslow, A. H. (1943), 'A theory of human motivation', *Psychol. Rev.*, 50, 370–96.

Maslow, A. H. (1954), *Motivation and Personality*, Harper & Row (chap. 5).

McGregor, D. M. (1960), *The Human Side of Enterprise*, McGraw-Hill.

Porter, L. W. (1961), 'A study of perceived need satisfactions in bottom and middle management jobs,' *J. appl. Psychol.*, 45.

Rodger, A. and Cavanagh, P. (1962), 'Personnel selection and vocational guidance', in *Society: Problems and Methods of Study*, ed. A. T. Welford, Routledge & Kegan Paul.

Wickert, F. R. (1951), 'Turnover and employees' feelings of ego-involvement in the day-to-day operation of a company', *Pers. Psychol.*, 4, 185–97.

CHAPTER 3

Human Abilities

Introduction and Overview

A trait analysis of personality proves useful in guidance and selection. There is evidence to show that it works; that is, there is evidence for its predictive validity, where predictions have been based on specific trait concepts. And with the development of trait theory and research, we grow in knowledge of why it works. With trait explanations of why certain people succeed, fail, like, dislike certain jobs and occupations, we will have a form of construct validity.

People do tend to see each other as bundles of qualities, anyway. Using a trait approach makes communication with the average manager easier in a guidance and selection situation. If the approach is valid, this provides an additional reason for adopting it.

Rodger and Cavanagh (1962) suggest that in guidance and selection we should be searching for 'general and persisting traits'. We might, for example, interview a young man for a job where he meets customers much of the time, and find him inhibited by shyness during the interview. If we think his shyness is peculiar to that selection interview situation, we need not concern ourselves. But if we feel he would always tend to be shy when other people are present, that his shyness is a 'general' trait, then it becomes more important. Similarly, if we are advising a school-leaver on choice of careers and he expresses an interest in things technical, before taking this seriously we would need to be confident the interest was likely to last—that it was a persisting trait. Thus Rodger and Cavanagh (1962): 'Traits of marked generality and persistence are, for selectors and advisers, characteristics of the utmost importance. They provide the main foundations for attempts to explain and forecast human behaviour.'

These general and persisting traits might usefully be seen in terms of Cattell's concept of source traits, examined in the previous chapter, and which Cattell divides into three categories, dynamic traits, temperamental traits, and abilities. In this chapter we are concerned with traits of ability—or talents, aptitudes, skills, capacities, as they have also been termed. This chapter explicitly adopts, therefore, a trait formulation of personality. We will start by referring again to faculty psychology. We will then examine the idea of correlation and the theories of ability which have emerged from statistical techniques of correlation—Spearman's two-factor, hierarchical group factor, Thurstone's primary mental abilities, and finally Guilford's structure-of-intellect model. Part of the following chapter will be concerned with the other sorts of traits, the dynamic, temperament, interests, preferences, attitudes, and inclinations type. The emphasis in both chapters is on a nomothetic analysis.

We adopt a historical approach here since in this chapter it helps to an understanding of relevant theory. We also indicate the applications of each theory in guidance and selection, which serves to relate closely theory and practice.

FACULTY PSYCHOLOGY

Theory

Faculty psychology was popular in the middle and later half of the nineteenth century, and is now abandoned. We have already referred to it in our discussion of Allport, but we re-introduce it here since it provides a basis for understanding subsequent explanations of human ability. According to the doctrine of faculties a man has a large number of faculties which enable him to function and to perform a repertoire of behaviour—a faculty of memory, of imagination, of artistic aptitude, etc. Usually it was thought each of these faculties was located in a special area of the brain.

The most well known of the faculty schools was Gall's phrenology which recognized many faculties such as an amativeness propensity, a combativeness propensity, and a conscientiousness sentiment. According to phrenology the presence, absence, or degree of any faculty was indicated by bumps on the appropriate parts of the skull. So a phrenologist could find out something about a man's personality by feeling 'the bumps'. Vernon (1961) suggests more realistically that 'the bumps on a man's skull tell you more about his wife's character than his own'.

The theory passed into academic history. After all, it said nothing—simply, that you remembered things because you had a memory faculty. Its supporters produced no evidence that faculties existed at all. If such faculties did exist, what evidence was there that they were independent of each other? For example, how do we know that my verbal reasoning faculty, assuming there is such a thing, is a different thing from my mathematical faculty? One faculty might be responsible for my verbal reasoning and my mathematical performance, which are both merely aspects of a more general, underlying 'faculty'.

Later the idea that faculties were based in certain areas of the brain received a severe blow from research on electrical stimulation of the brain. As Eysenck (1953) remarks, 'it was rather damaging to the claims of phrenologists to find that when the "area of amorousness" was stimulated the patient did not burst forth with lustful cries in pursuit of the nurses, but merely wiggled his big toe'.

Practical Applications for Occupational Guidance and Personnel Selection

In spite of the demise of faculty psychology, its ghost still walks. The assumption that faculties were independent of each other led to a sort of compensatory theory. The idea was that if someone is academically weak, he will be good at practical things; if he is not good with his head, he will be good with his hands. If he tends to be slow, he will make up for it by being accurate. If he is weak at figures, he will probably have a flair for languages. Such a 'compensatory theory' did not necessarily follow from faculty psychology. But if we regard faculties as independent of each other and hope that nature, God, or the environment goes in for some form of equitable distribution of faculties among the population, then this sort of compensation is both possible and likely.

Such a view of human ability as that of the faculty school suggests that the individual's behaviour is the result of his separate faculties. Adopting such a theory, guidance and selection become a process of determining which of these many faculties are required for various jobs and occupations, of assessing an individual's faculties, and then matching the two.

CORRELATION AND FACTOR ANALYSIS

In 1904 Charles Spearman published an article entitled ' "General intelligence": objectively determined and measured'. The application in psychology of statistical correlation techniques was with us. Now, the basic contention of faculty psychology that the many faculties were independent of each other could be examined.

For example, a faculty psychologist might explain mathematical performance by a number faculty, and performance in written work in terms of a verbal faculty. To check this the investigator could give tests of arithmetic and vocabulary to a number of children, and compare the two sets of results. In Figures 3.1–3.5 we give as graphs some of the different types of results he might possibly obtain. Both tests are scored on the basis of a possible 100.

The fictitious data plotted on the graph in Figure 3.1 state that the student who scored highest on mathematics also obtained the highest vocabulary mark; the student second on mathematics was second on vocabulary; and so on, with all the children having the

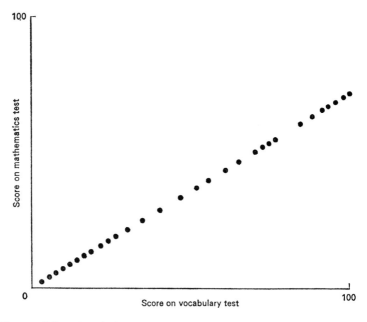

Fig. 3.1 The plot of children's mathematics and vocabulary test scores, indicating a perfect positive correlation of the sets of results

same position on one set of results as on the other. The correspondence or correlation on the two sets of scores is perfect. It would be reasonable to suggest with such data that performance on the mathematics test and on the vocabulary test are in some way related, and may indeed be a function of the same 'faculty'.

In Figure 3.2 there is still a correspondence or positive correlation between the two sets of scores, but it is by no means perfect. Those students who do well on the mathematics tend to do well also on the vocabulary; those who are about average on one are about average on the other; those who do badly on one seem likely to do so on the other. As with Figure 3.1, we could reasonably make the

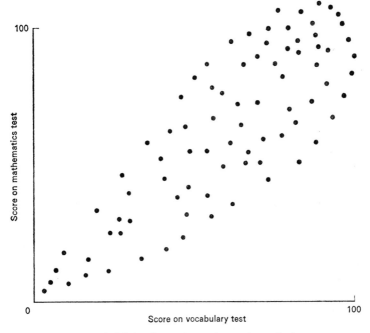

Fig. 3.2 The plot of children's mathematics and vocabulary test scores, indicating some degree of positive correlation in the two sets of results

assumption that the same faculty is involved in some way in performance on the two different tests, though here to a limited extent only.

The graph of Figure 3.3 indicates an absence of any correspondence or correlation between the two sets of scores. In the absence of a correlation it seems reasonable to assume that the two tasks, the mathematics and the vocabulary tests, involve different and unrelated faculties.

A correspondence in the two sets of results might be found where the mathematics scores go in an opposite direction to the vocabulary marks. The correlation would be a negative one, and

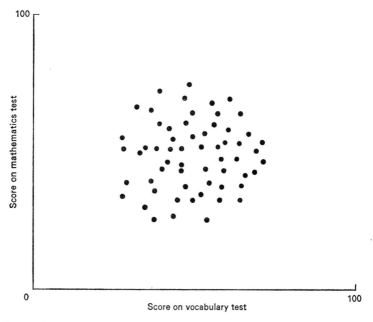

Fig. 3.3 The plot of children's mathematics and vocabulary test scores, indicating an absence of correlation in the two sets of results

the graph of Figure 3.4 plots data that tend to a negative correlation. The data indicate that where a child scores high on mathematics he will tend to score low at vocabulary, and vice versa. Such a correlation may be as significant, meaningful, and predictive as a positive correlation.

The graph of Figure 3.5 plots a negative correlation which is perfect.

In the above five figures we have merely represented on graphs possible relationships between two fictitious sets of scores. With the development of a measure of correlation, a correlation coefficient, it became possible to calculate the size of the correlation, and to determine how statistically significant and meaningful it was. The coefficient is calculated to vary from $+1.0$ where the sets of scores correlate positively and perfectly, as in Figure 3.1, through 0.0 where no relationship exists, as in Figure 3.3, to -1.0 where the correlation is again perfect, but is now negative, as in Figure 3.5.

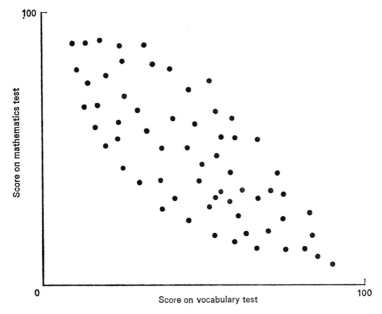

Fig. 3.4 The plot of children's mathematics and vocabulary test scores, indicating a degree of negative correlation between the two sets of results

In 1904 Spearman brought such statistical tools to the study of human ability. He raised the question of how we might interpret findings such as those plotted here in Figure 3.2, in the following way:

> Let us, then, consider the extent of connection between two series of things implied by this sole fact of their presenting a numerical correlation with one another; such a correspondence, when beyond the range of mere chance coincidence, may be forthwith assumed to indicate and measure something common to both series in question.

Using such techniques, investigators could obtain a number of correlations, as in Table 3.1. The data in this table are extracted from a study of over six-hundred ten-year-old schoolchildren, tested in elementary school subjects (Burt, 1939). It became possible by means of methods of what is termed factor analysis to calculate the size and extent of what is common to such sets of correlations. In Table 3.1, for example, where performances on all the tests correlate positively, a factor seems common to all the

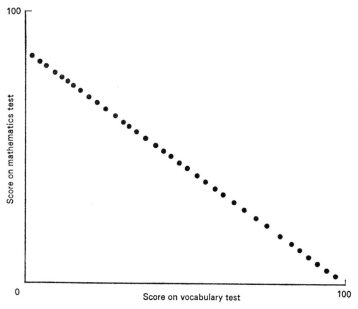

Fig. 3.5 The plot of children's mathematics and vocabulary test scores, indicating a perfect negative correlation between the two sets of results

TABLE 3.1 *Correlations between the performances of 613 children on a number of scholastic tests* (Burt, 1939)

TESTS	*Composition*	*Reading (comprehension)*	*Handwork*	*Drawing*
Composition		+0·723	+0·277	+0·263
Reading (comprehension)			+0·268	+0·198
Handwork				+0·521
Drawing				

66

test scores. Some factor, say factor x, is present, and factor analysts attempt to calculate the extent to which it is common in the four test performances.

But a similarity between two or more sets of scores may be the result of their having more than one factor in common. For example, certain crops may grow more plentifully in the south of a continent than in its northern region mainly because of the differences in climate. But there are further variations in fertility even within the south, partly because the quality of soil varies over the area. Over the whole continent these two factors operate, together with others, to produce a variation in the output of crops. In Table 3.1 the composition and reading comprehension correlate more highly with each other than either do with the other two tests. Similarly handwork and drawing correlate more highly with each other. This suggests that there is some factor common to all four tests, and in addition there is a second factor common only to the first two, and a third factor common only to the handwork and drawing. Factor analysis can calculate the size of the factor common to them all, of the factor common only to composition and reading comprehension, of the factor common only to the handwork and drawing, and what—if anything—is specific to each test.

The statistical techniques of correlation and factor analysis provided a new concept of human ability. They substituted these statistically derived factors for the rather armchair-derived faculties. This notion of ability is clearly stated by Vernon (1940): 'It [an ability] implies the existence of a group or category of performances which correlate highly with one another, and which are relatively distinct from (i.e. give low correlations with) other performances.' The reader may study correlation in any standard statistical textbook and factor analysis in Burt (1944) and Thomson (1951). It is essential to appreciate that many of our concepts of human ability, of personality traits and factors, many theories, much of the empirical data on personality, derive from such an approach to the study of behaviour. Cattell's sixteen Personality Factors, which we referred to in the previous chapter, are an example, based as they are on the factor-analytic approach. The work of Spearman, Burt, Vernon, Thurstone, Guilford, and many others similarly has a statistical basis.

SPEARMAN'S TWO-FACTOR THEORY

Theory

Spearman used correlational techniques with data from children's work at school, and in the 1904 article concludes 'that all branches of intellectual activity have in common one fundamental function (or group of functions), whereas the remaining or specific elements of the activity seem in every case to be wholly different from that in all the others'. This constitutes the basic statement of two-factor theory. There is, it suggests, one factor or fundamental function common to 'all branches of intellectual activity', and a second factor which is the element specific to a given situation. If a student learns Latin, maths, English, there is this one factor or general ability common to learning all of them; and there are these other factors, one which is specifically useful in learning Latin, another useful with maths, another with English, and they are not connected.

Spearman later developed and restated this in *The Abilities of Man* (1927):

> The one part has been called the 'general factor' and denoted by the letter g; it is so named because, although varying freely from individual to individual, it remains the same for any one individual in respect of all the correlated abilities. The second part has been called the 'specific factor' and denoted by the letter s. It not only varies from individual to individual, but even for any one individual from each ability to another.

Spearman's general factor or *g* is what we would popularly refer to as general intelligence. Spearman regarded a seeing of relationships as essentially characteristic of this *g* factor, 'the education of relations and correlates'.

The Abilities of Man has a section entitled, 'Discrepancies between theory and observation'. Spearman is simply saying that there are facts for which his theory does not quite account. It is important to appreciate the discrepancies he discusses under the heading, 'Overlap between specific factors', because hierarchical group factor theory emerges from Spearman's two-factor explanation and the problem posed for it by this specific overlap.

We take three tests, two very similar, the first involving the cancelling of all the a's on a printed page, and the second involving the cancelling of all the e's. The third test is, say, one of

68

geometry. Accepting Spearman's *g* we would expect to find some correlation between performances on all three tests, if a large number of schoolchildren did them. We find this, and find also, as common sense might predict, a greater correlation between the two cancelling tests than either has with the geometry test. Figure 3.6 gives a simple representation of this.

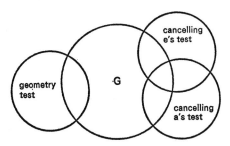

Fig. 3.6 A representation of the *g* factor common to performance on three tests, and of a further commonness or overlap between two cancelling tests

Spearman found that when he had allowed for (what is termed) the *g* loading of tests, there would still be a higher correlation between some tests than between others. It was this he saw as the overlap between specific factors, as here the two cancelling tests have something in common over and above what they share with the geometry and which can be explained in terms of a general factor of intelligence. Is this overlap, he asked, the result simply of the similar nature of specific tasks? But, as he points out, where do you draw the line 'between those performances which are and those which are not "quite different" '?

Early in his research work Spearman had found an overlap between the memorizing of syllables and of numbers. He had suggested (1904) that this might 'indicate the possibility of a rather extensive group of performances being so nearly related, that they might be gathered together as a more or less unitary ability under the concept of "memorization" '. Since this early suggestion he had investigated further the extensiveness of such broad specific factors, and in 1927 says: 'Overlapping specific factors have since often been spoken of as "group factors". They may be defined as those which occur in more than one but less than all of any given set of abilities.'

The question remained, therefore, of whether a simple two-factor model adequately accounted for these broader, specific factors—for types of ability less general than g, but not just specific to one task? This query about the Spearman model led to the hierarchical group factor explanation.

Practical Applications for Occupational Guidance and Personnel Selection

We will base our discussion of the relevance for guidance and selection of two-factor theory on Cyril Burt's 1924 article. It would seem from the model that with regard to ability general intelligence is the primary consideration in a guidance or selection situation. Burt quite simply says that 'of all psychological capacities, general intelligence is the easiest to measure; it is also the most significant for the purposes of vocational guidance'. He is concerned only with guidance, but much of what he says is relevant also to selection. General intelligence, whether evaluated by test, interview, school record, work history or whatever, determines the general level of occupation for the individual. Burt states this as follows:

> It is probable that for most occupations there is an optimal range of intelligence with an upper limit as well as a lower. One of the main tasks, therefore, of vocational guidance will be this: to draft each child into a job which corresponds as precisely as possible with his own level of intelligence, and requires neither a greater nor a less amount of mental capacity than he actually possesses.

It would be possible to stratify occupations and jobs according to the level of general intelligence the job occupant needs. We might do this simply, in terms of top 10 per cent, upper 20 per cent, middle 40 per cent, lower 20 per cent, and bottom 10 per cent, where placing a job in the first category means that only an individual whose intelligence level is in the top 10 per cent of the population could manage the work. With such a stratification scheme, measuring the individual's intelligence in guidance or selection immediately suggests his appropriate occupational level.

Burt in his article lays the foundations for a more differentiated stratification of occupations by intelligence. He derives this from data on intelligence quotient scores of people already in occupations. In the following two examples the 'mental ratios' referred to are I.Q. scores:

Higher professional (doctors, lawyers, lecturers, senior civil servants, higher business executives): mental ratios of above 150.

Lower professional (elementary teachers, high-grade clerks): mental ratios of about 130–50.

A second consideration the two-factor model would propose in guidance and selection is the matter of specific factors. We must assess an individual on the specific factors known to be relevant to the specific occupation or job we are considering. A series of money computations might measure a specific factor relevant to a task in accountancy, or an assembly test might assess some specific factor relevant to a part of this fitting job. But it would be wrong, according to the theory, to refer to ability with figures or to mechanical aptitude.

Burt suggests considerations other than those that relate to ability and two-factor theory. We need to consider the individual's 'temperamental qualities'—what we have previously referred to as dynamic and temperamental traits, interests, inclinations, etc.— and which largely determine a suitable type of occupation. We can develop from this a scheme for use in a guidance situation, based on a classification of jobs by level and type, as in Table 3.2, adapted from Rodger and Cavanagh (1962).

Specific factors relevant to individual jobs would be categorized in the appropriate boxes. A similar scheme could be adopted for personnel selection with greater emphasis on specific factors, on attainments, such as educational qualifications and occupational skills, and with less emphasis on interests and 'temperamental' factors.

TABLE 3.2 *A scheme of occupational classification by level and type* (adapted from Rodger and Cavanagh, 1962)

Type

Level of general intelligence		Office	Practical-constructional	Active-outdoor	People	Artistic
Top	10%					
Upper	20%					
Middle	40%					
Lower	20%					
Bottom	10%					

HIERARCHICAL GROUP FACTOR THEORY

This model of human ability was developed through the techniques of factor analysis principally by British investigators such as Cyril Burt and P. E. Vernon. We will first indicate its development from the two-factor explanation, briefly state the theory, then examine the model and its implications in more detail.

Group Factors

Spearman was troubled by the problem of 'specific overlap'. Subsequent research led Burt, Vernon, and others to suggest that such 'specific overlaps' were to be accounted for by types of ability which were not highly specific, but common to many situations, though not nearly so common and general in their functions as general intelligence. They were termed group factors. The data in Table 3.3, from the same source as Table 3.1 (Burt, 1939), gives a pattern of test correlations typically found.

The first three tests correlate more highly with each other than they do with the remaining three. Similarly the last three tests correlate more highly with each other than any of them do with the first three. Removing the intelligence loading from all six tests still leaves the first three with something in common, and similarly still leaves the second three with something in common. What remains here, when the g loading is gone, are the two most important of the group factors, namely the verbal-numerical-educational ($v:ed$) and the practical-mechanical-spatial-physical ($k:m$). Other group factors of less generality have been found, such as the artistic and musical.

Basic Theory

The theoretical model that emerged was characterized by hierarchical structure. At the summit of the hierarchy is the highly generalized factor, of prime importance, general intelligence (g). Remove this factor from an analysis of performance, and the remaining correlations fall mainly into the two groups we have just referred to, $v:ed$ and $k:m$, which are known as the major group factors.

Further analysis reveals the existence of differentiation within the major group factors. In certain performances, when g, $v:ed$, and $k:m$ were removed from the analysis, further correlations were

TABLE 3.3 Correlations between the performances of 613 children on six different tests (Burt, 1939)

TESTS	Composition	Reading (comprehension)	Science	Handwork	Drawing	Writing (quality)
Composition		+0·723	+0·461	+0·277	+0·263	+0·231
Reading (comprehension)			+0·426	+0·268	+0·198	+0·272
Science				+0·281	+0·037	+0·290
Handwork					+0·521	+0·498
Drawing						+0·403
Writing (quality)						

found, and the minor group factors postulated to account for these. Removing $v:ed$ leaves correlations accounted for by the minor group factors v and n. Removing $k:m$ leaves correlations accounted for by three minor group factors of mechanical information, spatial and manual. We will subsequently examine these.

There still remained variations in performance apparently specific to a task, which seemed the result of much-reduced versions of Spearman's specific factors. Table 3.4, adapted from Vernon (1961), illustrates this hierarchy of ability, but includes only those major and minor group factors just described.

TABLE 3.4 *Hierarchy of ability factors* (adapted from Vernon, 1961)

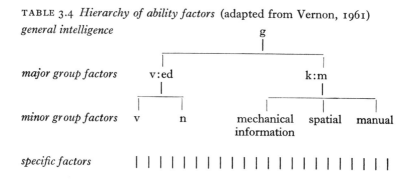

Major and Minor Group Factors

To describe the group factors, like describing intelligence or any other statistically derived concept, may be slightly misleading. A description attempts to say what a thing is or appears to be. The basis for an understanding of any factor-analytically derived concept resides in what performance it correlates with. A description of the concept follows from this. We will, therefore, relate our account of a group factor to test and other performances with which it tends to correlate.

Major Group Factor, v:ed, and Related Minor Group Factors. Verbal-educational-numerical, or $v:ed$, seems to be a general ability with language and number. This implies a relationship between language and number. Both are primarily symbolic activities. And one finds (Schiller, 1934) that tests of arithmetic reasoning and arithmetic computation correlate highly with a reading and a verbal intelligence test. As we have indicated on Table 3.3, composition, reading comprehension and science invariably have a *v:ed* loading.

This major group factor subdivides into two minor group factors, and not surprisingly one is concerned with languages and the other with number: *v*, concerned with language, is relevant to tests of vocabulary, spelling and comprehension; *n*, concerned with number, relates to tests of mechanical arithmetic and arithmetic comprehension. Within each the unity is considerable. Thus with army recruits (Vernon, 1961) tests of verbal ability, spelling, and dictation correlate about equally highly with each other. Part of the verbal ability test gave two words, and asked the testee to give a third word which rhymed with the first and meant the same as the second—thus 'bat', 'stout', and the required word was 'fat'. The test entailed a good vocabulary and verbal fluency, which might not be expected to correlate as highly with the spelling and dictation as it in fact did.

Major Group Factor, k:m, and Related Minor Group Factors. The factor *k:m* seems to involve the comprehension of spatial and mechanical relationships. 'It would appear to be', says Vernon (1961), 'not so much a positive practical ability as an aggregate of all non-symbolic capacities.' Numbers and languages are symbolic since they only have the meaning we care to ascribe to them. But activities such as hitting a nail with a hammer or pulling a lever are non-symbolic, since their significance can be directly grasped and is not dependent on any meaning we give to them.

What are the behaviours or tests that correlate with each other to constitute this major group factor? Raven's Progressive Matrices, the National Institute of Industrial Psychology Form Relations, and the typical 'squares' test, all appear to entail a direct perceptual manipulation of shapes and patterns, and are among the sorts of tests that intercorrelate to make up this group factor. A typical item in a squares-test requires the testee to divide a shape, such as Figure 3.7, into two pieces which can be fitted together to make a square, using only one straight line. Such *k:m* tests, the matrices, form relations, squares, etc., do invariably have a loading of intelligence.

Other types of tests with *k:m* loading are the various manipulative and assembly tests. Tests involving an appreciation of mechanical

75

relationships, such as the Morrisby Mechanical, usually have a *k:m* loading.

The factor *k:m* divides into minor group factors, mechanical information, spatial and manual. The *m* or mechanical or mechanical information factor involves an appreciation of mechanical principles, and seems related to factors of experience,

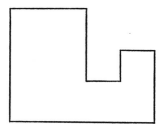

Fig. 3.7 In this squares-test the shape must be cut into two pieces by one straight line, so that the two pieces can be fitted together to make a square

training, and acquired information. A 'mechanical aptitude' test, such as the Morrisby, gives a measure of this factor, as also does a test of simple electrical and mechanical knowledge in certain situations.

The spatial factor, usually designated *k*, is concerned with the imaginative manipulation of shapes, as typically found in tests of the Progressive Matrices and squares sort. The manual or motor factor is small, and is involved in the actual physical manipulation of things. Pursuit and assembly tasks, and the various pegboard and other manual and finger dexterity tests entail, often only slightly, this motor factor.

General Points

Before relating the model to work, and to guidance and selection, a number of points need to be made. A theory may be seen as an elaborated hypothetical construct, as a system of general principles supported by a body of empirical data. But the supportive data are perceived in terms of the original principles, concepts, and constructs. This remains the case where the theory is based on a wealth of statistically derived findings. Statistical techniques of correlation and factor analysis perform certain quantitative operations on observed behaviours. Factor analysis does not tell us what the structure of ability is 'really' like, but provides one from a number of possible descriptions of it. Hierarchical group factor theory and the other statistically based theoretical models in this chapter are like any other theory, in that they attempt merely to explain what happens in terms of a set of laws or general principles. Vernon (1961), for example, says of his diagrammatic representation of the hierarchical structure of ability, which we have adapted for Table 3.4, that it is 'a hypothetical integration of all the factorial investigations that have been carried out, rather than an established fact'.

Emerging from this is the point that there exists a certain arbitrariness in the hierarchical model or, indeed, in any similarly derived model. There is no significant difference between a specific and a minor group factor, between a minor group factor and a major group factor. The difference is only quantitative, and one has to draw the line somewhere.

As with a computer, the data fed into the factor analysis largely determine what emerges. The absence of group factors in Spearman's work possibly results from his populations being small and mainly of brighter schoolchildren. So it becomes relevant that much of the empirical work that provided the basis for hierarchical theory comes from the field of education. One has to ask if the model provides a definitive account of human ability, or only describes that face of ability that presents itself in the educational situation. The model may possibly present only those aspects of ability that relate to academic performance, and so provide an inadequate account of personality factors relevant to success and failure in the employment field.

Another point is whether the hierarchical group factor theory assumes that ability is largely hereditarily or environmentally determined. The theory seems not necessarily to support one or the other viewpoint, though its protagonists may often have done so. Its concepts, and this applies also to the other theories discussed in this chapter, describe what is observed to operate, but make no necessary implication about how the structures originate. For example, the major group factor $v:ed$ may be cohesive and intercorrelating because of a hereditary and genetic basis. Alternatively, the common culture and similar education of Western society may work to produce a grouping of cognitive processes into a cohesive factor.

The hierarchical model, like two-factor theory and any explanation which postulates a broad, general factor, largely invalidates the compensatory theory of common thought. 'He's not good at his books, so he'll probably be clever with his hands.' At the same time there is some validity in the popular dichotomy between the academic and the practical, since they approximate to the two most important of the major group factors, $v:ed$ and $k:m$.

Finally, the overall importance of g may be modified not only by group and specific factors, but also by opportunity, practice, experience, and by the effects of interest and motivation which we will consider in the next chapter. For example, Mr Smith, the carpenter, is better at woodwork than Mr Jones, the manager, but as a schoolboy Jones showed more potential in the carpentry class than did Smith.

Abilities and Work
The following re-analysis of the hierarchical model in work terms is from Vernon (1961), who bases it partly on investigations during the 1939–45 war (Vernon and Parry, 1949). Vernon makes three general propositions, derived mainly from these studies in the armed forces but seemingly applicable in the field of civilian employment.

First, a very important determinant of occupational success is a general occupational ability which seems constituted of g, $v:ed$, and a motivational factor of some sort. The motivational factor, which we can classify as interests, dynamic personal dispositions, needs, source traits, or whatever, we will examine more fully in the next chapter. This general factor Vernon refers to here appears akin to Jaques's concept of capacity (1961), which is central to the model Jaques proposes as a basis for equitable payment.

Secondly, with the exception of $v:ed$ the major group factors play only a small part in job success. The $k:m$ complex, for example, is of limited importance and much of what the layman ascribes to a 'mechanical aptitude' is usually attributable to training, experience, interest, AND g.

The evidence suggests that anyone can learn any job provided he has sufficient g, interest, and no relevant physical disabilities—and is taught properly. The role of the major group factors is probably only supplementary. The writer's experience in guidance and selection situations illustrates the point. Individuals with low scores on tests of *k:m* but above average on intelligence tests successfully completed training in engineering trades such as fitting, milling, and grinding. Similarly individuals successfully completed training whose intelligence test scores appeared too low for a particular trade, but whose *k:m* scores had been above average.

Rodger (1952) clearly puts the position on group factors or special aptitudes, as he refers to them:

> It is, indeed, convenient to regard all special aptitudes as talents supplementary to general intelligence in certain restricted fields: they are available to 'help' the general capacity when material of a particular kind—mechanical, manual, words, figures, drawing, music—is being handled. They are rather like auxiliary engines, whose usefulness really depends on the extent to which the main engine is powerful and effective. Where the main engine is good, the scope for the use of auxiliaries is poor.

Thirdly, specific factors, and some minor group factors, may sometimes play an important part in work performance. One example is the specific factor, whatever it is, involved in adding up a row of figures, a task that will obviously be found in a cashier's job. Other examples are driving, a task found as a specific component in a number of jobs, and the finger control needed by the watch-mender.

Illustrative of Vernon's first proposition above is the experience in the armed forces with recruits who failed in a service job. When they were transferred to jobs at a similar level, and in which they expressed interest, they usually failed again. They normally were successful only when moved to jobs requiring a lower level of general ability and application. Vernon illustrates the second proposition by pointing out that men with a general engineering background in civilian life often did no better on naval ordnance or as engine room mechanics than did men with a non-engineering background, such as retailing. Similarly a mechanical background did not appear to be any advantage for radio and electrical mechanics. If a major group factor such as *k:m* was important, we might expect some sort of carry-over from civilian to service occupation. Such carry-over as there was proved small and tended to be of a specific nature. Such specific carry-over illustrates the third proposition. Vernon and Parry (1949) found, for example, that previous experience of driving as a civilian proved an excellent predictor of success as an army driver—better than any test. Such specific and directly relevant previous experience in other areas, with clerks, telegraphists, and some tradesmen, proved highly relevant to success in army jobs with similar tasks. Specific job factors seemed important.

The following diagram, Figure 3.8, taken with only minor modifications from Vernon (1961), illustrates this pattern of occupational abilities, still essentially a hierarchical structure.

Practical Applications for Occupational Guidance and Personnel Selection

What are the implications of adopting hierarchical group factor theory as a basis for guidance and selection? Our suggestions are based on Vernon (1961).

1. It is important to establish the level of general intelligence, since within limits this determines the appropriate level of occupation.

2. It is useful to measure the major group factors, $v{:}ed$ and $k{:}m$, and others like musicality, since these may supplement the workings of g. But other than $v{:}ed$, which supplements general intelligence over a broad area, the relevance of major and some minor group factors in many situations is limited, as Rodger again clearly indicates (1952):

> We can rarely, if ever, claim that a special aptitude is 'needed' in an occupation. All we can say, usually, is that *if*, in that occupation, special competence is required in understanding mechanical things, in manipulative operations, in using words, in handling figures, in drawing or in music, *then* the possession of relevant special aptitudes will help to make up deficiencies of other kinds, especially in general intelligence.

3. It is important to assess the relevance of the individual's previous experience to the job or occupation being considered. This may be seen as an aspect of specific factors.

4. It is important to evaluate motivational factors, whether they are of a general nature or are specific and relate to an individual

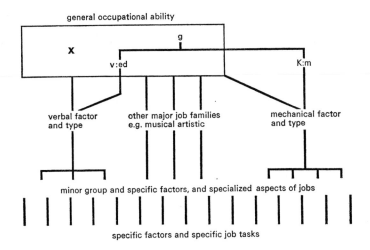

Fig. 3.8 Diagram of the hierarchical structure of occupational abilities (taken with minor changes from Vernon, 1961). X refers to a general motivational factor

job or occupation under consideration. This we will examine in the next chapter.

5. In a selection situation it is desirable to use work-sample tests to investigate any specific and minor group factors relevant to the job being filled. It is hardly possible to give an indefinite number of such tests for guidance purposes. In guidance it only becomes practicable to investigate such factors when the range of possible occupational choice has been considerably narrowed for the individual.

PRIMARY MENTAL ABILITIES

Theory
Thurstone (1938), in an article on the structure of human ability, reported that he had given 56 tests to 240 students of the University

of Chicago and factor-analysed the results using a technique different from that of most British investigators. On the basis of his data Thurstone suggested there was no such thing as *g*; there was no general ability running through all or most cognitive activities. Clearly this was a complete break with Spearman and Burt.

Thurstone suggested there were a number of distinct and separate mental abilities. He had found seven, possibly nine, of these main primary factors. His 1938 list—there were subsequent modifications—was as follows:

1. *V, verbal relations.* This ability was found in vocabulary tests, and tests of comprehension and reasoning involving language. An example in a V or verbal relations test might be: 'Which of the following relates to "hand" in the way "sock" relates to "foot"— cap, house, glove, finger?'

2. *N, number.* Simple arithmetic tests, involving arithmetic skill rather than reasoning with numbers, involved this ability. For example, testees were given straight additions which they had to indicate were right or wrong.

3. *S, spatial.* S ability was to be found in tests of visual-form relationships. For example, in Figure 3.9 one has to say which of the four forms in the second block are like the L in the first block, and which are different, that is, are backwards.

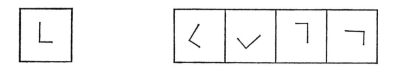

Fig. 3.9 Test of visual-form relationships

4. *W, word-fluency.* This seems involved where we need to think with words rapidly. Anagrams, finding words that rhyme with a given word, or simply listing in a specified time as many words as you can think of that begin with a certain letter. In the difference between W and V is the beginning of the distinction later developed by Hudson (1966), Guilford (1967) and others, between divergent and convergent thinking. For Thurstone a test

where you select a correct synonym from a list of words involves
V, and a test where you are asked to supply three synonyms for a
given word involves W.

5. *I, inductive reasoning.* This is found in simple tests of inductive
reasoning, but later Thurstone broadened this ability to R, a more
general reasoning factor. A typical item in an I test would require
the next letter to be given: b h c h d h e h ?

6. *M, (rote) memorizing.* This was involved in straightforward
tests of memory involving words, or numbers, or designs.

7. *P, perceptual factor.* Involved here was the perceptual
checking of numbers or shapes or words. Word and number
checking of this sort are typically found nowadays in any clerical
test. Speed is usually important in such a test. The following would
be a typical item in a P test: 'Underline the numbers with identical
digits to those in the first box.'

219		291	919	129	199	922	191

Thurstone regarded these abilities as distinct and separate,
and not in any way interdependent. So his theory of mental
abilities resembled in its structure, but not in its manner of
derivation, the faculty school of the nineteenth century. Its
critics slightingly referred to it as neo-faculty psychology.

Thurstone seemed to regard these mental abilities as fundamental and basic, in the sense of being irreducible. They were
the *primary* factors of human ability. Subsequent American
research has been characterized by an attempt to find such
irreducible and primary mental abilities.

Thurstone saw the mind working in a manner analogous to that
of the primary colours. The primary colours combine in a variety
of permutations to make all possible colours. Yellow and blue are
colours on their own, but they combine to give green. Similarly
the primary mental abilities, individually or in combination,
provide the basis for competence in all intellectual activities. The
intellect functions through a permutation of the primary mental
abilities.

Much of the work done subsequently in the United States

stems from Thurstone's original theoretical statement. We can see it as forking two ways. There has been further investigation of these primary mental abilities, with the result that Thurstone's original list has changed, and more particularly other factors, more detailed and specific, have been proposed. Guilford's structure-of-intellect model is one culmination of this sort of work.

The other development in America of Thurstone's original statement was towards the acceptance of some general factor of ability, and for this Thurstone himself was partly responsible. In subsequent research he found an overlap between factors. He explained such overlap and generality by the concept of 'second-order' factors. Originally he had suggested that Spearman's *g* factor, general intelligence, would have to be discarded, but later (1948) Thurstone stated: 'When the positive correlations between the primary factors are examined factorially, there appear second-order factors, and the most conspicuous of these second-order factors agrees well with Spearman's hypothesis.'

What Thurstone goes on to suggest is that we can explain intellectual performance in terms of these independent primary mental abilities, but that behind these separate factors is something they have in common. He continues:

> The primary factors represent different kinds of mental facilities such as several kinds of memory, several kinds of perceptual closure, several visualizing factors, and several verbal factors. These primary abilities may be regarded as media for the expression of intellect. . . . The second-order factors may represent parameters that are more central in character and more universal in the sense that they are not determined by the efficiency of each modality or imagery type.

What Thurstone is saying becomes clearer if we think of a structure of containers with paint in them (Figure 3.10). In the large central container is some wonderful, all-purpose paint that can be used for almost anything; this is a second-order factor. This paint, however, is not directly accessible to the painter, and comes to him only through pipes. These pipes are the primary factors, Thurstone's 'media for the expression of intellect'. But the paint, in the process of moving through the pipes, takes on a definite colour and can only be used for a limited range of objects. In other words, the intellect expresses itself in specific ways, as a number facility (N), a spatial facility (S), as word-fluency (W), etc.

In fact, some of the pipes may consist of a number of smaller pipes, which carry paint usable for a more limited range of articles. For example, there may be a main memory pipe, and in it are smaller pipes for visual memory, auditory memory, memory for ideas, etc. These again are primary factors but further reduced and more specific.

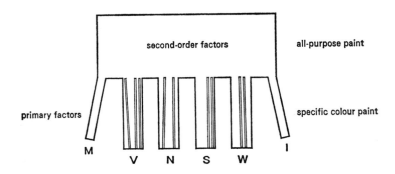

Fig. 3.10 Second-order and some primary factors represented as paint in containers

Practical Application for Occupational Guidance and Personnel Selection

The primary mental abilities model suggests that any job requires certain primary abilities to a specific degree. It is possible through job analysis to determine the specific requirements of a given job. In both guidance and selection we must evaluate the individual in terms of what primary mental abilities he has. In selection we then check these against the requirements of the vacant job. In guidance we consider the sorts of occupations that need the individual's kind of primary-ability profile.

In the United States the General Aptitude Test Battery has been developed within this theoretical framework. Among the aptitudes measured by the G.A.T.B. are verbal intelligence, numerical intelligence, spatial intelligence, clerical perception, form perception, manual dexterity, and finger dexterity. The three 'intelligence' aptitudes are not general ability factors such as is implied in the concept of g. Thus, a certain engineering maintenance or fitting job might need numerical intelligence, spatial intelligence, form perception, and manual dexterity. An accounts clerk position might require verbal and numerical intelligence, and clerical perception. What an occupational group or a specific job needs in reality can only be determined by research.

Within this theoretical structure a modified concept of general ability has sometimes been adopted, normally in terms of a general learning capacity or a scholastic aptitude. In such a theoretical context the approach is in the spirit of the axiom that there are more ways of killing a cat than choking her with cream. Thus Miss A could be a cashier because she has sufficient of this general ability; Miss B is low on general ability but could cope as a cashier because of her high level of clerical perception and number ability.

In both approaches special aptitudes and abilities are seen as important. Both approaches minimize the importance of a general factor and consequently neither adopts any concept of job levels such as that outlined by Burt.

GUILFORD'S STRUCTURE-OF-INTELLECT MODEL

Theory

The most well-known recent theoretical statement on human ability is Guilford's, fully given in *The Nature of Human Intelligence* (1967). All quotations from Guilford in this section are from his 1967 text. Reviewing American factor-analytic work on ability, he states that 'Almost no one reported finding a g factor', and later continues: 'Furthermore, there has been little or no tendency to find a few broader group factors (represented each by a larger number of tests) and a larger number of narrow group factors.' In denying, as he does here, the existence of a general ability, of major and minor group factors, Guilford is specifically rejecting the hierarchical group factor theory, and in fact any hierarchical view of ability, since he goes on to say, 'The factors appear to be about equally general in this respect, being strongly represented by small numbers, and relatively equal numbers, of tests.' Guilford regards the intellect as consisting of factors or abilities of more or less equal generality.

He sees the individual as operating intellectually in a number of ways. Different kinds of intellectual functioning are possible, so the intellect may be categorized in terms of the sort of cognitive operations involved. And on the basis of the relevant empirical data Guilford proposes five such operation categories: cognition, memory, divergent production, convergent production, and evaluation.

To illustrate the theory we will outline just three of these operations. Cognition Guilford defines 'as awareness, immediate discovery or rediscovery, or recognition of information in various forms: comprehension or understanding'. The two operations of divergent and convergent production are both essentially concerned with thinking, but their separation makes the distinction we have previously referred to. Divergent production embraces those thinking operations that are characterized by their fluency, their flexibility, and by their development and invention on existing information. It clearly relates to Thurstone's primary mental ability of word-fluency, and to Hudson's divergent thinking. Convergent production is concerned with those thinking operations which, on the basis of the provided information, converge on a unique right answer. This operation relates obviously to Hudson's convergent thinking, and to Thurstone's primary mental ability of inductive reasoning. The traditional intelligence test has frequently been accused of emphasizing convergent production, to the detriment of the divergent thinker.

Having categorized intellectual function according to the sorts of operations involved, Guilford states that such operations are affected by the nature of the information they deal with. Memorizing shapes is not the same operation as memorizing words, and involves a different intellectual ability. Guilford categorizes the content of the operation in four ways, according to the nature of the information involved. His categories are figural, symbolic, semantic, and behavioural.

By figural is meant shapes and patterns. Content is symbolic when signs and symbols are used to denote some other thing; numbers would be symbolic content. Semantic content is where words are used. Some intellectual performance which would be explained, in hierarchical group factor, by *v:ed*, is accounted for by the structure-of-intellect model in terms of those intellectual abilities behind any operation with semantic content. The behavioural category is most easily understood in relation to an earlier concept of social intelligence proposed by Thorndike (1920). He referred to an ability 'to act wisely in human relations', which entailed some understanding of the behaviour of others. Similarly, Guilford describes behavioural content as 'information, essentially non-verbal, involved in human interactions, where awareness of attention, perceptions, thoughts, desires, feelings, moods, emotions, intentions, and actions of other persons and of ourselves is important'.

Each of the five intellectual operations may function, therefore, with four different types of content. A separate intellectual ability would probably be involved in every case, which would mean in all twenty different abilities.

The structure-of-intellect model has a third dimension. Information is conceptualized in a specific form, for example, as a unit or in terms of a relationship. Whether we are memorizing words or convergent thinking about symbols, information is conceived in certain ways, which in fact determine our manner of knowing the information. Guilford refers to these forms in which intellectually we operate as product categories, and lists six of them: units, classes, relations, systems, transformations, implications.

We will illustrate the meaning of just two of these products. If an individual is given an incomplete picture of, say, a horse, and asked to identify it, this would normally involve him in a cognitive operation, with figural information, in a unit product. Guilford describes units as 'relatively segregated or circumscribed items of information having "thing" character, perhaps equivalent to the gestalt "figure on a ground" '. However, we may be concerned not with thingness but with relationships, such as in 'mare and foal, bitch and puppy, cow and ——'. This connection or relationship in terms of some criterion between two or more items of information is an example of a relations product.

This third category completes the model, which is now three-dimensional, and can be represented as a cube. Figure 3.11 from Guilford (1967) represents the model. The cube contains 120 boxes, and Guilford sees each box as representing a separate and independent ability or intellectual factor.

Practical Applications for Occupational Guidance and Personnel Selection
We can only be tentative at present about the practical consequences of adopting such a theory. Presumably in guidance and

selection our approach would be similar to a procedure based on a primary mental abilities view of ability. Adequate performance of any task is not partly determined by some general factor, but depends wholly on a number of these hundred and twenty or so abilities. We would need to discover which of these many factors are relevant to success in any job or occupation. Job and occupational profiles might be established in terms of the model. Similarly we would need to evaluate an individual in terms of the factors.

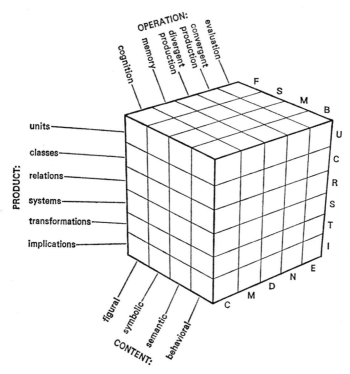

Fig. 3.11 Guilford's structure-of-intellect model (1967)

REFERENCES

Burt, C. (1924), 'The principles of vocational guidance', *Brit. J. of Psychol.*, 14.

Burt, C. (1939), 'The relations of educational abilities', *Brit. J. educ. Psychol.*, 9, 45–71.

Burt, C. (1944) 'Mental abilities and mental factors', *Brit. J. educ. Psychol.* 14.

Eysenck, H. J. (1953), *Uses and Abuses of Psychology*, Penguin.

Guilford, J. P. (1967), *The Nature of Human Intelligence*, McGraw Hill.

Hudson, L. (1966), *Contrary Imaginations: A Psychological Study of the English Schoolboy*, Methuen.

Jaques, E. (1961), *Equitable Payment*, Heinemann.

Krueger, F. and Spearman, C. (1906), *Zeit. f. Psychol.*

Rodger, A. (1952), The Seven-Point Plan, National Institute of Industrial Psychology Paper No. 1.

Rodger, A. and Cavanagh, P. (1962), 'Personnel selection and vocational guidance', in *Society: Problems and Methods of Study*, ed. A. T. Welford, Routledge & Kegan Paul.

Schiller, B. (1934), 'Verbal, numerical and spatial abilities of young children', *Arch. Psychol.*, 161.

Spearman, C. (1904), ' "General intelligence": objectively determined and measured', *Amer. J. Psychol.*, 115.

Spearman, C. (1927), *The Abilities of Man*, Macmillan.

Thomson, G. H. (1951), *The Factorial Analysis of Human Ability*, University of London Press.

Thorndike, E. L. (1920), 'Intelligence and its uses', *Harper's Mag.*, 140.

Thurstone, L. L. (1938), 'Primary mental abilities', *Psychometr. Mon.*, 1.

Thurstone, L. L. (1948), 'The psychological implications of factor analysis', *American Psychologist*, 3.

Vernon, P. E. (1940), *The Measurement of Abilities*, University of London Press.

Vernon, P. E. (1961), *The Structure of Human Abilities*, Methuen.

Vernon, P. E., and Parry, J. B. (1949), *Personnel Selection in the British Forces*, University of London Press.

CHAPTER 4

Human Motivation

Overview

In this chapter we first examine the interaction of ability and motivational factors within personality, and then indicate how the total personality interacts with the environment. The main body of the chapter considers the motivational aspects of personality under two headings, motives and needs, and motivational traits. Under motives and needs we discuss the concept of a general drive, relate needs to the idea of function introduced in Chapter 1, and refer to the work of Anne Roe. We conclude this section with a discussion of assessment, introducing the developmental method.

We begin the section on motivational traits by attempting to define attitudes, values, and interests. We then consider how such trait-elements interact within the personality, making particular reference to the classic Adorno study of the authoritarian personality. We next examine the relationship of traits, values, and interests to work.

In the concluding section we briefly suggest the nature of the relationship between personality and work, and its implications for guidance and selection. Finally we consider schemes which enable us to analyse the individual, and work, in terms both of needs and trait-elements.

INTRODUCTION

Interaction within Personality

We have looked at ability and performance. We will now examine the relationship between performance and those other personality factors we may broadly term motivational. But needs, drives, traits, interests, whatever concept we adopt to consider motivation, do not function independently of ability, nor does ability function in isolation from them; ability is not surrounded by a moat. The human individual strives to function as a whole, and within the personality system motivational factors and abilities interact. As Anne Roe says (1964), 'a person is divisible only conceptually'.

Young Smith has difficulty in remembering quotes from Shakespeare and simple chemical symbols, and because of this an imperceptive teacher might say he has a poor memory. But on Monday morning Smith can invariably recall most of Saturday's professional football results. A management committee, rigidly employing a concept of occupational and ability levels, describes one of the firm's machine-tool fitters as 'skilled craftsman level, might make shop-floor supervision, but unlikely to rise above this'. This same employee displays considerable flair in a small business concern he runs with his wife in his spare time. He is possibly quite capable of a technical sales job which relates to certain of his interests and social needs, and which the management committee places above shop-floor supervision in its hierarchy of job levels.

If we think of upper limits of performance determined by ability level, we should do so only in broad and flexible terms. The individual's operational competence and capacity is not the result of an addition of ability and motivation, but of a more dynamic and changing interaction between them.

Interaction between Personality and the Environment
What the individual does, his performance, depends not only on his personality. It is partly determined by his environment. Lewin (1952) expresses this simply as $B = f.O \times E$; behaviour is a function of the organism and the environment. This is another form of the older and better known $S \rightarrow O \rightarrow R$, where S is a stimulus, O is an organism, and R is response. We have previously suggested a number of the relevant aspects of the stimulus or environment of the job and of the organism, here the personality. In Table 4.1 we list some of these, together with various types of behaviour and response at work.

By work content we mean simply what the individual does in his job, his activities, duties, and responsibilities. Darley and Hagenah (1955) postulate the existence of a hierarchy of job titles, and suggest that our status and esteem in the eyes of others is in part determined by our position on this hierarchy. The title is, therefore, an important aspect of an individual's job because it becomes, they suggest, 'the hallmark of his status in society'.

Socialization and Identification need some explanation, and we will return to these concepts in later chapters. Here we simply refer to the process by which the employee learns, adopts and internalizes the standards and norms of his occupation, work group, or company.

TABLE 4.1 *Work behaviour as a function of interaction between personality factors and aspects of a job*

Stimulus ⟶	organism ⟶	response
JOB ⟶	PERSONALITY ⟶	WORK BEHAVIOUR
work content	abilities	job choice
physical layout	temperamental and	socialization and
organization	dynamic source traits	identification
informal	stylistic and dynamic	job satisfaction
relationships	common traits	work performance
supervision	needs, motives, drives	time-keeping, turnover,
job title	attitudes	absenteeism, fatigue,
incentives	values	accidents
	interests	

In the final chapter we will return to considering these environmental job factors and their interaction with personality. We will now consider factors of personality other than those of ability, examining them first in terms of motives and needs, and then in terms of traits.

MOTIVES AND NEEDS

Introduction

The simplest classification of needs is into the three categories of material, social, and personal. The needs for food, water, sex, and to maintain a certain bodily temperature, are examples of the material or primary needs. They serve a biological function for the individual or species and are primary in that they are necessary for the life of the individual or species. W. H. Auden makes the point in his poem, 'First Things First', with the line: 'Thousands have lived without love, not one without water.'

The social or secondary needs are those for love and belongingness. The personal or ego needs include a need for achievement, for recognition, for fulfilment in some sphere (such as one's job), and are more specific and personal to an individual.

The categories of Maslow's need hierarchy, discussed in Chapter 2, develop and elaborate on this basic threefold classification. But both provide only a very general framework for considering motivation in terms of motive and need in the work situation. Adopting either classification we would have to attempt to determine what needs and motives are important to a particular individual at a given time. An analysis of an individual in terms of his changing need structure at a certain point in his career would be primarily idiographic. A nomothetic analysis is sometimes also necessary. It may be important in guidance, selection, or other work situations, to determine how an individual compares with others on the strength of his needs and motives.

An ex-serviceman of thirty-five, married and with children, may seek guidance on choice of a civilian occupation. The vocational counsellor could usefully consider or guide the ex-serviceman to consider his position in terms of his present hierarchy of needs. For example, it might be wrong to guide him into a poorly paid job which involved work he would undoubtedly find socially and personally fulfilling, if for the individual his present need for a high and steady income took precedence over all others. A nomothetic analysis is also important because it may only be by a comparison with others that one is able to evaluate his internal need hierarchy meaningfully. A comparison with others may be a necessary realistic consideration when there is competition for the jobs the individual is considering. Methods of assessing the motives and needs of the individual clearly become necessary.

The Concept of General Drive

Hierarchical group factor theory postulates the existence of a broad ability, present in most if not all cognitive operations, general intelligence. The question arises—is there a similar general drive or motivational factor, analogous to general intelligence? The X in the diagram of occupational abilities taken from Vernon (see Figure 3.8) is some general drive factor. Such a concept suggests that an individual with high general drive would be characterized by highly motivated behaviour in most of his fields of activity.

It is possible that overall level of drive is partly a function of emotional responsiveness, and this in turn is related to a measure of anxiety (Taylor, 1956). Burt (1935) had earlier proposed a factor of 'general emotionality'. More recently Spence (1958) outlined a theory of emotionally based drive which suggests that the strength of an individual's response to a situation is a function of both a 'learning factor' and a generalized drive factor. The theory is particularly concerned with avoidance behaviour, where the individual is motivated to evade situations that are unpleasant and painful for him. The theory suggests that drive level, particularly in avoidance situations, is a function of 'a persisting emotional response in the organism . . . that is aroused by any form of aversive stimulation'.

Bendig (1960), factor-analysing various personality measures, found no distinction between anxiety and emotionality. Anxiety emerged as a manifestation of a general emotionality factor. So it is possible a general level of drive, especially drive to avoid unpleasant situations, is generated by a general emotionality, of which anxiety is a component part. This would be a personality characteristic of the sort measured as Factor C (dissatisfied emotionality) in Cattell's 16 P.F. (see Chapter 2).

The alternative is to conceive of motivation in terms of specific drives that relate only to certain environments. With such a view we would not see individuals in terms of general, high or low motivational levels, but as being highly or poorly motivated in relation to a specific situation. So someone might be very highly motivated in a situation or a job where there is considerable intellectual content, but manifest little drive in circumstances or an occupation where the content is mainly social. Such a view of motivation in terms of drives specific to specific situations is parallel to the primary mental abilities model. H. A. Murray, for example, postulated in his early writings (1938) twenty different 'manifest' needs, such as for abasement, for achievement, for dominance, for understanding, etc. Siegelman and Peck (1960) used Murray's system in a study of three occupational groups, graduate chemists, ministers of religion, and army and air force officers. In terms of Murray's classification of needs the investigators made suggestions as to what sorts of needs they thought the different occupations were likely to satisfy. Their study of the people in the three occupations did, in fact, confirm most of their predictions about the sorts of needs each occupation satisfied. Such a study tends to confirm the specificness of drives, as proposed in a theory like Murray's.

There may, of course, be both general and specific drive factors. This would necessitate some sort of hierarchical model of drive.

Needs and Functions

In Chapter 1 we discussed the manifest and latent functions of work. In discussing here the individual's needs we are examining the reverse side of the same coin, because when we say work or any cultural institution is functional we mean it fulfils needs. These needs may be those of all members of society or of a few in certain social groups. For example, in Chapter 1 we quoted Friedmann and Havinghurst (1954) as suggesting that association is one function of a job, and we have already given two classifications of needs which include social needs as one category. Similarly Friedmann and Havinghurst refer to meaningful life-experience as a function of work, and this would be fulfilling the personal/ego needs, or in Maslow's terms, the need for self-actualization.

The analysis of an individual's motivation, in terms of needs or traits, is key to an understanding of his personality. His job fulfils many functions, may satisfy many personal needs and may accord with many of his motivational traits. So people are attracted to certain types of jobs, and tend to remain in them, because those occupations 'fit' their personality structure. Roe (1956) goes so far as to suggest: 'Occupations may be sounder as taxonomic labels than any that we are currently working with in psychopathology.' Her point is that type of occupation may be a very significant and useful classification of people. The sort of job a person has may tell us a lot about him.

The Work of Anne Roe

Roe, mainly using the Rorschach Inkblot Test, has found a number of interesting differences between people in different occupational groups. The Rorschach is a projective test consisting of ten cards. On each card is a confused shape looking something like an inkblot, in black and white, or in colours. The individual is asked to say or to write down what he thinks each inkblot looks like, and the tester may question him to obtain more detail in what he says and possibly to evoke further responses.

The Rorschach is usually referred to as a projective test. Part of its rationale is that in looking at such unstructured shapes, what the individual perceives is highly subjective and is motivated by his inner needs. His reaction to the inkblot gives an account of his personality, since his response is an expression of his moods, feelings, and of his strongest and most urgent drives and personal needs.

Roe has used the Rorschach to study a number of professional groups. Her work is reported in a number of articles, and is generally summarized in *The Psychology of Occupations* (1956). The following extracts convey something of the flavour of her work.

Roe studied a small number of physical scientists who were regarded as men eminent in the research field (1951). She distinguished between those with theoretical and experimental orientations, and among her conclusions, derived largely from interview and projective test, are (1956): 'The psychosexual development of all of them was more often retarded than not, and few of them have any genuine social interests now.' Referring to their relationships with other people Roe says: 'For the most part, these are not close, and are relatively unimportant to them in the overall picture of their lives. This does not prevent them from being adequate husbands. . . .' She continues: 'Both groups have normal aggressive tendencies, but these are better controlled with the theorists and less likely to be handled by getting out of the provoking situation, or, if this is impossible, by explosive outbursts.'

In another investigation (1951a) she studied staff of university biological departments, and part of her summary, as given in the 1956 text, states:

> All biologists are more like other biologists than they are like physicists or social scientists. The anatomists are generally the least intellectually controlled; the physiologists seem to show more free anxiety and more concern with immediate personal problems than do the others. The botanists appear to be a generally rather well-adjusted group, and rather placid, with no particular deviant tendencies. The geneticists are a more colourful group than the others, with somewhat more emotional dominance, but this is of a sort different from that shown by the anatomists.

Roe's study of painters (1946) used the Rorschach and a second projective test, the T.A.T. She reports in the 1956 text:

> Both tests indicated a nonaggressive and rather immature type of social and sexual adaptation. There were many indications of insufficient freeing of emotional ties with parents, particularly mothers, and considerable confusion over their own sexual and personal roles.

97

Much of Roe's research is open to the usual criticisms levelled at work done with the Rorschach or other projective tests, that in the absence of completely objective measures and standards the interpretations of the individual's responses inevitably have some subjective element. The more basic question is whether, in fact, responses to a projective test provide any useful account of personality.

Roe's findings are stimulating and creative, but we must necessarily regard many of them as hypotheses which have only in a limited way been substantiated. To the extent they are confirmed, they provide further evidence of how choice of occupation and behaviour at work relate to and fulfil certain types of needs and wants.

The Assessment of Motives and Needs

So in guidance and selection we might usefully consider the individual in terms of motives and needs. They could prove helpful in an analysis of his internal personality dynamics and for comparing him with others. What means exist for assessing and measuring an individual's motives and needs?

Projective tests, such as the Rorschach and the T.A.T., constitute one method of evaluating drive and personality needs. They are too specialized a field to be dealt with in this text, though it is possible that such techniques may acquire a useful function in vocational counselling.

Assessment plans, interviews, application forms, are other means to the assessment of individual motives and needs. We will examine these in the following chapter. The interview and the application form are methods of collecting information. An assessment plan is merely a system for collating the information that has been collected. In guidance and selection one particularly useful approach to collecting information is through examining the individual's life history.

We are referring to what is essentially the biographical approach. We examine the individual's school history, his work history, and the history of his personal life if this seems relevant—as it often does in guidance. In such an examination of an individual's life history we attempt to find certain tendencies and trends, recurring themes, seemingly typical patterns of behaviour, which become especially significant and meaningful if analysed in terms of underlying drives, motives, and needs.

What we have briefly described here has been labelled by Super (1957) as the developmental or thematic-extrapolative method. 'The assumption underlying this approach', says Super (1957), 'is that one way to understand what an individual will do in the future is to understand what he did in the past.' This 'assumption' Super refers to as life pattern theory. We suggest it might prove particularly useful in guidance and selection to base the developmental method on some theory or model of personality needs, such as Maslow's. We would then try to categorize the trends and patterns in an individual's life history in terms of his attempts to satisfy physiological, safety, love, esteem, and self-actualization needs.

And here a rating scale would be useful, particularly if used as part of an assessment plan. For example, a slight modification of Maslow's categories would produce Table 4.2. The vocational adviser or personnel selector would complete the rating form on the basis of a developmental study of the individual's life history. The individual is graded on each need in comparison with other people. Such a comparison is useful in itself, and also provides an indirect evaluation of the relationships between needs within the individual.

TABLE 4.2 *Rating form for use in developmental method* (incorporating a modification of Maslow's need-hierarchy)

RATING FORM NEEDS	Grade A top 10%	Grade B next 20%	Grade C middle 40%	Grade D next 20%	Grade E bottom 10%
Economic					
Security					
Belongingness					
Esteem					
Self-actualization					

Alternatively we might assess the individual in terms of general drive or the overall level of motivation he appears to display in his life history. Such an approach might be coupled with an attempt to evaluate the individual on specific drives that relate only to certain environments. Table 4.3 gives the sort of rating form that might be used with this approach for, say, selection of applicants for a business studies degree course.

TABLE 4.3 *Section of rating form for use with developmental approach to business studies selection*
(concepts of general and specific motivation are incorporated)

RATING FORM	Grade A top 10%	Grade B next 20%	Grade C middle 40%	Grade D next 20%	Grade E bottom 10%
MOTIVATION					
1 Overall level of drive					
2 Specific drive for further study (for its own sake)					
3 Specific drive to obtain a degree qualification					
4 Specific drive to obtain a degree in business studies					
INTELLIGENCE					

Subsequent research might show that a high rating at initial interview on one in particular of the four motivation categories was especially predictive of success on this degree course. This would be useful information. The difficulty of obtaining comparability between different raters is usually considerable.

The development method attempts to analyse past behaviour in terms of tendencies and patterns of behaviour. It seems particularly useful to adopt concepts of needs, motives, drives, in such an analysis, possibly employing specific models or lists of needs proposed by theorists. The developmental method is essentially concerned with an analysis of the individual over a period of time. This sort of longitudinal approach contrasts with the cross-sectional nature of the trait analysis, with its emphasis on the present. We will now examine the trait approach.

MOTIVATIONAL TRAITS

Introduction

We have already examined personality in terms of traits, when in Chapter 2 we outlined the theories of Allport and Cattell and in Chapter 3 looked at human abilities. In this section we will examine further trait-type units of personality, other than those of ability, and attempt to see how they relate to work performance and satisfaction.

Among the trait-type concepts which seem to have some occupational relevance are Cattell's source traits, Allport's personal dispositions and common traits, all of which we have previously defined, and attitudes, values, and interests. We will now define the last three concepts.

Attitudes, Values, and Interests
Allport's (1961) distinction between cardinal, central, and secondary personal dispositions is useful but arbitrary. One can regard them as positions or areas on a continuum. We would place 'attitude' at the secondary personal disposition end of the continuum. Allport's cardinal and central dispositions and traits essentially have a certain generality, as in 'he is kind, aggressive, ambitious'. An attitude is specific, as is evidenced by its invariably having an object. We have earlier suggested that an individual has an attitude towards something—to comprehensive schools, to trade unions, to a political party. This point emerges in Secord and Backman's definition (1964): 'The term attitude refers to certain regularities of an individual's feelings, thoughts, and predispositions to act toward some aspect of his environment.' We might usefully think of attitudes as one kind of secondary personal disposition or common trait, rather similar in structure to the specific ability factors of hierarchical group factor theory.

If someone were asked what were the most important things in his life, his answer would say something about his values. Allport (1961) describes a value as 'a belief upon which a man acts by preference'. Among Smith's values might be the beliefs that 'all men are equal', 'all children should have equal educational opportunity', and that 'personal relationships are important in life'. Whereas Bloggs believes his country is better than others, that teachers should concentrate on the brightest children, and that making a lot of money is very important even at the expense of one's relationship with wife, children, and friends. These beliefs of Smith and Bloggs are values, and an individual's values indicate what he considers important in life and the order of their importance. Values, therefore, provide the individual with criteria by which to make his everyday but important decisions. Using the term, 'value system', Cooper and McGaugh (1963) summarize the significance of values:

> A value system is an individual's over-all life aspiration (what he really wants to achieve) which on the one hand gives direction to his behavior, and on the other hand is a frame of reference by which the worth of stimulus objects may be judged. In the value system sense, it is an elaborated and articulated organization of attitudes.

What is meant by 'interests' in most psychological studies probably differs little from popular use of the term. Many writers have avoided defining the concept, but the idea of 'expressed preferences' would have a place in most definitions. However, the apparent simplicity may be deceptive in that our medium or way of expressing such a preference is probably important. Super's (1962) classification of interests under four headings according to how they are expressed seems more than a methodological categorization. In each case because of the different method of expressing the preference what we obtain may be a different type of interest.

Super's four categories of interests are expressed, manifest, inventoried, and tested. Expressed interests are verbally stated preferences or interests, as a school-leaver may say in interview that he likes model-making or going to the cinema. We tend sometimes to rely on such verbally expressed interests in a guidance or selection interview, possibly a little dangerously. Such interests expressed in this way, often in response to a question from the interviewer, are as much a statement of hopes, expectations, even fantasies, as of what we normally mean by the term.

Manifest interests are shown not in words but in deeds; they are made manifest by what you do. If an individual actually is an active member of a political party, and canvasses at local and general elections for that party, then 'politics' is a manifest interest. However, though we may objectively note what the individual does, interpreting its meaning or what interest it really signifies is subjective. Is he active in politics because of a genuine 'political interest', because it gives useful business contacts, or because it provides some form of social life?

Inventoried interests are the measures of interests obtained from responses to a form of questionnaire, which usually asks questions on likes, dislikes, and preferences for certain types of activities. But they are not just questionnaires, as Super emphasizes:

The essential and all-important difference is that in the case of the inventory each possible response is given an experimentally determined weight, and the weights corresponding to the answers given by the person completing the inventory are added in order to yield a score which represents, not a single subjective estimate as in the case of expressed interests, but a pattern of interests which research has shown to be rather stable.

The Kuder Preference Record (Vocational) and the Connolly Occupational Interests Questionnaire are examples of interest inventories. Much of our present knowledge of interests which is useful in the guidance field comes from this area, and it is with inventoried interests we will concern ourselves.

Super's fourth category is an interesting though as yet little developed possibility. Here some form of attainment or information test is reckoned a measure of interest, on the basis that the individual acquires and retains knowledge in the areas where he is motivated by his active interests. Successful training in a number of engineering trades in the armed forces was frequently predicted by a test of simple electrical and mechanical knowledge (Vernon and Parry, 1949). This may have been because the test reflected relevant interests as well as some ability and knowledge.

Trait-Elements and the Actuarial Method

In future we will use the term trait-elements comprehensively to include the sorts of units of analysis we have been discussing, such as attitudes, values, interests, source traits, common traits, and personal dispositions. If we wish to refer specifically to any of these last three concepts, we will simply say traits or dispositions.

Such trait-elements provide the units for the cross-sectional analysis of what Super (1957) terms the actuarial method. The alternative to the longitudinal approach of the development method in guidance and selection is a study of the individual at the present point in time by the actuarial method. As we shall see, the actuarial approach has essentially been that adopted over the past fifty years in scientific guidance and selection. It consists of appraising the individual in trait-elements, of studying the requirements of a job or occupation in terms of trait-elements, and matching the two. The basis for the actuarial method is, as Super points out, essentially that of trait theory with, as part and parcel of it, the theory of individual differences. The individual can be usefully analysed in trait-elements such as interests, values, source traits, etc. Individuals differ significantly in the trait-elements they possess. These differences have important educational and vocational implications. Such a theoretical position, and the actuarial method based upon it, provide the framework for the following examination of trait-elements.

The Relationship of Trait-Elements within the Personality

We have already pointed out that 'a person is divisible only conceptually' (Roe, 1964), and have stressed the interaction of ability and motivation within the individual. Trait-elements such as source traits, values, interests, also should be seen as separate but interrelated parts of personality.

A dramatic illustration of this point is the study by Adorno and others of the 'authoritarian personality' (1950). The study began as an investigation of anti-Semitism by means of an attitude scale. The question then arose of whether an individual's anti-Jewish prejudice was an isolated attitude, or whether it related to other aspects of personality. A more comprehensive scale was developed which measured a belief in the superiority of one's in-group and hostility to those perceived as outsiders. The correlations between an individual's score on this measure of 'ethnocentrism' and on the anti-Semitic scale were sufficiently high to suggest a relationship between the two. In other words an anti-Jewish attitude tended to be found with prejudice against Negroes, a belief that other cultures, nations, classes, are inferior to one's own, and even (with men) that women are inferior. The study went further and found that these in turn correlated with what they termed a politico-economic conservatism, part of which was support for the *status quo*, resistance to social change, and preoccupation with power.

Finally it was found that all these correlated with an attitude scale, labelled the F or fascist scale, which ranged over a wider variety of items, such as 'sex criminals ought to be publicly whipped', 'there will always be war and conflict, human nature being what it is', 'obedience and respect for authority are the most important virtues children should learn'.

Among the attitudes investigated by this F-scale were those of strict adherence to conventional middle-class values, of uncritical submissiveness to authority, of obsessive concern with sexual matters, of preoccupation with power, of hostility to tenderness and feeling. The authoritarian personality can be thought of as a syndrome of traits which, whatever their origins, tend to go together. All this started with a study of hostile attitudes to one minority group, Jews. The investigation powerfully illustrates how apparently isolated trait-elements may closely relate to each other.

Whatever the origins of trait-elements in the individual, in the adolescent and adult they interact and relate within the personality system. Trait-elements and how they interact will change over time as the individual is affected by physical processes of growth and decay and by environmental influences such as the changing expectations society has of him.

A time-honoured undergraduate laboratory study illustrates a relationship between values and interests. A subject completes a values questionnaire, and scores, say, very high on religious values and low on economic. Words are then projected on to a screen at considerable speed so that he has difficulty in seeing them. Typically he will recognize and remember many 'religious' words such as priest and sanctuary, and very few of the 'economic' words. Postman, Bruner, and McGinnies (1948) adopting a similar approach gradually lengthened the exposure time of a word on successive trials until the subject recognized it. They found that the words relating to high values of an individual were recognized by him at shorter exposure times. This may be the result of values functioning motivationally to heighten the perceptual sensitivity of the individual or may merely be because he has acquired a greater familiarity with such words. In either case the finding illustrates that some deep value-structure, say, religious or economic, relates to and affects interests as indicated by our perception or knowledge of words.

Typical of a number of investigations in this area was that of Sarbin and Berdie (1940). Using the Allport–Vernon Study of Values and the Strong Interest Inventory with college students they found positive relationships between religious values and welfare interests, and between theoretical values and scientific interests.

Interests may relate not only to values but also to personality traits, as a study by Triggs (1947) illustrates. The investigator gave a number of college students the Minnesota Multiphasic Personality Inventory and the Kuder Preference Record, the first a clinical test of 'surface' traits and the second an inventory of vocational interests. He found several relationships between the two sets of scores, such as a positive correlation between schizoid tendencies and musical and clerical interests, between depression and clerical interest, with a negative correlation between depression and social-service interests.

Values and traits may also relate within the individual, as Adorno's authoritarian personality study illustrates. What we have quoted as typical aspects of the authoritarian individual are expressive of values, since each is indicative of 'a belief upon which a man acts by preference' (Allport, 1961). The authoritarian's unqualified approval of authority, his anathema on feeling and tenderness, his uncritical support for middle-class norms, his unquestioning assertion of the superiority of his own race or nation, constitute values or an expression of a value system. Adorno's study suggests that an individual's values may often originate not from rational, cognitive processes, but in the functioning of cardinal and central traits of personality.

Research has sometimes confirmed the common-sense expectation of relationships between interests and abilities in related fields, but rather surprisingly such relationships are often absent. Sartain (1946) found that scores on the mechanical and scientific scales of an interest inventory (Kuder) correlated slightly with performance on tests of mechanical and spatial aptitude (Bennett Mechanical Comprehension and Minnesota Paper Form Board). But Adkins and Kuder (1940), using the same inventory and the Tests of Primary Mental Abilities, found only one correlation, between computational interest and number ability, and this only with women.

If trait-elements interrelate, changes and developments in one area of the personality system may have repercussions in other areas. Bloggs becomes an accountant primarily because of his computational and business interests. We may find that years in the job not only deepen these same interests and develop his abilities which relate to the work, but also change his values away from those of his working-class parents to the values of this middle-class professional group, and even modify or possibly reinforce personality traits such as his praxernia (see Cattell), that is, his practical, and uncreative orientation. The changes occur through the process of the individual interacting within an environment.

Temperamental and Dynamic Traits (personal dispositions, source traits, common traits), and Work

Guilford (1952) investigated the personalities of a number of executives and supervisors using two personality inventories. His results suggest that the success of the executives is related to traits of masculinity, co-operativeness, sociability, and self-confidence. Similarly the more successful supervisors (in a big grocery concern) were characterized by co-operativeness, calmness, and emotional stability.

In two early studies Dodge (1938, 1938a) compared very successful with not-so-successful sales clerks, and concluded that they differed in a number of ways. The better sales clerks were more confident and self-sufficient, more aggressive, more social, more radical and unconventional, than the poorer sales clerks, and also less emotionally unstable, less self-conscious, and less resentful of criticism.

Kuder, in his Preference Record (Personal), adopts a different approach from that of attempting to relate specific traits to success. Through the normal inventory technique the Preference Record attempts to specify for the individual the sorts of work situations he would prefer along dimensions which seem likely to be related to personality traits. The five dimensions are:

A. Preference for being active in groups.
B. Preference for familiar and stable situations.
C. Preference for working with ideas.
D. Preference for avoiding conflict.
E. Preference for directing others.

Such preferences may relate, in Cattell terms (see Chapter 2), to surface traits, not to source traits.

Kuder has compared the scores of a number of satisfied and dissatisfied people in certain occupations, for example, comparing lawyers who like their work with lawyers who do not. In his manual (1953 edition) he reports on eight occupations. In the first six the study was concerned only with men. Satisfied accountants and auditors score significantly higher on scales B and D than do dissatisfied men in the same occupations. With lawyers and judges no differences were found. Satisfied public school superintendents (similar to a headmaster) scored significantly higher on A and E. Retail managers who were satisfied scored higher only on A.

Satisfied insurance salesmen scored significantly lower on C and D. Satisfied mechanics and repairmen scored significantly higher on B than did similar dissatisfied employees, and lower on E. With women grammar schoolteachers he found that those satisfied scored lower on E. Satisfied housewives were higher on B and D, but lower on E, than were the dissatisfied housewives.

Data are accumulating on the relatedness of Cattell's main source traits to work behaviour. Some of these data appear in the various 16 P.F. *Handbooks*, and many of them are given in the Institute for Personality and Ability Testing publications.

Earlier attempts to relate personality traits to work behaviour met with only limited success. One reason for this is the nature of the personality measures used which were frequently clinically derived. What emerges from factor analysis or most statistical techniques depends on what goes in. If the bits of behaviour that were statistically processed related to mental health, or educational success, then the trait factors which emerged would not necessarily have much occupational relevance. In more recent work investigators such as Cattell have sampled a wide range of behaviours, while Kuder has adopted broader personality dimensions, more operationally stated in terms of work situations.

There is also the problem of the categorization of jobs. We shall return to this, and it is sufficient to make the point here that an occupational category such as accountancy can cover a multitude of jobs. One accountant may need to be a highly sociable office-manager, while another works alone in a quiet corner preparing balance sheets and management reports. Three lecturers may have essentially differing roles, of teacher, researcher, and administrator. Even where the job itself is identical, individuals may experience satisfaction or dissatisfaction because of factors extraneous to the work itself. In Chapter 1 we stressed that the nature of the organization, the social relationships in the firm, the sorts of incentives provided, and other factors, may impinge on the occupant of a job.

Finally, if we accept the unity of personality and the interaction in practice of many trait-elements, it seems unlikely that many one-variable relationships, such as that good salesmen are more assertive than poor salesmen, will be found. It would appear more probable that what affects occupational choice, success, failure, satisfaction, and length of stay in a job, are certain configurations or patterns of personality traits. We are back to the Gestalt, and this would suggest that even a trait analysis is most useful when essentially holistic as well.

Values and Work

The latent and manifest functions of work satisfy needs. Above the biological level an individual's values will affect the importance he places on different needs. In this way values relate to the functions of work. Quite simply, I may place different values on high status, on a sense of personal achievement, on money, etc., and this will affect the functions work has for me. It will partly determine my choice of occupation and what I seek to obtain from my work activity.

In the following chapter we will examine the Allport–Vernon Study of Values; here we will briefly refer to three investigations. The business executive was investigated by Henry (1949) who suggests that in the United States, where the study was made, the role of the business executive is clearly defined and well known to most people. This would mean that anyone who becomes a business executive does so knowing full well what is involved. The position provides many economic and social rewards and Henry suggests: 'The successful executive represents a crystallization of many of the attitudes and values generally accepted by middle-class American society.' He goes on to say what these are: 'The value of accumulation and achievement, of self-directedness and independent thought, and their rewards in prestige and status and property, are found in this group.'

The Work Values Inventory developed by Super provides fifteen value categories, such as creativity, achievement, surroundings, security. Subjects must state their preference for 'work in which you—organize and direct the activities of others (Management); make something beautiful (Aesthetic); help other people (Altruism)', etc.

Normile (1967) in the United States studied a number of professional occupational groups using the inventory. A hierarchy of work values derived from the inventory discriminated between certain groups. There were a number of specific differences, such as altruism being ranked high by priests, teachers, psychiatrists, psychologists, and low by lawyers, accountants, and engineers. Priests valued the aesthetic category higher and economic returns lower than did the others. Similarly teachers tended to be significantly high on their ranking of security and low on management.

The Super Work Values Inventory was used by Carruthers (1968) in a study of students at university and other colleges in Glasgow. There were several different student groups, such as management studies, ordinary arts, and honours science, and men and women were investigated separately. A number of students were also compared on subsequent choice of job. In all 195 comparisons were made, since 11 pairs were compared on the 15 value categories of the Super Inventory (see Table 4.4). Of these 43 showed differences significant at the five per cent level or beyond. At this level of significance it is reasonable to regard differences between the two sets of scores as probably meaningful, and unlikely to have occurred by chance.

Clearly, as Carruthers emphasizes, the results are not conclusive. But they provide evidence that diverse occupational groups and students on various courses may be differentiated by their work-value hierarchies. Such findings suggest the potential usefulness of value inventories in guidance and, possibly, selection.

There is sometimes in practice an interesting difficulty. If the individual answers honestly we can obtain some useful assessment of his values. But there is the phenomenological problem of how an individual perceives a specific job. Raylesberg (1949, given in Super, 1957) found that some student engineers saw engineering as a scientific occupation, others as materialistic, and others as social welfare. In practice, therefore, it is not only important to know an individual's values; we should know also how he sees different jobs and occupations as enabling him to implement certain values.

In fact our perception is culturally mediated, so individuals within a common culture tend to perceive the same object in similar terms, and this is true also of how we regard occupational roles. In Britain most people would see nursing as high in altruism and service. But there will be individuals and sub-groups within a given culture with different perceptions of jobs and occupations. More important, with broad occupational groupings such as engineering, law, etc., different people may perceive them in different terms which make them consonant or at odds with diverse value systems. Smith becomes a lawyer because it pays well and

TABLE 14 [Significant] Groups on Separate Values of the Super Work Values Inventory

(Carruthers, 1968)

	Intellectual stimulation	Creativity	Management	Achievement	Surroundings	Supervisory relationships	Way of Life	Security	Associates	Aesthetic	Prestige	Independence	Variety	Economic returns	Altruism	No. of values showing a difference
Men																
By course of study																
Honours science v. honours arts	>.05													(H) >.01	>.05	2
Ordinary science v. ordinary arts																—
Ordinary science and arts v. management studies			(H) >.001			>.05										3
Ordinary arts v. management studies			(H) >.001			>.05			>.05						>.05	4
By subsequent job choice																
Literary/soc. science research v. physical science research																—
Teaching v. physical science research		(H) >.05														1
Business v. physical science research	(H) >.05	(H) >.05						(H) >.001								3
Teaching v. business	(H) >.05							>.01								1
Women																
By course of study or occupation																
Ordinary science v. ordinary arts		(H) >.01														1
Ordinary science and arts v. occupational therapy students	(H) >.02		>.01			>.01	(H) >.001	(H) >.001	(H) >.01				>.05	(H) >.001		8
Ordinary science v. occupatinal therapy students	>.01					(H) >.001	>.001		(H) >.01			(H) >.05		>.001	(H) >.001	6
Ordinary arts v. occupational therapy students	>.05	(H) >.001	(H) >.001			>.01	>.01		(H) >.02					>.001	(H) >.001	8
Ordinary arts v. occupational therapy practice	>.01	(H) >.01				>.05	>.02					>.05	>.01	>.01		6

Entries in cells shows the level of probability (chi square) where $P \geqslant 0.05$.
(H) The second group of a pair had the higher median score.

E

he values economic returns highly. Jones, a deeply committed socialist, enters law because he regards it as a powerful instrument in social change.

Interests and Work

A number of studies have indicated that inventoried vocational interests relate to such aspects of work as occupational choice and job satisfaction. Levine and Wallen (1954) found significant relationships between the inventoried interests of schoolboys in their teens and subsequent choice of occupation. The Kuder Preference Record (Vocational) was completed by 215 youths while they were at school. About eight years later a questionnaire was sent to them, and the replies analysed. The investigators classified the jobs of those who had replied into what the Kuder manual indicated as the appropriate interest areas. Those who according to the Kuder categories were in the same sort of occupation were compared with the others on their Kuder interest scores. Comparisons were made on seven of the Kuder scales then in use, and in six of them significant differences were found. Men who were actually in jobs related to the mechanical, scientific, computational, literary, persuasive, or clerical interest areas, were found to have scored more highly on the related interest scales, the eight or so years previously, than did men who were not in related occupations. The social service interest scale failed to correlate in this way, but the sample for this scale was small.

Similarly Connolly (1954) using the Connolly Occupational Interests Questionnaire found that scores of structural engineering draughtsmen in certain interest fields differed significantly from those of a general population sample. These were experienced draughtsmen from a variety of firms, and their scores were higher in Connolly's Group E (natural sciences) and his Group L ('working with tangible things . . .'). The draughtsmen's scores indicated significantly lower interests in F ('people as individuals . . .') in H ('words, verbal concepts . . .'), and in K ('codifying, classifying and arranging data'). Connolly reports other such differences with various occupational groups.

We will examine the Kuder Preference Record (Vocational) in the next chapter. We need to indicate here a number of classifications of interests that have been proposed by investigators, and suggest their usefulness for simple classificatory models in

TABLE 4.5 *Classification of interests*

From G. F. Kuder, Kuder Preference Record (Vocational)	*From* T. G. Connolly, Occupational Interests Questionnaire (1954)	*From* D. E. Super's synthesis, *Psychology of Careers* (1957)
0 Outdoor	E 'Natural sciences'	1 Scientific
1 Mechanical	F 'People as individuals'	2 Technical or material
2 Computational	G Influence the attitudes of people	3 Humanistic or social welfare
3 Scientific	H Words and verbal concepts	4 Systematic or business detail interest
4 Persuasive	J Music, drama, visual arts or design	5 Business contact
5 Artistic	K Codifying, classifying data	6 Literary
6 Literary	L Working with tangible things, tools and materials	7 Musical and Artistic
7 Musical		
8 Social Service		
9 Clerical		

guidance. Table 4.5 lists three classifications of interests, and indicates their sources.

Two basic questions arise in relation to interest inventories and their classifications of interests. First, are such interest categories psychologically meaningful? Do they reflect real groupings in the individual personality of certain likings and preferences which tend to go together? They should. If they do, then we can *adapt* Vernon's account of ability (1940), given in Chapter 3 above, to describe an interest category or dimension: 'It implies the existence of a group or category of expressed preferences which correlate highly with one another, and which are relatively distinct from (i.e., give low correlations with) other expressed preferences.'

The second question relates to validity. The interest categories may be psychologically coherent, and enable us to describe an individual's motivation on meaningful dimensions. But this only helps if we know that relationships exist between scores on these interest categories and work behaviours such as job choice and satisfaction. An interest inventory needs to be validated, and this has been done with many inventories, such as the Strong Vocational Interest Blank (1943, 1955). There have been two approaches to such validation. First, the inventory is given to people already in various occupations, and the investigator analyses the results to see if typical profiles emerge for certain occupations which are significantly different from interest profiles of other job groups. The second approach is longitudinal. The inventories are completed by young people, probably while they are at school. Subsequently the investigator follows up these individuals to see what jobs they enter, and how satisfied and competent they are in them. The data are then analysed in an attempt to discover relationships between the earlier interest scores and the later work behaviour. This second was the approach adopted in the Levine and Wallen (1954) study we have referred to; the Connolly data were obtained by the first, cross-sectional method.

With such a classification of interests and with whatever model of human ability we choose to adopt, we are in a position to formulate a scheme for provisonally categorizing individuals and jobs for guidance and placement purposes. In Table 3.2 we gave one such scheme. In Table 4.6 below, the two dimensions are level of general intelligence required and kind of interests relevant, using Connolly's seven interest areas. The job or occupation we are analysing or the individual we are guiding may need to be placed in more than one box in the scheme.

Clearly we might adopt alternative classifications of interests for describing the job or individual by kind or type. Similarly other ability concepts might be adopted for the horizontal dimension, such as one or a number of the primary mental abilities.

Interest inventories are normally constructed so that choosing one item means rejecting another. High scores on some interest categories necessarily entail low scores on others. As a result an individual's scores on an interest inventory may indicate the likely direction of his motivated behaviour, but say nothing of the degree of his motivation compared with that of other people. If, adopting a concept of general drive, we consider Smith to have three times the drive of Taylor, then Smith's low score on artistic interest might still seem to reflect higher motivation in that area than does Taylor's high artistic score. What we do know is that Smith will probably be even more motivated in those areas where his interest scores are higher than his artistic score.

Guidance based on an assessment of interests is frequently confronted with the danger of the self-fulfilling prophecy. The young man whom we are advising has limited experience, because he is young and possibly also because of a culturally narrow background. Faced with an interest inventory he completes it on the basis of his limited experience, and we, guided by the interests he expresses, advise him on possible occupations. He enters one of them, is reasonably happy and successful, and our advice or prediction is seen to be justified. The danger is that our prediction, success and satisfaction in a certain occupation, has come to pass only partly because of the grounds on which we made it, his inventoried interests. The prediction was fulfilled partly because we predicted it; this is the self-fulfilling prophecy. Because the individual has interests XYZ we immediately direct him to occupation XYZ. But in a different environment there might have emerged other interests which his youth and his restricted background have never allowed to develop. These potential but unexpressed interests ABC might have led to an even more suitable occupation, even more in accord with the individual's abilities, cardinal and central personal dispositions, and basic values. The danger is that in guiding any young person on the basis of the interests he has already developed into work appropriate to

TABLE 4.6 A scheme for classifying job and individual by level and type (level categorized in terms of general intelligence, types in terms of Connolly's interest groups)

Fields of interest

	E	F	G	H	I	K	L
Level of general intelligence	Natural Sciences	People as individuals	Influencing people	Words and verbal concepts	Music, drama, visual arts, design	Codifying, classifying data	Working with tangible things
Top 10%							
Upper 20%							
Middle 40%							
Lower 20%							
Bottom 10%							

those interests, we tend to preclude the possibility of other, different interests developing.

The danger, particularly with young people, may be reduced but not eliminated by making more use in guidance of negative interests or dislikes. What a person is very hostile to doing, whether it be figure work or ball games, may be important and very constant over time. Tyler (1959) in analysing the interest scores of some doctors found that it was primarily the pattern of their dislikes which had remained unchanged over time. In many situations guidance, based on an individual's expression of definite, experienced dislikes, may often function most usefully as a process for determining what sorts of jobs the individual should avoid.

CONCLUSION

Personality and Occupation

We have mentioned that one approach to determining the relevance of certain interests to specific occupations is that of analysing the interests of people already in those occupations. This approach has also been adopted for investigating the values and personality traits of particular occupational groups. Such a cross-sectional approach does not answer a basic question. Is any typical pattern of interests and values found among, for example, accountants, the result of people with similar interests and values entering that profession? Or do different sorts of people become accountants, but a typical interest and value profile emerges because of their socialization and common experience within the same occupation? With regard to interests, Darley and Hagenah (1955) assert that their interpretation of the relevant research leads them to conclude: 'The individual's occupational interests are well determined before job experience. Interest measurement merely translates existing motivations and satisfactions into the vocabulary of the world of work.' If we agree with this, then the danger of the self-fulfilling prophecy we have referred to is negligible. It only remains to decide by what age 'occupational interests are well determined'.

Alternatively it is possibly more useful to regard interests and values in the child, adolescent, and adult—personality traits are another matter—as the product of a continuing interaction between personality and the environment. The environment has presumably more influence in earlier years, but the situations of adolescence and adulthood may modify or develop interests and values, or make manifest those that are latent in the individual personality. Studies of the Levine and Wallen (1954) kind are undoubtedly convincing but not conclusive. The fifteen-year-old with 'accounting type' interests is happy and successful in an accounting job ten years later. The prophecy is fulfilled (his own, his parents, or his counsellor's) simply because it was made and implemented. He might have been as happy and successful (or more so) in a number of other occupations. The Morse and Weiss (1955) study referred to in Chapter 1 suggests we make the best of the job we have, as would be expected from dissonance theory (Festinger, 1957). The point may apply particularly to those individuals whose patterns of interests and values are not occupationally distinctive, and be less relevant to people with highly specific occupational interests and value profiles.

Schemes for Analysing the Individual and Work
At some stage the individual must choose, at least provisionally, a certain type of job. When we advise in guidance and placement, what models exist to help us, by their relating interests, values, traits, drives, needs, etc., to relevant occupations? We have already examined the basic threefold classification of needs, and have listed Maslow's drive-hierarchy. We have referred to Cattell's categorization of source traits, and have given a number of divisions of interests along various dimensions. In the next chapter we will examine a division of values into six categories.

What might prove useful for occupational purposes, and particularly for guidance and selection, is a model which relates personality types to relevant occupational classes. This has been attempted by Holland (1959, 1962) in his theory of vocational choice. Holland provides six categories which relate both to the individual ('pattern of personal orientations', 'personality types', 'model orientations'), and to employment ('occupational environments'). The model orientations of these six personality types are realistic, intellectual, social, conventional, enterprising, and artistic (the names are those given by Holland in the 1962 article). For illustration we will include Holland's account of the intellectual: 'The model type is task orientated, intraceptive, asocial; prefers to think through rather than act out problems; needs to understand; enjoys ambiguous work tasks; has unconventional values and attitudes; is anal as opposed to oral.'

The term, personality type, is misleading, in that no one is, say, either intellectual *or* realistic. Holland, in fact, thinks of the individual as having a hierarchy of preferences for the six orientations, and of vocational choice being determined by whichever orientations head the hierarchy. We can assess this hierarchy of orientations within the individual, says Holland, by means of 'interest inventories' broadly conceived as 'personality inventories which reveal information such as the person's values, attitudes, needs, self-concept, preferred activities, and sources of threat and dissatisfaction' (1959). Such an assessment might suggest that the individual's chief orientation is, say, intellectual, which makes it likely he will seek intellectual occupational environments. Holland gives the occupations of physicists, anthropologists, chemists, mathematicians, and biologists, as examples of this type.

Various classificatory grids are also useful, particularly for guidance purposes. We gave schemes in Tables 4.6 and 3.2, adapted from Rodger and Cavanagh (1962), for classifying the individual and job by level and type. No individual or occupation is likely to be satisfactorily described in terms of one 'type' only, and it may be necessary to categorize them under two or three headings, indicating the order of importance.

Super proposes a similar sort of grid (1957), but the classification is threefold, by level, field (type), and enterprise. This last is according to the sort of institutional setting within which the occupation is pursued. Thus an accountant might work for a finance company, or a manufacturing concern, or the Civil Service, and these may all affect the job in some way. Super's scheme is given in Figure 4.1.

The self concept also provides a framework for considering the individual's motivation in terms both of needs and trait-elements. In Chapter 2 we introduced Allport's proprium and in Chapter 6 we will discuss the self at greater length, but we are simply suggesting here that we may usefully think of the individual as having two selves, the apparent and ideal. The apparent self is what the individual perceives himself as really being. The ideal is the self he would ideally like to be. The individual experiences any discrepancy between the two as dissonant and uncomfortable. He strives to reduce this discomfort and dissonance by making his

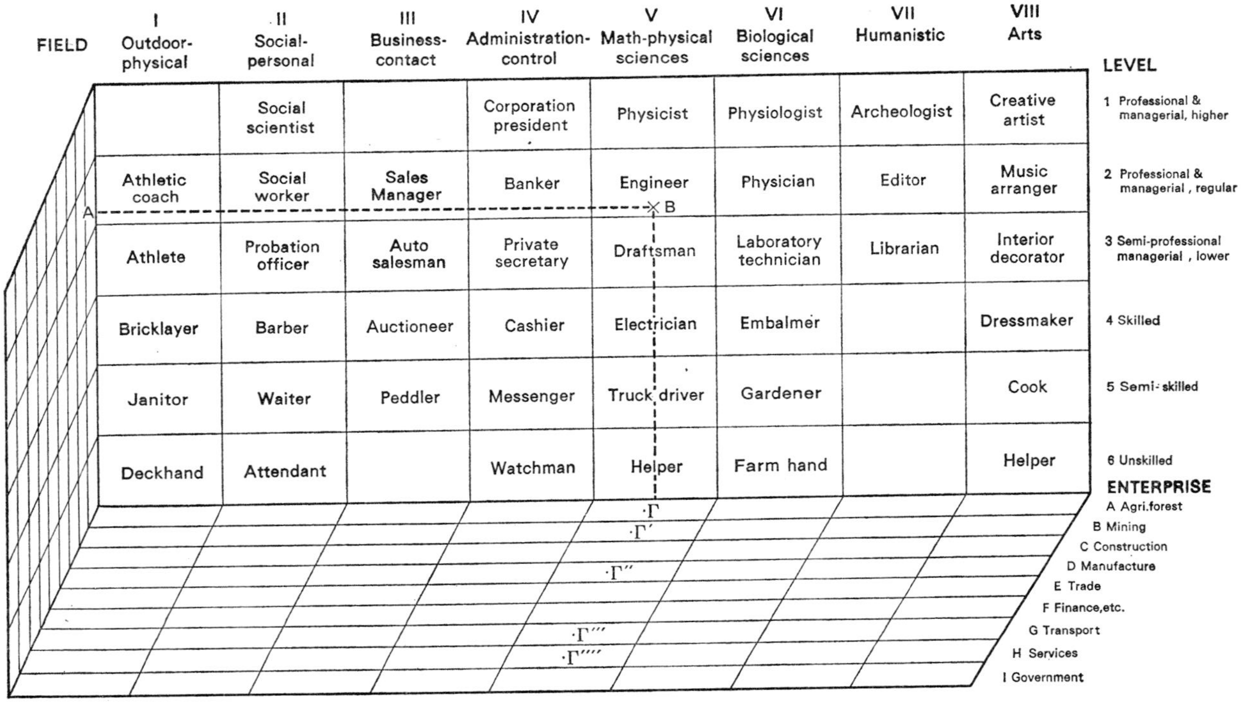

Fig. 4.1 A scheme for classifying occupations by level, field, and enterprise (Super, 1957)

apparent self more like his ideal self; in this way the discrepancy he perceives between his two selves becomes a source of motivation. Alternatively he might, by some internal process, bring his ideal self into better accord with his apparent self.

This overall discrepancy between the two selves is a source of general drive and motivation, such as we earlier discussed. But the individual also sees himself in relation to specific aspects of his environment. As regards work he might see that his apparent and ideal selves do not accord in relation to his job, or its pay, its physical environment, surrounding organization, or informal social relationships. For example, an accountant might be in a certain job and so see himself in a certain way (his apparent self). This may partly accord with his ideal self, since the job enables him to see himself as the sort of person he wants to be in terms of income, associates at work, and the prestige of the company. But the actual content of the job, its duties and responsibilities, are dissonant with his perception of his ideal self. He 'knows' he is a backroom accountant, producing mundane reports that no one ever reads. He likes to see himself as an assertive executive, influential in determining company financial policy (his ideal self). Here the discrepancy between his two selves, and the motivation it generates, are specific.

Interest and value questionnaires, tests of personality traits, interviews and other measures of needs and drives, may variously provide some account of how the individual perceives himself. We need to refine such techniques so that we can distinguish between these two aspects of the self, and so obtain another sort of measure for general and specific motivation, embracing analyses in terms of both trait-elements and needs.

REFERENCES

Adkins, D. C. and Kuder, G. F. (1940), 'The relation between primary mental abilities and activity preferences', *Psychometrica*, 5.

Adorno, T. W. *et al.* (1950), *The Authoritarian Personality*, Harper & Row.

Allport, G. W. (1961), *Pattern and Growth in Personality*, Holt, Rinehart & Winston.

Bendig, A. W. (1960), 'Factor Analysis of "Anxiety" and "Neuroticism" Inventories', *J. of Consulting Psychol.*, 24, 2.

Burt, C. (1935), *The Subnormal Mind*, Oxford University Press.

Careers Research and Advisory Centre (1968), *Interests and Occupations. An introduction to the design and use of the Connolly Occupational Interests Questionnaire,* Cambridge: CRAC.

Carruthers, T. E. (1968), 'Work values and chosen careers', *Occup. Psychol.*, 42, 111–17.

Connolly, T. G. (1954), 'A Contribution to the Measurement of Occupational Interests', Ph.D thesis, University of London.

Cooper, J. B. and McGaugh, J. L. (1963), *Integrating Principles of Social Psychology*, Schenkman.

Darley, J. G. and Hagenah, T. (1955), *Vocational Interest Measurement, Theory and Practice,* University of Minnesota Press.

Dodge, A. F. (1938), 'Social dominance and sales personality', *J. appl. Psychol.*, 22, 132–9.

Dodge, A. F. (1938a), 'What are the personality traits of the successful salesperson?', *J. appl. Psychol.*, 22, 229–38.

Festinger, L. (1957), *A Theory of Cognitive Dissonance,* Harper & Row.

Friedmann, E. A. and Havinghurst, R. J. (1954), *The Meaning of Work and Retirement*, University of Chicago Press.

Henry, W. E. (1949), 'The business executive; the psychodynamics of a social role', *Amer. J. Sociol.*, 54, 286–91

Holland, J. L. (1959), 'A theory of vocational choice', *J. Counseling Psychol.*, 6, 35–43.

Holland, J. L. (1962), 'Some explorations of a theory of vocational choice: 1. One- and two-year longitudinal studies', *Psychol. Mon.* 76, 26.

Kuder, G. F., *Kuder Preference Record—Personal, Administrator's Manual*, 1953, Chicago: Science Research Associates.

Levine, P. R. and Wallen, R. (1954), 'Adolescent vocational interests and later occupation', *J. appl. Psychol.*, 38, 428–31.

Lewin, K. (1952), *Field Theory in Social Science*, Tavistock.

Morse, N. C. and Weiss, R. S. (1955), 'The function and meaning of work and the job', *American Sociological Review*, April.

Murray, H. A. (1938), *Explorations in Personality*, Oxford University Press.

Normile, R. H. (1967), 'Differentiation among known occupational groups by means of the Work Values Inventory', unpublished dissertation, Washington, D.C.

Postman, L., Bruner, J. S., and McGinnies, E. (1948), 'Personal values as selective factors in perception', *J. abnorm. soc. Psychol.*, 43, 142–54.

Raylesberg, D. D. (1949), 'Personal values as a frame of reference in the perception of some aspects of an occupation', doctoral dissertation, Teachers' College, Columbia University.

Rodger, A. and Cavanagh, P. (1962), 'Personal selection and vocational guidance', in *Society: Problems and Methods of Study*, ed. A. T. Welford, Routledge & Kegan Paul.

Roe, A. (1946), 'The personality of artists', *Educ. Psych. Measurement*, 6.

Roe, A. (1951), 'A psychological study of eminent physical scientists', *Genet. Psychol. Mon.*, 43.

Roe, A. (1951a), 'A study of imagery in research scientists', *J. Pers.*, 19.

Roe, A. (1956), *The Psychology of Occupations*, Wiley.

Roe, A. (1964), 'Personality structure and occupational behavior', in *Man in a World of Work*, ed. H. Borow, Houghton Mifflin.

Sarbin, T. R. and Berdie, R. F. (1940), 'Relation of measured interests to the Allport-Vernon Study of Values', *J. appl. Psychol.*, 24.

Sartain, A. Q. (1946), 'Relation between scores on certain standard tests and supervisory success in an aircraft factory', *J. appl. Psychol.*, 30.

Secord, P. F. and Backman, C. W. (1964), *Social Psychology*, McGraw-Hill.

Siegelman, M. and Peck, R. F. (1960), 'Personality patterns related to occupational roles', *Genet. Psychol. Mon.*, 61, 291–349.

Spence, K. W. (1958), 'A theory of emotionally based drive (D) and its relation to performance in simple learning situations', *Amer. Psychologist*, 13.

Strong, E. K. (1943), *Vocational Interests of Men and Women*, Stanford University Press.

Strong, E. K. (1955), *Vocational Interests 18 Years after College*, University of Minnesota Press.

Super, D. E. (1957), *The Psychology of Careers*, Harper & Row.

Super, D. E. and Crites, J. O. (1962), *Appraising Vocational Fitness*, Harper & Row, and John Weatherhill, Inc.

Taylor, J. A. (1956), 'Drive theory and manifest anxiety', *Psychol. Bull.*, 53, 4.

Triggs, F. O. (1947), 'A study of the relationship of measured interests to measured mechanical aptitude, personality, and vocabulary', *American Psychologist*, 2, 296.

Tyler, L. E. (1959), 'Distinctive patterns of likes and dislikes over a twenty-two year period', *J. Counseling Psychol.*, 6, 234–7.

Vernon, P. E. and Parry, J. B. (1949), *Personnel Selection in the British Forces*, University of London Press.

CHAPTER 5

Techniques of Personality Assessment and Measurement

INTRODUCTION

Reliability and Validity

In the last three chapters we have considered personality. We need to examine now some techniques for assessing and measuring personality, particularly those which seem relevant to guidance and selection. In guidance and selection we wish to be able to predict, on the basis of our assessment of personality, so that when we say 'you will like that sort of work' or 'he will be suitable for this job', subsequent events will prove us to have been right. Personality assessment serves also a diagnostic function in guidance and selection; this is particularly useful for the counselling approach to guidance which we will outline in Chapter 6.

The predictive capacity of any personality assessment remains important. But for a technique to be predictive it must first be reliable, which means it has to be able to give the same results on different occasions. It must be consistent. Thirty centimetres on a rubber ruler, which stretched or shrunk according to heat and usage, would be different on different occasions. The ruler, an intelligence test or an interest inventory, need to be consistent over time and place, or at least we must know why and to what extent they vary.

If a technique gives consistent results, our next question relates to our first point—do the data predict? To put this another way, has the technique validity? Which is to say, does it measure what it is supposed to measure? At the end of Chapter 2 we introduced predictive and construct validity, and we wish briefly to return to this idea of construct validity.

A standard dictionary definition of a technique might refer to 'a skill or method based on systematic application of accepted principles or theory', and this approximates to the idea of a technique adopted in much of the chapter. A technique is a method of analysing the data of a problem into categories on the basis of some theory. The very form of the analysis implicitly determines the nature of the solution to be adopted for the problem; it will be a solution in terms of the underlying theory. It we use tests of general intelligence and specialized aptitudes to select engineering apprentices, then already implicit is the adoption of some form of hierarchical group factor theory. This would normally mean we should select those applicants who do sufficiently well on tests which seem, in terms of the theory, most relevant to success in engineering. When we predict in this way, on the basis of ideas, constructs and theoretical explanations, and our predictions subsequently correlate with appropriate criteria, we have construct validity.

In this chapter, and in the book, we are primarily concerned with the construct validity of techniques. Explanation, prediction, and testing are the steps of construct validity, and essential to the proper use of a technique; they are, of course, the distinctive features of scientific method. Using a technique such as a personality test in guidance, we need to be aware of the personality theory it embodies; on the basis of the information the technique provides we make predictions in terms of the theory; subsequently we test or validate those predictions against the observed data, observed in terms of the original theory. If the predictions prove right, technique and theory continue to be useful. If some or all the predictions prove wrong, we should abandon or modify theory or technique.

Overview, and Four General Points

A job analysis scheme is an important technique for guidance and selection; this has been discussed in Chapter 1. We will specifically examine here assessment plans, such as the Seven-Point Plan, which frequently constitute part of a job analysis. In this chapter, then, we will examine the following techniques of personality assessment: assessment plans; the interview; tests of ability; interest inventories; value questionnaires; application forms. There are other techniques which will not be discussed here, such as the group selection procedure (see N.I.I.P. Paper No. 5) and the 'country-house' type of assessment.

We wish first to make four points which run as themes right through the chapter, since all are relevant to the consideration of each of the techniques.

First, the really critical part in solving any guidance, selection, or even training problem consists in the study and analysis of the whole problem, and in deciding the appropriate procedure. If the problem is seen as one of guidance, or selection, or training, then the job analysis will indicate what the procedure should be. The job analysis might suggest that numerical aptitude, good appearance, and an interest in selling are necessary. A knowledge of techniques helps us decide if these can be observed in an individual, and if so, what techniques are likely to reveal and evaluate them—a test for this, an application form and interview for that. In other words we must first determine the overall procedure, and only then decide what part different techniques might have to contribute to that procedure.

The layman's approach is frequently the reverse, and starts not with an overall analysis of the problem and consideration of an appropriate procedure, but with the chance selection of a technique. The psychologist and the personnel selection consultant are frequently presented with a problem such as—'Our key punch trainees never seem to stay very long. Can you find us an aptitude test which shows us which ones are most likely to stay?' Here a decision on technique has preceded any analysis of the problem or any consideration of appropriate procedure. In fact, if the consultant investigates Firm X he may find that high turnover among the key punch operators is a result of poor supervision. Similarly he may find at Firm Y it is indeed a selection problem, and a new procedure for selection is required. But what emerges is a more careful screening of applicants for key punch positions with regard to certain details in their job histories, and an attempt to provide them with more information on the job at interview. An aptitude test has no part to play in the new procedure.

Techniques exist for a particular purpose, and embody a certain theoretical viewpoint. This is our second point and clearly relates to the first. A tennis racket is designed for playing tennis, and is not suited for hitting a golf ball, nor for playing cricket except with children in the garden. A technique, like a tennis racket, has a specific function, and so an aptitude test might give limited but useful information in a specific area, but no information at all that is relevant in some other area. The lay approach, therefore, of using techniques as general, all-purposive instruments can be ineffective and even dangerous. For example, a manager, selecting for engineering student apprenticeships, might reject an applicant with a high intelligence level on the grounds of his low score on a test of 'mechanical aptitude'.

Our third point has already been developed in the previous chapter. In guidance and selection we attempt a form of analysis and diagnosis of personality, and there are, suggests Super (1957), two different types of approach. The first is that of the actuarial method, based on trait theory; the second approach is that of the developmental or thematic-extrapolative method, based on life pattern theory. We have already outlined both methods and their underlying theory. In this chapter we can usefully consider how a technique might contribute to one or both of these two approaches.

Our fourth point relates to general criteria for techniques and procedures. Rodger (1955) suggests that in attempting to solve a manpower problem there are three considerations. The solution must be technically sound, administratively convenient, and politically defensible or socially acceptable. This would apply specifically to our choice of techniques in guidance and selection. Most of the text is concerned with considerations that come under the heading of 'technically sound'. In guidance and selection our scheme for classifying jobs or the job analysis are key to these technical considerations: What are we looking for in the individual? Can we observe it? What technique would most effectively reveal and measure it?

Under administrative convenience come considerations of whether this procedure with these techniques can be implemented with the facilities, time, and staff available. Cost is a prime criterion; normally there would seem more justification for an expensive procedure to select senior managers than for a costly selection procedure for semi-skilled operators. The advantage of an interview over the construction of a new battery of tests consists sometimes principally in this, that the interview is more convenient and cheaper. But the interview does frequently have a second advantage; it is more acceptable to candidates than tests are. Since in guidance and selection we are dealing with people, techniques not only need to be technically sound and administratively convenient; they must also be acceptable to those concerned.

The Seven-Point Plan

In 1924 Cyril Burt, in an article entitled 'The principles of vocational guidance', asked 'What qualities are to be assessed in making recommendations for vocational guidance?' He answered his own question, and suggested six (Burt, 1924): (a) physical and medical; (b) educational attainments; (c) general intelligence; (d) vocational attainments and capacities; (e) special abilities; (f) temperamental qualities.

These practical suggestions are based on an acceptance of Spearman's two-factor theory, as becomes evident in Burt's discussion of items c, d, and e. Burt says, for example, (1924):

> Of all psychological capacities, general intelligence is the easiest to measure; it is also the most significant for the purposes of vocational guidance ... In other directions we seem confronted, not with a general power of memory, a general power of attention, or a general power of manual skill, but rather with specific and relatively independent forms of each of these several functions which share a common name.

However, there are signs of hierarchical group factor theory on the horizon, since Burt continues:

> Even if (as upon theoretical grounds, some are inclined to suppose) there really are, underlying these various cognate capacities, certain undiscovered 'central' or 'group' factors, nevertheless no adequate test for them has in any case been established or devised.

In fact Burt's list of six qualities is the origin of the Seven-Point Plan. The following year Burt, writing in a rather different field, in his classic study, *The Young Delinquent* (1925), proposed what he called a 'psychographic scheme', which was a schedule for examining the delinquent. Its relationship to the Seven-Point Plan has become more obvious.

Part of the theoretical sub-structure of this practical schedule consists again in concepts of general ability and highly specialized abilities, and these are regarded as innate. Similar assumptions are made with regard to the 'temperamental' characteristics of personality. Burt, in his main division, history and present

TABLE 5.1 *The 'psychographic scheme' for examining the individual*
(slightly abbreviated from Burt, 1925, with corresponding categories
from the Seven-Point Plan indicated)

Seven-Point Plan	*Psychographic scheme*
	I HISTORY:
	A Family history
	B Personal history
	II PRESENT SITUATION:
7	A Environment
	B Personality:
1	1. Physical characteristics
	2. Mental characteristics
	a Intellectual:
	i inborn capacities:
3	(a) general ability (intelligence)
4 (now major and minor group factors	(b) special abilities (attention, memory, verbal facility, manual dexterity, etc.)
2	ii acquired attainments:
	(a) general cultural level
	(b) special educational and vocational attainments (reading, spelling, etc.)
	b Temperamental:
	i inborn tendencies:
	(a) general emotionality
(6)	(b) special instincts and emotions (sex, anger, acquisitiveness, etc.)
	ii acquired tendencies:
5	(a) general sentiments (including habits and interests)
	(b) special complexes (including moral conflicts and neurotic states)

situation, stresses the importance of studying both the individual's
past and contemporary situation. This parallels the distinction
between life pattern theory with its developmental method, and
trait theory with the actuarial approach.

It is from Burt's conceptualization of what is relevant in examining the individual and attempting to determine the causes of
his behaviour that Rodger, as he states (1952), derived the N.I.I.P.
Seven-Point Plan. In Table 5.2 the categories of the Seven-Point

Plan are given, Table 5.1 having shown the number of each category from the Seven-Point Plan placed against those items in Burt's scheme from which they appear to be derived.

TABLE 5.2 *The Seven-Point Plan*

(Rodger, N.I.I.P., 1952)

1 PHYSICAL MAKE-UP
   defects of health or physique:
   agreeableness of
appearance	A B C D E
bearing	A B C D E
speech	A B C D E

2 ATTAINMENTS (AND PREVIOUS EXPERIENCE)
   type of education (school and later)
educational level reached	A B C D E
occupational training and experience	
occupational level reached	A B C D E

3 GENERAL INTELLIGENCE
ceiling assessed by test	A B C D E
level ordinarily displayed	A B C D E

4 SPECIAL APTITUDES
mechanical aptitude	A B C D E
manual dexterity	A B C D E
facility in use of words	A B C D E
facility in use of figures	A B C D E
talent for drawing	A B C D E
talent for music	A B C D E

5 INTERESTS
intellectual	A B C D E
practical-constructional	A B C D E
physically-active	A B C D E
social	A B C D E
artistic	A B C D E

6 DISPOSITION
how acceptable	A B C D E
how influential	A B C D E
how steady and dependable	A B C D E
how self-reliant	A B C D E

7 CIRCUMSTANCES
   domestic circumstances:
   family occupations:
   special openings:

In Chapter 4 we discussed the concept of a broad drive factor, which relates to Burt's general emotionality. Rodger omits this. The special aptitudes of the Seven-Point Plan are broader than Burt's special abilities, and this reflects the change in underlying theory. Spearman's two-factor view has been supplanted by the hierarchical group factor model. Lastly, history, one of Burt's two main categories, seems largely incorporated under Rodger's point 2, attainments and previous experience.

The Seven-Point Plan is concerned with abilities, with motivational (or 'temperamental') factors, and with opportunities. It is outlined at length elsewhere (Rodger, N.I.I.P., 1952), and here we need only to discuss a few points. Such an assessment plan as the Seven-Point, Munro Fraser's Five-Point or any other, does not serve as a technique of personality assessment in the same way as tests or interest inventories do. Assessment plans propose relevant categories within which to consider the individual in a guidance or selection situation. We have argued that techniques are normally most useful when fulfilling specific functions in a total procedure. The most important function of an assessment plan is to provide a framework within which to decide on an appropriate overall procedure. When we use the Seven-Point Plan we are saying that in order to select well or give good guidance we normally need to have information on the individual under the seven headings. Having determined what we need to know, we can choose the tests, interviews, inventories, etc., that will give us this information.

Assessment plans have also a second, more specific use, as an aid to interviewing. Prior to seeing the individual we decide in terms of the plan what information we should obtain from interview. This will suggest how we might handle the situation, and act as a check-list while we are interviewing—'by the end of the half hour I need to know this, that and that about him'.

We will conclude this outline of the Seven-Point Plan with a few specific comments. Burt's separate category of history has vanished, and we might regard it as subsumed under point 2. This would seem to emphasize a contemporary, cross-sectional approach to the individual, and favour a trait rather than a life-pattern analysis. However, Rodger in discussing the Seven-Point Plan does stress the importance of a biographical analysis under point 2 (1952).

The Seven-Point Plan does not give motivation a central place;

this is true of most schemes which emphasize a trait analysis. Interest (point 5) and disposition (point 6) are in some sense a measure of motivation, but only obliquely. Munro Fraser, as we shall see, provides motivation as a separate heading. It is certainly possible to incorporate in the scheme, possibly under disposition, the consideration of dynamic and stylistic traits. However, the previous chapter would suggest that the relationship between cardinal or central temperament traits and work behaviour is still unclear.

We can, of course, query part of the theory underlying the Seven-Point Plan. Guilford holds there is no factor of general intellectual ability. Are the categories of interests satisfactory? The practitioner can, if he wishes, replace Rodger's fivefold classification with Kuder's ten categories, Connolly's seven, or Super's seven, listed in Chapter 4.

Munro Fraser's Five Categories

As we have seen in Chapter 1, Munro Fraser proposes five headings under which we can both describe a job and specify its requirements of the job occupant (1962, 1966). The same headings serve also as an assessment plan. We have, therefore, five categories which are seen as relevant when we analyse and assess an individual for guidance or selection purposes:

1. First impression and physical make-up.

   Here we are concerned with physique, health, appearance, and other similar aspects of the individual.

2. Qualifications.

   Relevant education, training, and experience are considered.

3. Brains and abilities.

   Fraser (1962) stresses under this heading the relevance of tests. We might also attempt to evaluate ability through an analysis of the level of his past performances; such a biographical analysis is part of the developmental method.

4. Motivation.

   Fraser suggests that evaluating his past performance through biographical analysis remains the best approach.

5. Adjustment.

   Here we are concerned with the individual's stability, his reliability, and the amount of pressure he can tolerate in a work situation.

Fraser's framework is one of both categories and levels. Each of these five dimensions are divided into levels, A B C D E , which are subdivided to form twenty levels, with equal intervals between them. In the two texts referred to, Fraser provides considerable guidance on the meaning of the different levels, and stresses the importance of a clear idea of the 'average' in any category if consistency and agreement over different occasions and with different assessors is to be obtained. Table 5.3 gives Fraser's five categories and twenty levels.

Fraser's assessment plan provides a useful framework in selection, but possibly to a lesser extent in guidance. His categories are mixed. The first three are static concepts, and refer to limited aspects of the individual. Motivation and adjustment are more comprehensive concepts, which relate to total personality function.

Conclusion

Seven points, five points, or any good assessment plan functions as an aid in interviewing. More important, an assessement plan provides a framework within which to develop guidance and selection procedures appropriate for a specific situation. Decisions have to be made. To test or not to test? What tests? What sort of an interview? What do we want from an interview? Would interest inventories help? Is a medical examination necessary? etc. An assessment plan suggests, provisionally, what are the significant and relevant questions to ask about an individual in guidance and selection. Such a plan usually embodies a theory, which may be simple or highly developed. We need to be aware of this theoretical position.

THE INTERVIEW

Introduction

'The evidence shows that interviews are useful/useless, reliable/ unreliable. . . .' Blanket condemnations or approvals of the interview, common though they are, would seem to be meaningless. First, we need to qualify such a statement by specifying what the interviews are for. An interview may be for selection, guidance, for diagnosing psychiatric illness, for finding the causes of high staff turnover, etc. Even this sort of category will subdivide,

TABLE 5.3 *Munro Fraser's Five-Category Assessment Plan (1960)*

ASSESSMENT SHEET	Grade E 10% Very much below average				Grade D 20% Below average				Grade C 40% Average				Grade B 20% Above average				Grade A 10% Very much above average			
	1	2	3	4	5	6	7	8	9	10	11	12	13	14	15	16	17	18	19	20
IMPACT ON OTHERS Appearance, (speech and manner, health, etc.)																				
QUALIFICATIONS (General education, vocational training and previous experience)																				
BRAINS AND ABILITIES *Verbal*																				
Perceptual																				
Numerical																				
Mechanical																				
Spatial																				
MOTIVATION (Level of goals, realism and consistency in following them up)																				
ADJUSTMENT (Acceptability, sense of responsibility, reliability and leadership)																				

since we can interview to select apprentices, or managers, or salesmen.

Second, is the interviewer trained or untrained, adequately or inadequately briefed? Third, in a selection interview, the homogeneity of the applicants becomes very relevant. The task is obviously easier when there are real differences between applicants than when there is not much variation between them anyway. Fourth, if an interviewer is clear about what he wants from the interview and has the help of an assessment plan, he is more likely to conduct a useful interview than when his objectives and procedure are vague. The reliability and validity of an interview depend on factors such as these.

The first of our original four points suggested that a technique contributes usefully only as an appropriate part of a relevant, overall procedure. In considering the place of an interview in a guidance or selection procedure, we need to ask two questions. First, what are we looking for in the individual? The job analysis and the job classification scheme (see Chapter 4) answer this for us in selection and guidance. Normally we would specify what we are seeking in the individual in terms of an assessment plan. Secondly, we ask in what way the interview might help us assess and measure what seem the relevant aspects of the individual. For example, we might feel in guidance it is essential to determine the individual's level of intelligence and the direction of his interests. Can the interview help us with this?

Our second point was that techniques exist for a specific purpose, and we can usefully think of the interview as having two main purposes whenever it is used. First, the interview can provide additional information, like a test or interest inventory. In a selection situation we might already know an applicant's work history from his application form, and have character references and test scores for him. But the job specification has indicated that a good appearance and a friendly, acceptable manner are essential for the job. An interview would seem the obvious way for assessing the applicant on these. Alternatively the interview may have an integrating function. Here we have all the relevant information, but it still needs to be structured and made meaningful. We use the interview to make sense of what we already know. In practice an interview usually functions both to provide additional information and to integrate all that one knows of the individual.

The third point relates to a consideration of techniques in terms of the actuarial and developmental methods. Does one regard the interview as a sample of an individual's behaviour, providing like tests a cross-sectional analysis of his personality? This would be to use it as part of an actuarial approach. Or alternatively should one use the interview more as a method for finding out about an individual's past behaviour in real-life situations? Here the analysis would be mainly historical, as in a biographical application form, and typically a developmental approach. In practice the interview can be a combination of both, with the interviewer attempting to analyse the individual in terms of trait and life pattern theory together.

The fourth point relates to Rodger's three criteria, and on two of them the interview does well. The interview is here to stay, and simply for no other reason than that it is administratively convenient, being flexible, able to deal with all manner and level of applications, and easy to arrange. The interview is also socially acceptable, to interviewer and interviewee. Its technical soundness provides the main area of criticism, and is what we will now examine, in terms of reliability and validity, taking our examples mainly from interviewing for assessment purposes.

Reliability

Is the interview reliable? That is, do interviewers agree and are they consistent? Counsel for the prosecution inevitably refers to an early study by Rice (1929). A large number of destitute people applying for relief were interviewed by two individuals. One of the interviewers was a socialist and the other an advocate of temperance. The socialist 'found' that with 39 per cent of those interviewed their destitution was attributable to industrial conditions, and with 22 per cent their destitution was caused by drink. The advocate of temperance regarded the destitution of only 7 per cent the result of industrial conditions, but with as many as 62 per cent drink had been the cause of their present state.

Hollingworth (1929) provides further evidence for the prosecution. Twelve managers interviewed independently fifty-seven applicants for sales positions. Every applicant received rankings most of the way from the top to the bottom of the list. An applicant placed top of the list by one interviewer was ranked last by another interviewer.

From these early studies onwards we can quote a number of investigations with low levels of agreement between interviewers. But our original point stands. Such data are evidence of the unreliability of certain interviews, with certain interviewers, in specific situations. We cannot make bold generalizations on the strength of such data.

What evidence is there for the defence? Vernon and Parry (1949) report on an officer-selection study, where two teams of experienced staff observed and interviewed 125 candidates. The two teams, and members with the same functions in the different teams, achieved some considerable agreement on their evaluation of candidates. For example, the ratings of senior army officers, who had sat in on each other's interviews, correlated positively to the extent of 0·65. Two psychiatrists independently interviewing the same candidates also obtained a correlation on their ratings of +0·65. The agreement between the total ratings of one team with another, based on a knowledge of test scores, on observation of group situations, and interviews, was +0·80.

Munro Fraser (1966) provides evidence on a smaller scale from what is more typically an interview situation. Twenty mature, part-time students acted as interviewees. They were in the main supervisors, junior executives, and workers' representatives, from local industry. Four personnel officers gave them tests and then interviewed them, knowing their test scores. Each personnel officer was to assess all twenty students along four of Fraser's categories, impact on others, qualifications, motivation, and adjustment, and indicate his assessment by placing them at one of the twenty levels (see Table 5.3). The first interviewer's judgments were compared with those of a second interviewer; and the judgments of the other two interviewers were compared. This made eighty comparisons, which are given in Table 5.4. The data in Table 5.4 show agreement within two points of less (10 per cent of the scale) for 84 per cent of the comparisons.

These and similar studies provide evidence that interviewers sometimes agree, which does not mean that what they agree upon is right. Whether or not the interviewer is right relates to the question of validity.

Validity

Has the interview validity?—that is, does it measure what it is

138

TABLE 5.4 *Assessments by different interviewers compared*
(Interview assessments of twenty students, made by four different interviewers on a twenty-point scale, a total of eighty comparisons: A's
assessments are compared with B's; C's assessments are compared with
D's)

	No. of times	Percentage
Exact agreement on	21	26
1 point difference on	27	34
2 point difference on	19	24
3 point difference on	9	11
4 point difference on	4	5
	80	100

supposed to measure? Are interviewers right and accurate in their
assessment and predictions? In considering the evidence we need
to retain the distinction between the interview as a technique for
gathering additional information and its integrating function.

First, the evidence against, and of course data on the unreliability of the interview, such as the Hollingworth study (1929),
are evidence also of its invalidity. Vernon and Parry (1949) report
that during the war there were many instances when the interview
had a lower correlation with the chosen criterion than did a test
score, even though the interviewer would usually have made his
interview and assessment knowing this test score. For example,
730 army personnel were selected to train as drivers, and the
criterion of success was whether they passed or failed on the
training course. The correlation between the Selection Officers'
assessment in interview and success on training was 0·234. But the
validity of the Bennett Test proved higher, 0·294, and a straight
correlation of success with age produced a coefficient of 0·288 (the
younger the man, the more likely was he to pass training). In other
words the individual's age or Bennett score were better predictors
of success than was the selection officer's interview assessment,
even though he interviewed knowing the candidate's age and
Bennett score. There were similar findings with the selection of 411
naval radar plot operators, where the criterion was final course
results. Selection officers' assessments correlated with criterion
at +0·374, and scores on the S.P. Test 2 also produced a positive
correlation of 0·416. The statistics are complicated by the fact

that men were actually selected on the selection officers' assessment. Allowing for this, validities are, according to Vernon and Parry, about the same.

A similar study in a different field, student selection for undergraduate courses, produced the same sort of result (Himmelweit and Summerfield, 1951). Interview judgments by a board of university teachers showed zero validity against degree marks one and two years later. A battery of aptitude tests gave small positive correlations.

The first piece of evidence for the defence is substantial, though the correlations are small (Vernon, 1950). The study investigated the selection of candidates for the Civil Service by the Civil Service Selection Board. The procedure lasted two or three days, and used examination, tests, *curricula vitae*, exercises, interviews, and a final selection board. In the follow-up a number of criteria were used. One criterion consisted in assessments of the work of selected applicants as assistant principals by their superiors one and a half to two years later. Each candidate had three interviews, first a 20-minute viva with an 'observer', and a longer interview with a psychologist and then with the chairman. Interviewers were supplied with a considerable amount of information on the candidate. Most interview ratings correlated positively with the criteria. For example, the interview predictions by 'observer', psychologist, and chairman for 202 administrative officers correlated positively with a composite, overall criterion at 0·419, 0·408, and 0·476. The correlations, usually of around 0·4, added only slightly to correlations derived from the tests and various observed exercises. The Final Selection Board, fully briefed on a candidate's performance in the selection procedure, made a last interview, as a result of which they might modify the candidate's final assessment and mark. Their amendment was usually an improvement. For example, the predictions of the 'observer', the psychologist, and the chairman above, changed to produce improved correlations of 0·436, 0·485, and 0·486. The overall correlation for the Administrative Class rose from around 0·4 to 0·563.

Other examples of 'valid' interviews are found again in Vernon and Parry (1949). In a study of 503 Royal Navy Volunteer Reserve cadets the criterion adopted was assessment at the end of training. The cadets were rated in interview prior to training, by psychologists interviewing with full knowledge of their test scores. The psychologists' interview assessments correlated with criterion at $+0.57$, whereas test scores gave a correlation of only $+0.24$.

Munro Fraser (1966) provides further supporting data on a small account in a follow-up of a personnel officer's interview assessments. The personnel officer was involved in the selection of 39 staff for clerical, sales, drawing office, research, and marketing positions; a few were employed against his advice. He used a biographical interview as the basis for his assessment, and no tests. The criterion was an assessment by a supervisor six months after the applicant had started work with the firm, with the following results: 28 applicants assessed as suitable at interview proved suitable; 6 applicants' weaknesses diagnosed at interview later became evident. Thus in 34 out of 39 cases (87.5 per cent) the assessment and prediction was correct. With 2 out of the remaining 5 cases the interviewer's prediction proved completely wrong, and the remaining 3 individuals were found satisfactory, as predicted, but left because they did not like the jobs. Impressive though this is, we do not know if equally good or better results could have been obtained with, say, tests or by scoring items on the application forms.

Most guidance and selection studies which present evidence for certain validities will have an interview somewhere as part of the guidance or selection procedures. This applies to the studies we will examine in the next two chapters. But where a procedure is successful and, for example, reduces by better selection the failure on a course by 10 per cent, we cannot evaluate the contribution (if any) of the interview. Success may be due to factors other than the interview, such as information from tests and interest inventories.

Enough evidence exists to show the interview can be reliable and valid. It is more likely to be technically sound when its function in a guidance or selection procedure is clearly defined, and when the interviewer is trained or experienced, and uses some suitable job classification scheme or an assessment plan based on adequate job information. Such an interview may contribute by providing supplementary data, or by integrating existing information, or by both.

But the interview remains irreplaceable, whatever its validity, especially as far as the candidate is concerned. The interview is not just socially acceptable; to omit it remains socially unacceptable.

The Useful Interview

The interview, like any other technique, is likely only to be useful as an appropriate part of a well-planned guidance or selection procedure. We achieve this by answering two questions. What are we looking for in the individual? We can specify our answer in the categories of an assessment scheme, such as the Seven-Point Plan. Secondly, can we observe and evaluate in the individual these relevant traits, interests, needs, etc., by means of an interview? In this way we decide the specific objectives of an interview, which determine its form and content.

In a selection interview we may choose a developmental or actuarial method, or a combination of the two. The biographical approach which proves so useful in employment interviewing is primarily developmental; we examine the individual's past behaviour as a basis for predicting his future behaviour. But the biographical approach may implicitly be actuarial also; we evaluate the applicant in, say, abilities and interests on the manner, style, and competence with which he describes his school and work record.

We will now discuss interview method considering it under four headings, rapport, content, guidance of interview, and reporting.

Establishing Rapport. If we want from an interview information on the applicant's background, education, and work record, and at the same time to assess his 'normal' way of behaving, it is important to have him talking easily and naturally about himself. The real roles in selection interviewing, interviewer and interviewee, are dominant and subordinate. There is really a power relationship, if the applicant wants the job, since the interviewer will normally have some say in who is offered the post. But in most selection situations and invariably in guidance an apparent reversal of roles is required, with the interviewee the dominant talker and the interviewer the interested, impressed listener. Dealing with the obvious points about the situation, such as giving the interviewee a comfortable seat, beginning the interview on time, and having no interruptions, does provide the right circumstances.

The opening should be easy to cope with, possible factual; not 'why do you want this job?' or 'what sort of work do you want when you leave school?', but more suitably 'can we just get the facts about your G.C.E. results cleared up?' and 'your present job seems very relevant to this vacancy, so can you tell us something about it?' Once the interview is begun, questions should be open, and aimed at launching the individual on a flow of talk, rather than inviting a short reply. For example, 'the job you are doing—what does it entail?' will normally find out more than 'I suppose you are responsible for all Machine Shop Inspection in your job?' Encouraging remarks and noises, 'good, hmm, that must have been interesting', have a useful place in most interviews. Challenging or critical remarks have their uses, but in many situations, in guidance and in selection, a hint of criticism will stop the flow of information. 'Did you find your school work interesting?' is likely to discover more than 'I get the impression you were lazy at school—was this so?' Obtrusive note-taking by the interviewer may inhibit conversation, and it is wise to put down the pencil or biro when the interviewee is about to say something personal.

Content of Interview. At the pre-interview stage we must decide what we want to learn from the interview; this is where an assessment plan is helpful. If we are clear about what we want to know, then questions tend to suggest themselves, and may be appropriately structured around an exploration of the individual's education, experience, and interests. During interview an assessment plan acts as a quick reference list of relevant headings which serve to remind the interviewer what information he needs.

Job applicants and people receiving guidance want facts on the vacant post or on various occupations. Advertisements, job write-ups, career pamphlets, can help with this by providing general information. In interview we can tell the individual what seems particularly relevant to him, and he can ask questions.

Guiding the Interview. Interviews can be conducted with varying degrees of control. It may be useful to exert less control in guidance than in selection, especially if the guidance interview has a counselling orientation. But time is always limited, and an unobtrusive pushing from less to more profitable interview content may sometimes be necessary. For example, when an applicant is providing excessive detail on a job he has had, the interviewer might say: 'I think I've a pretty good idea now what that job entailed; could you tell me something about your next job?'

Reporting the Interview. An assessment plan provides the framework for the report on the individual. Ratings and comments along the various dimensions, such as 'level of intelligence, motivation, mechanical interests, etc.', might be supplemented by an overall pen-picture. Assessment and ratings along the different dimensions provide a useful basis for comparing candidates. It helps also to avoid the 'halo effect', whereby one good, or bad, characteristic of an individual influences us to rate him consistently high, or low, in all other areas. Other examples of forms for rating were given as Figures 2 and 3 in Chapter 4.

TESTS OF ABILITY

Tests of aptitude and intelligence are too specialized a subject for detailed treatment in this text, but our four points concerning techniques in general still apply. These sorts of tests have no magic about them; they contribute in guidance and selection only as an appropriate part of a well-planned procedure.

Tests exist for a fairly specific purpose, and usually embody a certain theoretical position. The test, like an interview, attempts to take a representative sample of behaviour. A test score is a measure of an individual's performance on this sample. If we know through correlation coefficients that a test score correlates with a certain performance in a given area, we are in a position to make limited predictions. If we know also why the correlation exists—we have a theory—we can make broader predictions and they are more likely to be correct. We have already discussed in Chapter 3 the main theories embodied in ability testing, hierarchical group factor, primary mental abilities, and Guilford's structure-of-intellect model. Test scores, therefore, need to be interpreted in terms of their underlying theory.

With large numbers of applicants tests may be used on the basis of minimum and maximum cut-off points, with those scoring above or below the cut-offs not being considered further. In selection, decisions are needed on appropriate cut-off positions, and also on what other group of people we should compare a test score with. This problem of norms exists in both guidance and selection. Shall we compare the scores of these applicants or of this individual in guidance with those of a typical cross-section of the population, or with the scores of engineering craft apprentices or university undergraduates? Shall we compare them with test results of people from the same age group, or from a wide spread of ages? We can answer the question if we are clear on why we are using the test and on what sort of information we want from it.

Though intelligence and aptitude testing originated mainly in the field of education, evidence has now accumulated on their reliability, validity, and usefulness in the employment situation, both for guidance and selection purposes. Much of the evidence is published in a comprehensive text edited by O. K. Buros, *The Mental Measurements Yearbook*. This text is constantly in revision, and embraces not only ability tests but all other sorts, such as personality measures, interest inventories, value questionnaires, etc.

Our third point is the actuarial-developmental distinction. If a test embodies a trait analysis, then it is actuarial in its method, and is attempting to make a cross-sectional analysis of the individual at one point in time. An attainment test, such as a set of mathematics problems, is more developmental in its approach, since it measures obliquely an individual's behaviour in the past. But the distinction between attainment and ability tests is not precise since an individual's knowledge is affected by his past ability, and his past experience affects his ability.

Some tests are technically sound, and others less so, and some not at all. Their reliability and validity coefficients are a measure of this. If tests already exist which are relevant in a specific situation, then they are administratively convenient in a number of ways; for example, where there are a very large number of applicants, and cut-off points are applied, numbers to be dealt with may be reduced to more manageable proportions. The social acceptability of tests varies with a number of factors, such as age and level of jobs. In selection, tests are more readily accepted at an apprentice level than at senior management; a sixteen-year-old copy-typist might happily take a test while a middle-aged typist may regard it as demeaning to do so.

Testing

Part of the meaning of a test score arises in its relation to the scores of other people. So differences in the scores of a number of individuals should reflect underlying differences in those individuals; they should not be an outcome of different situations in which the tests were taken. Test-giving needs to be standardized. We attempt to achieve this by providing a test situation which enables the individuals to give their best performance. They should be motivated, but not anxious. The room in which they take the test should be ready beforehand; it should be well-lit, comfortable, and provide satisfactory desks. Trainees must be able to hear the instructions, and these should be given clearly and confidently. Most tests and inventories provide a standard set of instructions which the tester should speak out slowly and precisely to the testees. Testees must be in a condition to give of their best to the various tests. If they are unwell or tired, test or inventory scores may give no real indication of their true potential or of what they really feel and think.

INTEREST INVENTORIES

Whatever the derivation of an individual's interests, however static a concept that of interests appears to be, however peripheral interests might seem to personality structure, inventoried interests frequently prove significant in work behaviour. Over the past forty years much data have been accumulated which differentiate between different occupational groups, such as doctors and lawyers, on the basis of interests. We can also, to a limited extent, predict choice of occupation and satisfaction in a certain occupation using inventoried interests. The evidence tends to suggest it is interests which in part cause the choice and satisfaction, and not the work and occupation which determine the interests. Though the concept of interests might fail to convey the dynamic nature of motivation, the static quality of the concept does reflect the stability of the direction of motivation at work. An individual's inventoried interests appear to change very little after adolescence.

There exist a number of reliable interest inventories about which there are data on their occupational relevance, such as the Strong Vocational Interest Blank, the Rothwell–Miller, the Kuder Preference Record (Vocational) and the Connolly Occupational Interests Questionnaire. In Chapter 4 we referred briefly to data on the Connolly and Kuder, and will now examine the Kuder in more detail.

The Kuder Preference Record (Vocational)
There are three Kuder Preference Records in use, Vocational, Personal, and Occupational. The Occupational is concerned with

relationships between various expressed preferences and specific occupations, such as newspaper editor and electrical engineer. We have referred to the Personal in the previous chapter. Here we are concerned only with the Vocational (see *Administrator's Manual, Kuder Preference Record—Vocational*).

In the booklet the individual is given, activities are listed grouped into threes. He must indicate those activities he most and least prefers, as in the following example from Kuder: 'Visit an art gallery / Browse in a library / Visit a museum.' No time limit is placed on such inventories, but usually this one takes about 50 minutes to complete. It is simple to score, and this can be done by the individual himself.

The Kuder Vocational has ten interest categories, which we listed in Chapter 4, and an accuracy check. We suggested in Chapter 4 that there are two important questions that arise in relation to the classifications adopted in an interest inventory. First, are the categories psychologically meaningful? Secondly, if they are, then what do they correlate with? This last is, of course, the question of validity again.

An outline of how Kuder constructed the inventory helps answer the first point. The approach is similar to one method of constructing an attitude scale. First, a large number of items, such as the above three, are assembled. Each item is put into the category which looks to the investigator about right, scientific, persuasive, etc., so 'Browse in a library' might be assumed to be literary. This first classification of items is on the investigator's subjective judgment, but only temporary. Next, several hundred people complete the inventory. The data are then examined for internal consistency or inconsistency. For example, an item that is provisionally classified as mechanical is selected. If people who have scored high on 'Mechanical' express interest in this item, and people who scored low on 'mechanical' have no interest in this item, then the item is consistent with those others placed in the same category, and is retained. If the reverse occurs, and the high mechanical scorers have no preference for the item, and the low mechanical scorers have a high preference for it, then the item is obviously not consistent with the rest, and is scrapped. The same procedure is followed with all other items. This results in there being within each interest category only those items which are grouped together by people's preferences.

Developing his inventory in this way Kuder has modified his original, provisional scheme, and provided most of his interest categories with an empirical basis. Such a procedure meets our first query, since it ensures that an interest category in an inventory, such as scientific interest, does represent a psychologically meaningful grouping of preferences in the individual. Each classification of interests indicates preferences that tend to go together in an individual, and to be separate and distinct from other groups of preferences. Different sets of norms need to be established for the different categories, and this Kuder has done.

The next and final step, and this deals with our second requirement of an inventory, is to determine what these 'psychologically meaningful' categories mean. What real-life behaviour correlates with these expressed preferences? And here we return to validity. With the validity of interest scales established we may use them for diagnostic and predictive purposes.

Validity. First, to what extent are Kuder scores predictive of choice of occupation? Levine and Wallen (1954) found significant relationships between vocational interests of adolescents and their subsequent choice of a job. In this study, which we referred to in Chapter 4, 215 men, who had completed a Kuder while at school, were sent a questionnaire between seven and nine years later, the majority of which were completed and returned. The Kuder used nine scales at the time, and the jobs these men were now in were classified into their appropriate interest areas on the Kuder. Had they, years previously, scored significantly higher in that appropriate interest scale, related to their present occupation, than had the others who went into different sorts of jobs? With six of the scales this was the case, mechanical, computational, scientific, persuasive, literary, clerical, and the differences were statistically significant. And so, for example, men now in 'mechanical' jobs were found to have scored on average significantly higher in mechanical interest than had those now in 'non-mechanical' work. Of the remaining three categories social service, with a limited sample only, was not found significant, while artistic and musical had too few people involved to make comparisons meaningful.

The study is impressive. Here, with most Kuder scales, a preference score proved predictive of the sort of occupation an individual would enter. But choice of job is not the ultimate in criteria. Are inventories predictive also of success and satisfaction in a job?

A study by Lipsett and Wilson (1954) is representative of a few investigations into Kuder scores and job satisfaction: 108 individuals who had received some guidance and counselling rated themselves on their job satisfaction. The investigators then compared their high Kuder scores against their present jobs. If they were in occupations which seemed appropriate in terms of their two highest Kuder scores, this was classed as satisfactory, and a division was made on this basis: 59 were in jobs appropriate to their Kuder scores; 19 of these regarded their job as the best possible one for them. Only 3 actually disliked or were indifferent to their job. The rest had less extreme views on their jobs. This difference is statistically significant. The rest of the 108 people were in occupations which seemed inappropriate and unsuitable in terms of their inventoried Kuder interests. Of these 49 only 4 reported considerable job satisfaction; 16 were indifferent or disliked their jobs, and the rest rated it centrally as regards satisfaction. The difference is again statistically meaningful. People in jobs appropriate to their expressed Kuder preferences tended to like them more than did people whose jobs were inappropriate to their high Kuder scores.

The evidence of relationships between interests and success is by and large slimmer, and this might be expected on common-sense grounds. Individual performance is a function both of ability and motivation, and interests provide a measure of motivation to a limited extent only. In the employment situation other motivational factors, social and economic, may sometimes be so important as to minimize the motivating force of any interests.

Some studies, however, have found a relationship between success and interests, and that of Lattin (1950) is a good example. He did a follow-up of 595 students who, fourteen years previously, had graduated in hotel administration. Lattin took as the criterion of success remaining and progressing in this field of employment, and classified the students accordingly as successes or failures. He found that the successful students had higher persuasive and musical interest scores than did the failures. The failures had higher mechanical and computational interest scores than did the successes. The *post hoc* interpretation is that hotel work makes social demands, and these conflict with a preference for activities that are object-oriented and not people-oriented.

Uses. Kuder has classified a large number of occupations according to the major interest or interests of the individuals in them (*Administrator's Manual, Kuder Preference Record—Vocational*). A number of these classifications are based on actual data; some are based on 'presumptive evidence', that is, the duties involved in these occupations would appear to be appropriate to certain interest categories. Such classifications prove most useful in guidance.

If we contend that interests exist prior to entry and satisfaction in a certain occupation, we can say to the individual in the guidance situation: 'People with these sorts of interests tend to enter and find satisfaction in these sorts of occupations. Your interests are . . .' In fact the three studies we have quoted support this position.

If our theoretical position is less certain, and we are unsure whether interests cause occupational choice and satisfaction or vice versa, we can make a more guarded statement: 'People in these sorts of occupations are found to have these sorts of interests. They are the sort of people you would tend to become like. Your interests are . . .'

As we will indicate in the next chapter, Rodger and Cavanagh (1962) contend that guidance has positive and negative aims; the Kuder Vocational can help with both. First, it helps suggest to counsellor and client occupations which seem consonant with the client's inventoried interests. Second, its negative function is to guide the individual away from jobs which seem alien to his expressed preferences. At least it should ensure that he considers carefully the choice of an occupation apparently dissonant with his inventoried interests.

Conclusion

We will now discuss interest inventories with reference to our four general points on techniques. First, such inventories only contribute as an appropriate part of a satisfactory procedure. They are normally useful in guidance and counselling situations, but rarely in selection since job applicants will tend to express those interests they think will get them the job.

Techniques exist for a specific purpose. Interest inventories evaluate aspects of motivation expressed in an individual's preferences for certain activities. But in their jobs people are motivated not only by these sorts of preferences. A woman's first consideration in choosing a job might be the sort of people she will work with. Money, the size of the pay packet, is the dominating motive with some men. The Morse and Weiss study (1955) referred to in Chapter 1 indicated the existence of class differences here. In giving their reasons for working, middle-class men spoke of interests and related factors, whereas manual workers talked more of needing activity and of being bored without employment. In other words, the motivating force of the preferences expressed as inventoried interests may often be small.

Thirdly, interest inventories provide essentially trait analysis and are appropriate to the actuarial method. We suggest that the trait information they provide helps mainly to predict job choice and satisfaction. We suggest that job performance is better predicted by a trait analysis of ability, but even more satisfactorily predicted by a developmental approach based on life pattern theory. In other words, if we wish to evaluate the likely success of someone in a job, we should assess his past behaviour by means of application form, biographical interview, and some test of attainment. Past performance seems a function of motivation interacting with ability and experience, and for this reason probably is highly predictive of job success.

The data on a number of interest inventories used in guidance confirm they are technically sound. They are also administratively convenient. A careers officer might have a whole class of impending school-leavers complete a Kuder or Connolly, and so obtain for all of them the sort of information he would have from one person only in a 20-minute interview. The completed inventory could provide the basis for a useful guidance interview. Interest inventories are socially acceptable; completing such an inventory is sometimes experienced as useful by the individual, helping him to a clearer view of himself.

VALUE QUESTIONNAIRES

We have previously quoted from Allport (1961) that 'a value is a belief upon which a man acts by preference'. Values are central to personality and to an individual's perception of himself. Any accurate assessment of a man's values says what he considers important, and describes his aspirations, his orientation to life, and the frame of reference or criteria by which he makes decisions. If we know this about someone we know something of the likely direction of his motivated behaviour. As we saw with two studies in Chapter 4, Super's Work Values Inventory differentiated between occupational groups, and between students on various courses of study.

The Study of Values

Probably the best-known questionnaire technique for investigating this aspect of personality is the Allport, Vernon, and Lindzey Study of Values (1965). The test is derived largely from a sixfold classification of values by Spranger. In his book *Types of Men* (1928) Spranger suggested the individual is best understood through a study of his values, which he classified into six categories —theoretical, economic, aesthetic, social, political, and religious. As with any typology, like extrovert-introvert, there exists a danger of regarding the individual as essentially one or the other. Spranger's types are more usefully seen as six dimensions along which an individual should be considered. So we find, for example, that Mr X scores high on religious and social values, and very low on economic and political. Mr X remains uniquely himself, but is characterized by certain values and value orientations.

The authors of the Study of Values describe, in the manual, each of these six value types. They point out that implicit in Spranger's typology is a flattering view of people. He omits as a separate category any purely hedonistic orientation to life, one concerned with obtaining sensual pleasures. They suggest also 'he does not allow for formless or valueless personalities'. This last point, however, seems as much a criticism of 'value' as a generally useful concept. Personal dispositions or traits (in the narrow sense) are what everyone has. But values, in our earlier sense of 'articulated organization of attitudes' (Cooper and McGaugh, 1963), are possibly not part of every individual personality structure.

Description. The Study of Values divides into two parts, with thirty items in Part 1 and fifteen in Part 2. Each item presents a number of possible choices, and the individual indicates his preference. The test is untimed, but takes about 20 to 30 minutes to complete.

The completed test gives, therefore, a score on each of six values, and provides a value profile on an individual. With it we can study the individual in terms of the relative strengths of his different values, an idiographic analysis. Such an intra-individual analysis needs to be placed in the perspective of how values are patterned in the total or a comparable population. For example, in analysing the value profile of a particular woman, it would be relevant to know that women generally score higher on religious value than on political. Such a nomothetic comparison is possible, since the authors provide percentiles and average profiles for men and women. An example is given in Figure 5.1.

Reliability and Validity. The manual for the Study of Values provides evidence on the reliability of the test both in its stability over time and in the internal consistency of its items. It also gives data on validity, with a study by Mawardi (1952) as its main source, which show relationships between value scores on the test and choice of jobs or courses of study. Mawardi's unpublished investigation found with the old version of the study that the test, completed in college, predicted with some accuracy the subsequent careers of graduates five to fifteen years later.

Some findings are as expected. The average score of clergymen and theological students on religious value is usually in the top ten per cent of the male population, and the social value of these groups tends also to be high. Compared to the rest of the male population engineers score low on social, and relatively high on economic and theoretical values. Businessmen and students of business administration tend to score high on economic and political values. Artists score high on aesthetic values.

Among the data cited in the manual are findings that were not so predictable. Medical students, both men and women, have high theoretical and political scores, but are a little low on social. Similarly the around average social values expressed by nurses, personnel and guidance men, and social workers, do not fit their popular image.

The manual gives tables of average value scores for different occupational groups. Most of the data are from American populations, and much of them with students on vocational and professional, usually undergraduate, courses.

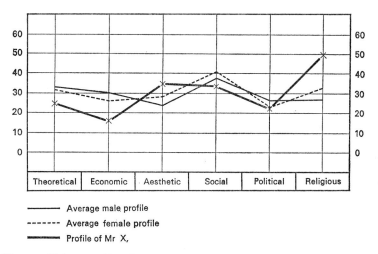

Fig. 5.1 Value profile of Mr X, 25 years of age, graduate in English literature, compared with average profiles for men and women (the schema and averages are from Allport, Vernon and Lindzey, 1965)

Conclusion

A value questionnaire, such as that of Allport, Vernon, and Lindzey, or Super's Work Values Inventory, can provide useful information in most vocational guidance and counselling situations. Some, such as the Study of Values, are appropriate only to the better educated and more intelligent client, because of the nature of the items and the level of vocabulary adopted.

A test like the Study of Values could be used in guidance to provide an appraisal of the individual in trait terms, just as an interest inventory does. Some data exist on how certain values relate to certain occupations which would provide the basis for tentative career advice. But in examining values we are measuring traits that are broad, deep and, in Allport's terms, propriate. In the counselling situation, which we will discuss in the next chapter, scores on value questionnaires and value profiles might be used to help the individual develop in awareness of himself. As he comes to know what he really values, the individual grows in that awareness of self which is essential to successful counselling.

APPLICATION FORMS

An application form is a kind of questionnaire used in selection which asks certain information of the individual. Some of the points we make about application forms are relevant also to the biographical record the client completes in guidance. The nature of the questions and categories in any such form determine the information we obtain, so we should attempt to make them relate to what we wish to predict, be it job competence or satisfaction, length of stay, etc. What, therefore, are the questions, categories, dimensions, in an application form that usefully diagnose and predict? They will presumably vary from situation to situation.

Fleishman and Berniger (1961) tried to find out, through analysing the items in an application form, why secretaries left an organization. They found that secretaries who still were with the organization after two years differed significantly in three ways from those who had left. Those who stayed tended to be over thirty-four years of age; had children at high school (secondary school); and lived in the town.

Interestingly two of these factors refer not to the person, but to her situation. Had the investigators concerned themselves only with personality factors, whether in trait or life pattern terms, they would have missed the facts that the secretaries' length of stay was a function of where they lived and their children's schooling. Such social considerations are frequently important, but techniques such as intelligence and aptitude tests, interest inventories, and value questionnaires, take no account of them in a guidance and selection situation, since such techniques are concerned directly with the personality system. It would be absurd in practice to ignore such social factors in the individual's environment. An unqualified housewife with a husband, three young children, and a home, might seek re-employment. Tests and inventories suggest teaching or senior administrative work. But her situation would need also to be taken into account in deciding if she should train for teaching or if she should be offered some responsible administrative post. In the total context neither might be suitable. Allowance is made for such considerations in the Seven-Point Plan, since its last category is circumstances, originating from Burt's distinction between environmental and personality factors in the 'present situation'.

Information on personality which the application form attempts to obtain can be seen, as with other techniques, in terms of life pattern and trait theory. The biographical data the form elicits are used on the basis of life pattern theory, which simply states that how a person has behaved in the past is a guide, possibly the best guide, to how he will behave in the future. Some application forms seek information also on hobbies, interests, and spare-time activities, and this data can be readily analysed in terms of trait theory.

The value of biographical data typically found in application forms will vary. Much importance is frequently attributed to how long an individual has stayed in his previous jobs. In selection this is often taken as predictive of how long he would stay in the post for which he is an applicant. Wickert (1951) in a study of turnover among girl operators and service representatives with a telephone company found that their length of time in previous jobs did not differentiate between those who stayed and those who left over a given period. In a similar study Morea (1965) found that previous job history had very little power in predicting stayers and leavers on weekly-paid staff. Wickert, in fact, found that stayers and leavers were differentiated by the extent to which they had felt involved in their jobs. In this case again the relevant factor, involvement, seems a function of the situation, and not the personality, or possibly of an interaction between the two.

Vernon and Parry (1949) report a number of wartime studies which show the usefulness of various application form items. In the Navy, the job of radio mechanic was exacting, and selecting suitable individuals for training proved difficult, with tests giving useful but only small correlations. The investigators assembled a questionnaire type of application form, taking account of the intellectual and educational demands of the training and the subsequent job. In a study of 500 the following were found significantly associated with good course results:

1. Staying on at school past the age of fifteen years.
2. Some attendance at further education, such as evening classes in accountancy, insurance, or a technical subject.
3. Having passed any examination.
4. Obtaining a credit or distinction in the then School Certificate or Matriculation, as opposed to passing or merely 'attaining a school certificate standard'.

5. Obtaining School Certificate or Matriculation in mathematics and/or physics.

6. Indicating an interest in metalwork, house repairs, radio or electrical repairs, or photography.

Certain explanations for the predictiveness of these factors suggest themselves, in terms of various motivational and ability concepts.

REFERENCES

Allport, G. W. (1961), *Pattern and Growth in Personality*, Holt, Rinehart & Winston.

Allport, G. W., Vernon, P. E., and Lindzey, G. (1965), *Manual for the Study of Values*, revised for British National Foundation for Educational Research, by arrangement with Houghton Mifflin.

Buros, O. K., ed., *The Mental Measurements Yearbook*, Rutgers University Press.

Burt, C. (1924), 'The principles of vocational guidance', *British J. of Psychol.*, 14.

Burt, C. (1925), *The Young Delinquent*. University of London Press.

Cooper, J. B. and McGaugh, J. L. (1963), *Integrating Principles of Social Psychology*, Schenkman.

Fleishman, E. A. and Berniger, J. (1961). 'Using the application blank to reduce office turnover', in *Studies in Personnel and Industrial Psychology*, ed. E. A. Fleishman, Homewood, Ill.: Dorsey.

Himmelweit, H. T. and Summerfield, A. (1951), 'Student Selection', *British J. of Sociol.*, 2.

Hollingworth, H. L. (1929), *Vocational Psychology and Character Analysis*, Appleton.

Kuder, G. F., *Kuder Preference Record, Administrator's Manual*, Chicago: Science Research Associates.

Lattin, G. W. (1950), 'Factors associated with success in hotel administration', *Occupations*, 29, 36-9.

Levine, P. R. and Wallen, R. (1954), 'Adolescent vocational interests and later occupation', *J. appl. Psychol.*, 38, 428-31.

Lipsett, L. and Wilson, J. W. (1954), 'Do "suitable" interests and mental ability lead to job satisfaction?' *Educ. Psychol. Measmt.*, 14, 373-80.

Mawardi, B. H. (1952), 'The Allport–Vernon Study of Values as a tool in vocational guidance with liberal arts college women', unpublished M.A. thesis, Wellesley College, Wellesley, Mass.

Morea, P. C. (1965), 'Studies of the usefulness of routine staff selection procedures in an industrial firm', unpublished M.A. thesis, University of London.

Morse, N. C. and Weiss, R. S. (1955), 'The function and meaning of work and the job', *American Sociological Review*, April.

Munro Fraser, J. (1962), *Industrial Psychology*, Pergamon.

Munro Fraser, J. (1966), *Employment Interviewing*, Macdonald & Evans.

Rice, S. A. (1929), 'Contagious bias in the interview: a methodological note', *Amer. J. of Sociol.*, 35.

Rodger, A. (1952), *The Seven-Point Plan*, National Institute of Industrial Psychology Paper No. 1.

Rodger, A. (1955), 'The effective use of manpower', address to British Association, reprinted in *Advancement of Science*, No. 46.

Rodger, A. and Cavanagh, P. (1962), 'Personnel selection and vocational guidance', in *Society: Problems and Methods of Study*, ed. A. T. Welford, Routledge & Kegan Paul.

Spranger, E. (1928), *Types of Men*, Stechart.

Super, D. E. (1957), *Psychology of Careers*, Harper & Row.

Vernon, P. E. and Parry, J. B. (1949), *Personnel Selection in the British Forces*, University of London Press.

Vernon, P. E. (1950), 'The validation of civil service selection board procedures', *Occup. Psychol.*, 24.

Wickert, F. R. (1951), 'Turnover, and employees' feelings of ego-involvement in the day-to-day operations of a company', *Personnel Psychology*, 4.

CHAPTER 6

Occupational Guidance and Vocational Counselling

Overview

There are two approaches to giving careers advice, and we have labelled them occupational guidance and vocational counselling. We will begin with a case study where the appraisal approach of occupational guidance is adopted, and then examine the principles and procedures that underlie such an approach. We will then refer to a well-known study in guidance, and conclude the section with an attempt to summarize the theory and practice of occupational guidance.

Vocational counselling is examined under different section headings which detail its characteristics, and a case study is also used. We attempt to summarize the theory of vocational counselling, and suggest what it entails in practice.

Having listed some of the differences between the guidance through appraisal and the counselling approaches to giving careers advice, we outline their common ground.

OCCUPATIONAL GUIDANCE

A Case Study

Brian Jones was big, strongly built, a single man of thirty. His parents' income had been low, and he had left grammar school at fourteen to bring in a wage, just prior to the school-leaving age being raised. From then on he did a variety of jobs, all physically active, and mostly unskilled or semi-skilled. A 'slipped disc' was the cause of his having to stop such heavy work, and at this stage he received occupational guidance. A medical report stated that his disc trouble should not prove serious, that he would be able to lift and carry moderately heavy objects, but that really heavy work was no longer possible. Just previously he had been in a temporary job as a grave-digger.

During the first interview Jones stressed that even prior to the back trouble he had been seriously considering trying to 'get a better job'. There seemed nothing in his past history to suggest any higher level of ability, other than his scholarship to grammar school. He had worked as a machine operator, a fitter's mate, and generally as a labourer.

Jones completed a number of tests before interview. The battery consisted of a verbal and non-verbal test of general intelligence; of one test of practical-mechanical aptitude (that is, of *m*); of a mathematics test, and another of trade knowledge. We have referred to the ability tests in terms of hierarchical group factor theory. Jones consistently obtained scores in the top 20 per cent, sometimes top 10 per cent, of the general population. The test scores suggested he was justified in wanting to raise the level of his employment.

The two tests of intelligence placed him just in the population's top 10 per cent. The level of his conversation in interview also suggested he was an intelligent individual. His score on the test of practical-mechanical aptitude came high, but did not fall within the top 10 per cent. In interview he said his best job had been that of fitter's mate, since 'it was the only job where I used my brains'. After a short while as a mate he had been classed as semi-skilled. Jones had clearly a high level of ability.

His interests, dynamic and temperamental traits, the direction of his motivation—however these might be conceptualized—now needed to be assessed in order to determine what type of a job might be suitable for him. His hobbies were of a physically active nature, such as sport and mountain climbing. He read a lot, but in no particular area. Personality tests and interest inventories had not been used, but his high score on the test of trade knowledge seemed a pointer. His work as a machine operator and as a fitter's mate must have increased his knowledge in this area, but the question arises of why he had chosen these jobs. He previously indicated that fitter's mate had been his best job. Discussion in interview subsequently confirmed he had strong interests in electrical and mechanical things. Table 6.1 suggests his likely position in an occupational grid, using Kuder's interest categories (*Kuder Preference Record—Vocational*).

Having assessed Jones's ability and the direction in which his

TABLE 6.1 *Representation of occupational level and type : B. Jones (interest categories from Kuder Preference Record—Vocational)*

Direction of interests

Level of general intelligence	Outdoor	Mechanical	Computational	Scientific	Persuasive	Artistic	Literary	Musical	Social service	Clerical
Top 10%	X									
Upper 20%		X		X						
Middle 40%										
Lower 20%										
Bottom 10%										

energies tended, it was necessary to see realistically what openings and opportunities existed for him. It seems likely that Jones might suitably have obtained an O.N.C. or H.N.C. qualification in a science subject or some area of engineering, and worked as a technologist. But this was not immediately possible since he had no entry qualifications, nor did he have the time in which to study over some years for entry requirements and then to complete the course. A suitable job or a short, suitable technician training seemed more realistic. It was proposed to Jones that he train for radio and television servicing and repair. He expressed a keenness for the idea, had a two-week trial on similar work, and started the training which he successfully completed over the nine months.

Since Brian Jones had never worked in any really suitable job there was nothing in his work history to indicate the level of his abilities, nor where his interests lay. Apart from his fitter's-mate experience, an account of his past seemed to give no prediction for the future nor to provide any clue as to suitable future employment. Here, careers advice had to be based on an assessment and appraisal of abilities and interests, an appraisal in terms of personality traits. Such an analysis suggested as one possibility a high-level mechanical or electrical job, physically active, but not strenuous in view of the disability. Preferably the work should contain a theoretical component to make it intellectually satisfying for Jones. Radio and television servicing seemed one possibility, and training was available.

Occupational Guidance—a Trait Appraisal of People and Jobs
The approach of occupational or vocational guidance is essentially one of appraisal. Parsons's basic statement, though made over sixty years ago (*Choosing a Vocation*, 1908), is still valid. He speaks of 'three broad factors', and they are:

  1. a clear understanding of yourself, your aptitudes, abilities, interests, ambitions, resources, limitations, and their causes;
  2. a knowledge of the requirements and conditions of success, advantages and disadvantages, compensations, opportunities, and prospects in different lines of work;
  3. true reasoning on the relations of these two groups of facts.

It is from this sort of approach that the actuarial method, based on trait theory, and illustrated in the case of Brian Jones, has been derived. We will now discuss the development of each of Parsons's three factors.

In regard to the first, there is frequently adopted in guidance a division of the individual's characteristics into two categories, aptitudes and preferences, abilities and interests, etc. This is, of course, the division this book adopts in its distinction between Chapters 3 and 4. Our knowledge of the area of ability has developed tremendously over the past sixty years, as becomes apparent in studying the work of Spearman, Thurstone, Burt, Vernon, and Guilford. Our knowledge of what we have termed motivational traits, which embrace interests, values, Allport's stylistic and dynamic personal dispositions, Cattell's general and dynamic factors, has also developed considerably over the same period. But the approach in guidance remains essentially one which conceptualizes a man in terms of bundles of qualities. These qualities may be relevant over a wide work area, such as intelligence, or highly specific to certain jobs, as is a musical aptitude. They may be of the ability sort, as are these last two, or motivational and refer to the direction of interest in the employment area, such as a business interest or social value. Over the past sixty years we have developed better techniques for assessing the individual in these terms, and in Chapter 5 we outlined a number of such techniques.

Implicit in Parsons's second point is the need to categorize jobs in some way. It would be absurd to attempt to evaluate an individual in terms of the many thousands of jobs that exist, and so schemes of classification have been proposed. We have already looked in Chapter 4 at a number of occupational classifications, usually based on interests or on general personal orientations. Much work has yet to be done in relating specific jobs to the various categories.

To implement Parsons's third factor we need a framework for our 'true reasoning on the relations'. Assessment plans normally provide such a framework. We need also criteria by which to evaluate the relations between 'these two groups of facts', and the criterion normally adopted in guidance is the satisfaction of the individual.

In the real situation we must consider, besides Parsons's three factors, the constraints on the individual's choice of occupation. The practitioner has to determine in guidance what openings and opportunities exist for an individual; these would be considered under circumstances in Rodger's Seven-Point Plan.

Rodger and Cavanagh, in a more contemporary account of such an approach to guidance (1962), state the following:

> In the circumstances, there is much to be said for envisaging the basic vocational guidance task as a double one with both positive and negative aims. The negative aim is gently to steer people away from work likely to prove unsuited to their capacities or inclinations or both. The positive aim is to supply information about apparently suitable occupations, and to foster an attitude of 'planned procrastination' in the consideration of them.

This negative aim of guidance (and selection) needs to be stressed. It often becomes apparent in research that there is no ideal type of person for many jobs. For example, there might be many ways of being a good sales manager, so it would be pointless to attempt to develop profiles of sales managers. On the other hand sales managers who have proved unsuccessful may have something in common, in which case it would be possible to identify characteristics likely to predict unsatisfactoriness generally in sales management or (in selection) probable failure as a sales manager with Firm X. This is probably one reason why, as Rodger and Cavanagh suggest (1962), the occupational misfit is likely to provide a fruitful source of information on jobs.

In guidance it is often difficult when we have assessed the individual to determine the type of work for which he is definitely suited. This seems to be so not because of the imprecision of our measuring instruments, the tests, inventories, etc., but because there is not only one ideal job for the individual. He might obtain success and satisfaction in several different types of work. The difficulty arises also from there being a number of ways of doing a job as we have suggested. Psychologists have long since rejected Gilbreth's concept of 'the one best way', even for simple operator tasks.

The statement from Rodger and Cavanagh (1962), and their article generally, provides an account of the position usually adopted on guidance in the United Kingdom. The adviser's function is to help the individual avoid choosing an occupation that would prove disastrous for him, and to help him explore a variety of occupations apparently compatible with his personality (that is, not obviously incompatible), at the same time encouraging him to postpone making irrevocable job choices.

In the United Kingdom there has been very little attempt to base guidance on any precise measurement of the individual. It seems preferable to classify only broadly in ability and occupational levels. Attempts at precision, as when, we confidently describe someone as suitable for employment at a clerical or technician level, have their dangers. Whatever the precision of our measurement of ability, in real life it is ability interacting with motivation that determines level of performance. Secondly, the danger of the self-fulfilling prophecy arises out of such attempts at precision. In suggesting to a school-leaver he is suitable for work at (only) a clerical or technician level we make it more likely that this and this only is the level he will achieve. He will tend to fulfil the expectations placed on him.

Similarly with guidance in the United Kingdom the tendency has been, as we suggested above, to think broadly and tentatively in terms of types of occupations and the direction of motivation. The self-fulfilling prophecy may occur again when we attempt to be specific and definite here. For example, a science graduate may be directed prematurely into teaching, not a disastrous choice for him nor incompatible with his personality. He makes the best of it, and is genuinely satisfied; but he might well have found technical sales even more to his liking.

An Experiment in Guidance

An excellent early study is Rodger's investigation of guidance with an intake of youths to a borstal (1937). The young offenders, committed to a borstal instead of a prison, were allocated to work-parties where they received different training. It was thought that many of them were being allocated to training which was inappropriate, and so the National Institute of Industrial Psychology was consulted in an attempt to improve this allocation procedure.

The Original Procedure. The practice normally adopted was simply for each youth to have a talk with his housemaster about possible training, after he had been a month on general duties. What sort of work-party and training the youth was allocated to was determined by this informal interview, and the vacancy position. Constant complaints from training instructors about the unsuitability of some of their trainees, and complaints from some of the young men themselves about their training being unsatisfactory, indicated the inadequacy of the procedure.

The New Procedure. The procedure then introduced consisted of a number of appropriately selected tests and a planned interview. The tests used were the N.I.I.P. Group Test 34, the N.I.I.P. Form Relations, the N.I.I.P. Memory for Designs, the Cox Manual Dexterity, the Stenquist Mechanical Assembly, the Cube Construction Test, and the Dearborn Formboard. These tests would provide an appraisal of (the hierarchical group factor model is used): general intelligence; major group factor, $k:m$; minor group factors, mechanical (m), spatial (k), and the manual or motor factor.

An interview lasted about 45 minutes, and usually at the start the youth was given the Dearborn Formboard and the Cube Test to attempt. There might be two or three interviews. The interviewer would already have biographical data, mainly on the individual's home, his schooling, and the offences he had committed, and the interviewer would normally begin by asking the individual about his past. Some of this biographical analysis would be concerned with his employment experience; what jobs he had been in, what training he had received for them, what he had liked about them, what disliked, what he had found hard about them, what easy, etc. The interviewer moved on to a consideration of the present and future; present training possibilities, their attractiveness, unattractiveness, likely job openings for him after borstal, etc.

The Study. The study attempted to cover the whole of one year's intake, about four hundred youths in all. All the intake were to follow the new procedure, but only the alternate ones (one out of every two) were to enter the training actually recommended by the new method; these would constitute the experimental group. The rest were to enter training recommended by their housemaster, which was the original procedure. These constituted the control group. Since each section could take only a limited number of trainees, two or three recommendations needed to be made for each individual, in case the first or second recommendation was for a training group already full.

The Follow-up. A criterion was needed against which to evaluate the training recommendations for the control and experimental groups. Over a period the borstal authorities reported on the youths, and attempted to judge the 'boy's satisfactoriness in the work assigned to him'. This rating, made on a simple scale, was used to grade the placing as A or B, according to how satisfactory it seemed. 'A' indicates the placing is very satisfactory. The experimental group, those recommended by the National Institute of Industrial Psychology investigators, had a far higher degree of success than did the control group, recommended by the housemaster. The figures are given in Table 6.2.

TABLE 6.2 *Comparison of placement procedures*
(satisfactoriness of placement: Grade A more satisfactory placing than Grade B)

	New procedure (experimental group)	Old procedure (control group)
Grade A	110	73
Grade B	48	87
Total	158	160

The existence of only a limited range of training possibilities acted as a constraint on the vocational adviser, since he might regard an individual as suited to work for which there was no training in the borstals. This makes the findings, confirming the effectiveness of the new procedure, even more impressive.

The Theory and Practice of Occupational Guidance
The appraisal approach of guidance has been criticized for its lack of theory (Hopson and Hayes, 1968). Guidance does have a theoretical base, though its derivation was rather *post hoc*. Practitioners used its methods long before any theoretical rationale was articulated.

Occupational guidance is based on trait theory and the theory of individual differences (Super, 1957). Individuals may be analysed in terms of traits. People differ in the degree to which they possess various traits. Traits can usefully be divided into ability traits, such as intelligence and various special aptitudes, and motivational traits, such as interests, values, and some dynamic and temperamental factors. Many traits are relevant to satisfaction and

performance in different occupations. Occupations may be categorized according to the various traits relevant to success and satisfaction in them; people may be analysed in terms of the traits
they possess which are occupationally relevant. In guidance, using
various techniques, we obtain trait information on people and jobs,
and diagnose and predict on this basis.

Occupational guidance has, therefore, a theoretical base, which
is not to say the theory is adequate. As we shall see, vocational
counselling adopts an approach which attempts to avoid the
inadequacies in the appraisal process of guidance.

VOCATIONAL COUNSELLING

Holism and the Whole Person

Any trait analysis of the individual is open to the criticism that
it ignores the unity and wholeness of personality. It assumes we
can extract and examine, say, someone's aggressiveness in the
way we would a relay from an electrical circuit. The relay remains
the same out of the circuit, and if we substitute an identical unit
the circuit will function just the same. We discussed this in Chapter
2 where we pointed out that holistic theorists contend one cannot
meaningfully extract bits of personality in this way. An individual's
aggressiveness would be unique, as Allport stresses in his concept
of the personal disposition. His aggressiveness can also only be
understood in relation to the rest of his personality. We return
here to an emphasis on the idiographic analysis, also discussed in
Chapter 2.

Vocational counselling rejects the reductionism of the trait
approach. It views personality as a dynamic organism, tending
always to function as a whole, in the work situation as in any other.
In Chapter 1 we considered the importance of work for the individual. Within the limits to opportunities set by the economic
and social system, the choice of an occupation, training in it,
finding frustration or satisfaction in a job, doing it well or badly,
are a function of the whole personality. In turn work will tend
to influence and modify the whole personality and the style of
life that emanates from it.

If we are concerned with the whole person it becomes constrain-
ing to consider only his relationship to his employment. Work
may influence him extensively, but there remain other sides to

his life. It becomes more useful if we are orientated to a general counselling of the individual, within which vocational counselling functions as one important process. Counselling has originated in the work of the psychotherapists, and is a process by which a counsellor helps an individual grow in his adjustment to himself and to his environment, and through this growth helps him make personal decisions. In the area of vocational counselling we are primarily concerned with adjustment and decisions that relate to the individual's work.

A Case Study

S.N. was in his mid-twenties, married with two children, and working as an estimator. He seemed in a good job, with a salary high in relation to his age and modest qualifications. He had, however, sought occupational guidance because of dissatisfaction with his work, wanting, as he said, 'a job where there was more contact with people'. It soon became apparent in interview that other problems existed.

S.N. obviously thought he was far more able than his test scores and his school and work record would suggest. Over-estimating his own ability seemed by itself unimportant, though the extent to which he was exaggerating was somewhat disturbing. But throughout interview he maintained an opinionated manner that rapidly became defensive when any statement of his was questioned. Ironically, in view of his dogmatism throughout interview, he had described himself in the occupational guidance form as 'attempting always to see the other man's point of view'.

S.N. appeared also to have marriage problems. During interview he suddenly stated, for no apparent reason, that he had married too young and his wife was not the sort of person he should have married. Later in the same interview, again for no obvious reason, he said it seemed wrong a man should promise to love and honour a woman for the rest of his life before he was old enough to know what it all meant. Subsequently he mentioned his parents were divorced.

In a narrowly conceived appraisal approach to guidance there seems little to be done. In terms of his abilities and interests S.N.'s present occupation looked suitable, and his dissatisfaction more an expression of personality and marriage difficulties. In the report on the case appears the following comment:

It is difficult to know how the occupational guidance expert should deal with such a problem. His first reaction is to consider referring the individual to a psychiatrist, marriage guidance specialist, or priest, since much of his problem lies within their fields and not that of the vocational adviser.

The approach of vocational counselling rejects such a statement. The counsellor is concerned with the total person, and will deal if necessary with general problems of adjustment and decision-making, before dealing specifically with such problems in relation to work.

S.N. would seem to illustrate how personality functions as a total system. Anxiety originating presumably in personal mal-adjustment and marriage problems expressed itself in a dissatisfaction with his job. His marriage problems may also have been not a cause, but a result again of his personality difficulties.

The Whole Person and a Decision on Work.

If personality functions as a whole and work is so important to the individual, then career-decisions will involve the total person. In which case such decisions will not be cool, cerebral appraisals for the individual that Parsons's 'true reasoning on the relations' would suggest. They are or should be processes of the total personality, involving the individual's attitudes, traits, emotions, fears, fantasies, etc., as much as might the choice of a marriage partner. Choosing an occupation (and a wife) will probably benefit from calm, rational reflection, but counselling stresses also the value of the more feeling and intuitive responses.

We need, therefore, to consider the whole person in vocational counselling, and in the adjustment and decision-making that counselling involves. A number of theoretical models enable us to consider the total personality. A Freudian analysis would do so, but seems hardly relevant in other ways to the work situation. The self concept provides a comprehensive view of personality, and has now emerged as a key construct in vocational counselling.

The Concept of Self

In Chapter 2 we introduced Allport's proprium, 'the me as felt and known' (1961), and suggested in Chapter 4 that the self provides a framework for considering motivation. The concept has a long history. In 1892 William James distinguished between the I and the Me, his Me proving in some ways the antecedent of the self concept. Later Mead (1934), in a further analysis of Me, emphasized the role of learning in its growth, stressing particularly the importance of social factors and social experience in its development.

But it is largely through the more recent work of Carl Rogers that the usefulness of the self concept in the field of counselling and therapy has become recognized. Through Donald Super's writings we have come to appreciate its specific value in vocational counselling. Rogers appears to reject James's distinction between the I and the Me (1959):

> Self, Concept of self, Self-structure. These terms refer to the organized, consistent conceptual gestalt composed of perceptions of the characteristics of the 'I' or 'me' and the perceptions of the relationships of the 'I' or 'me' to others and to various aspects of life, together with the values attached to these perceptions. It is a gestalt which is available to awareness though not necessarily in awareness.

In Chapter 4 we distinguished between the apparent self, which the individual perceives himself as really being, and the ideal self he would like to be. We can also think of a social self which refers to how a person perceives other people as seeing him. In the counselling or analytic situation the client might make this clear by saying: 'This is just the Me I let other people see. I'm really not like that at all.'

In what way, then, is the self a key concept in vocational counselling? We have already suggested in Chapter 1 how important work is for the individual, affecting his status in society, his income, the sort of friends he has, where he lives, etc. At another level, but related, his work affects and is affected by his traits, interests, values, attitudes, and the way he perceives himself. In a phrase, his work is related to his self-concept. The individual, says Rogers (1959), 'has the capacity and tendency to keep his *self-concept* congruent with his *experience*'. The more consonant his experience is with his self-concept, the greater is likely to be his adjustment and satisfaction. If they are dissonant, he will tend to be dissatisfied. Because his employment impinges so comprehensively on his self-concept and his style of life, the individual attempts to choose a job which is consonant with his self, or at least with that aspect of his self he accepts. If the role prescribed for Smith's job requires tough, assertive sales behaviour, but this is not how he sees himself, he will experience dissatisfaction and uncreative tension. But if this accords with his concept of self, he is likely to be satisfied and involved in the job.

It becomes apparent how much is implied in vocational choice, and how the self concept helps us usefully analyse the process of choice. As Super says (1957): 'In choosing an occupation one is, in effect, choosing a means of implementing a self-concept.' Involved in this choice is a decision not only on the sort of person one 'really' is, the apparent self, but also on the person one wishes to become, the ideal self. The self affects choice of occupation, and once in employment the job probably affects the self. With most people the influence works both ways.

There is a further complication. As Starishevsky and Matlin (1963) point out: 'People differ both in their self concepts and in the ways in which they translate self concepts into occupational terms.' It is not enough in counselling to be able to clarify with an individual what his self-concept is. People see jobs differently. Raylesberg (1949), in a study we quoted in Chapter 4 from Super (1957), found that different engineering students regarded engineering in different ways, some as materialistic, others as a scientific occupation, and others as a social-welfare activity. So in vocational counselling it needs to become apparent not only how the individual perceives himself, but also how he perceives occupations.

Life Stages, Work, and Continuous Counselling
In 1932 Macrae (*Talents and Temperaments*) stated that 'vocational guidance cannot be divorced from educational guidance; rightly conceived, it is merely the culmination of a continuous process of advising throughout the child's school life, the logical conclusion of the whole business of education.' Part of what Macrae says here is about guidance being a continuous process, though continuing only over a limited period, and terminating presumably when the individual is fitted into a suitable occupation. Rodger's concept of 'planned procrastination' (1961) develops this, since it implies that the search for a satisfactory job should be continued in the employment situation. But it may be argued as an even further development that there is never a final, once-and-for-all decision on occupation and career, and there should not be. The individual's decisions about his

career continue throughout his lifetime, so vocational counselling should be a continuous process.

That individuals do have to make many career decisions during their working life is a matter of common observation. Businessmen become academics, craftsmen take semi-skilled jobs on a production line, policemen train for nursing when they retire from the force in their late forties (see *The Times*, 29 June 1970), research and production men turn to technical sales, farm labourers find work as tradesmen's mates. Individuals change, as do their circumstances. Their abilities and attainments develop and decline. They acquire new attitudes, needs, values, new ways of seeing themselves; self-concepts alter. Their situations change, as new opportunities and jobs present themselves, and other avenues are closed.

If we examine people's lives and careers we will find that these changes occur in typical stages, each characterized by certain needs, values, activities. Super, for example, adapting Buehler (1933), suggests we may usefully conceive of vocational development occurring in five stages. They are growth, exploration, establishment, maintenance, and decline. Miller and Form (1964) propose five slightly different stages, which are preparatory, initial, trial, stable, and retirement. Interestingly they suggest there exist differences in the characteristics of the various life stages at different occupational and socio-economic levels.

Vocational choice and development extend over a lifetime, and are usefully analysable into certain stages. Vocational counselling needs to be a continuing process, as might be expected of an approach so nearly related to psychotherapy. Over fifty years analysts of different schools have emphasized not the attainment of specific goals and objectives, but the commitment to a process, a process which can only occur over time, and may lead anywhere. For this reason in analysis and counselling we have to talk vaguely in terms of self-actualization or personal growth. Certainly S.N. seemed unlikely to profit from any appraisal and immediate advice given by the guidance expert; he might have benefited from vocational counselling over a period.

Non-Directive Counselling and the Growth of Self

Girl-friend: Still depressed, Jimmy? I think I know your problem. Your problem is that you're you.

Jimmy: Well, what do you suggest I do about it?
Girl-friend: It's not up to me to advise you. I'm just pointing out your problem.

In occupational guidance we speak of the vocational expert's appraisal and his recommendations. He will normally involve the individual at all stages of the analysis and appraisal, and attempt to arrive at a set of recommendations through discussion and agreement with the individual. But the guidance expert will play an active, directive role; after all, he is the expert.

But, argues the vocational counsellor, for a decision to be really meaningful for the individual it must be his. The decision must proceed from insights, perceptions, feelings, he has himself experienced. Counselling merely provides a situation where the individual can experience, test out, and work through these insights, perceptions, feelings, usually about himself. Vocational counselling is essentially client-centred, and attempts to be non-directive. Here again is the influence of psychotherapy.

Advising an individual and suggesting a course of action, as is done in guidance, helps him in a direct way, and so may reinforce habits of dependency and feelings of inadequacy. Sometimes what the vocational expert says may not be accepted by the individual for this reason. When the interviewer tactfully suggested to S.N. that his dissatisfaction at work might be caused in part by other sorts of personal worries, he hastily and emphatically rejected the idea. Counselling, vocational or otherwise, like psychotherapy, provides a situation within which an individual may work through his difficulties and problems himself, and find his own solutions. In vocational counselling we provide conditions which enable an individual to work through the difficulties and problems that relate to his employment, and to arrive at his own decisions about his job. Such a process does not lead to dependency or inadequacy, but facilitates personal growth.

The Developmental Method and Work
We have already discussed in Chapters 4 and 5 life pattern theory and the developmental method that derives from it. An emphasis on the predictive and explanatory value of a developmental study of the individual is characteristic of vocational counselling. Since the approach adopts a longitudinal analysis, seeking to identify significant themes and meaningful trends in the individual's

past, it contrasts with the actuarial appraisal typical in occupational guidance. However, even in the basic trait appraisal of guidance there is usually some developmental analysis, as evidenced by its interest in biographical data.

A difference in emphasis becomes apparent if we re-examine the case of Brian Jones. On the basis of a trait evaluation the vocational expert had no hesitation in advising him to aim at some active, technician job, and in recommending training for radio and television servicing. With a consideration in life pattern terms some doubt remains. For ten to fifteen years Jones had worked at a consistently low level with regard to his abilities, with apparently no sustained attempt to progress to a level of job more appropriate to his ability. Did the difficult circumstances of his home background adequately explain this? Was there an absence of drive? In what way would this past behaviour be predictive of future performance? These considerations might lead the counsellor to question not the choice of radio and television servicing, but the process by which the decision was made. The vocational expert recommended this training, and Jones enthusiastically welcomed the idea. But it should rather have been Jones's own decision, made after working through the significance of his fifteen years of 'drifting', after consideration of how he now saw himself, and after reviewing his hopes for the future realistically with regard to the limitations of his personality and circumstances. We could have greater confidence that Jones would enter and remain in more satisfactory employment through the training, if it were essentially his decision, and the decision were grounded in this sort of process.

Vocational Counselling in Practice

In the vocational counselling of an individual we try (1) to help him with immediate decisions that are necessary in the short-term; (2) to develop his growth in knowledge and acceptance of himself; (3) to encourage him to see and experience more meaningfully the world of work and his role in it; (4) to help him in this process of testing and satisfactorily implementing his self-concept in the real situation; (5) to provide him with the opportunity of learning satisfactory ways of making decisions.

We will illustrate vocational counselling by discussing the place of Parsons's first two 'broad factors' in the counselling process. Parsons's two factors are concerned with a knowledge of the individual and a knowledge of occupations. What place do they both have in vocational counselling?

In counselling we are concerned with experience. Information and data have little value and relevance in themselves; it is how they are perceived and experienced by the individual himself that proves significant. The position is in a sense phenomenalist; reality consists simply in what we perceive and experience.

Information about work and occupations means something to the individual only if perceived and experienced by him as relevant to a felt personal need. The experience of personal needs, growth in the awareness of them, and development of a sense of personal identity, are necessary before information has meaning for the individual. Parsons's 'clear understanding of yourself, your aptitudes', etc., has, therefore, to be of this personal and experienced nature. In counselling the individual's growth in self-awareness comes in part through his interaction with the counsellor. Tests, of intelligence, special aptitudes, and dynamic and temperamental personality traits, can also be used as part of the situation which the individual usefully experiences. Typically in occupational guidance the expert selects and gives a number of tests, then conveys the results to the individual or simply recommends to him appropriate employment partly on the basis of test scores. But vocational counselling functions as a process of self-discovery relevant to work. So the client should participate in the selecting of tests; after all he is the one who knows what areas of his self he remains ignorant of and wishes to understand more clearly. The client should seek out the test results from the counsellor, and attempt to see their significance for himself, with the counsellor acting primarily as the technical expert on tests. Even the individual's fears and anxieties about the use of tests, or any reluctance to accept their findings, become material for the counselling situation, grist to be ground in the counselling mill.

As the individual grows in self-awareness he is better able to benefit from Parsons's second factor, 'a knowledge of the requirements and conditions of success, advantages and disadvantages, compensations, opportunities, and prospects in different lines of work'. But information about jobs has also a function in the actual process of exploration, reality-testing, and personal growth. In reviewing occupations and work the individual can come to perceive and experience some as meaningful to him, others as having no personal significance, and in this way become more aware of his needs, values, aspirations, anxieties, limitations, in fact, of his self-concept. Similarly outside the counselling situation the straight descriptive lecture to school-leavers is often replaced by a group discussion on jobs. In the group discussion, where feelings, anxieties, hopes, are all expressed, information about jobs seems more likely to facilitate the necessary growth in self-knowledge. However, the use of occupational information to help with actual choice and decisions about work needs to be subsequent upon growth in occupational self-awareness. With such information the individual can provisionally decide whether some specific occupation might enable him to implement his developing concept of self.

CONCLUSION

In this chapter we have polarized occupational guidance and vocational counselling, and as practised they are frequently very different. They can, of course, be used together as one approach to helping people choose and develop in a job. Their differences originate in the different ways they view and conceptualize the problem. We will illustrate this. Rodger and Cavanagh (1962) refer to the importance in guidance of 'the Interviewer's Search for General and Persisting Traits'. They suggest that by examining an individual's background, history, and present behaviour we try to determine how he normally behaves, what he 'is "usually" like'. Using this information we make inferences about underlying traits, and have the basis for the appraisal approach to guidance. We might alternatively regard the same sort of information through other conceptual spectacles, such as those of life pattern theory which provide the basis for vocational counselling. Thus Super (1957): 'In the life pattern approach, the individual's behaviour and his roles over a period of time are analysed to ascertain persistent and recurrent themes or trends.'

Similarly the idea of life stages and of continuous vocational counselling views and attempts to meet the same sort of problem which Rodger is concerned with in his concept of 'planned procrastination'. Inventoried interests and values, seen in guidance as units of preference and belief, might alternatively be regarded as an expression of how an individual perceives his self-concept. The emphasis of vocational counselling remains idiographic. But individuals work in a world of other people and the nomothetic comparisons of guidance cannot be ignored. Becoming an actor completely accords with Smith's perception of himself, but there are a thousand others with more acting ability and only a hundred acting vacancies. Allport's affirmation of the idiographic in his concept of personal dispositions, and his acceptance with the notion of common traits that comparisons are possible and sometimes necessary, provides the way to a solution.

REFERENCES

Allport, G. W. (1961), *Pattern and Growth in Personality*, Holt, Rinehart & Winston.

Buehler, Charlotte (1933), *Der menschliche Lebenslauf als psychologisches Problem*, Leipzig: Hirzel.

Hopson, B. and Hayes, J. (1968), *The Theory and Practice of Vocational Guidance* (p. 5), Pergamon.

James, W. (1892), *Psychology: Briefer Course*, Henry Holt.

Kuder, G. F., *Kuder Preference Record, Administrator's Manual*, Chicago: Science Research Associates.

Macrae, A. (1932), *Talents and Temperaments*, Nisbet.

Mead, G. H. (1934), *Mind, Self and Society*, University of Chicago Press.

Miller, D. C. and Form, W. H. (1964), *Industrial Sociology*, Harper & Row.

Parsons, F. (1908), *Choosing a Vocation*, Houghton Mifflin.

Raylesberg, D. D. (1949), 'Personal values as a frame of reference in the perception of some aspects of an occupation', doctoral dissertation, Teachers' College, Columbia University.

Rodger, A. (1937), *A Borstal Experiment in Vocational Guidance*, Report 78 of the Industrial Health Research Board, H.M.S.O.

Rodger, A. (1961), 'Occupational Versatility and Planned Procrastination', Inaugural Professorial Lecture at Birkbeck College, University of London.

Rodger, A. and Cavanagh, P. (1962), 'Personnel selection and vocational guidance', in *Society: Problems and Methods of Study*, ed. A. T. Welford, Routledge & Kegan Paul.

Rogers, C. R. (1959), 'A Theory of Therapy, Personality, and Interpersonal Relationships, as developed in the Client-Centred Framework' in *Psychology, A Study of Science*, vol. 3, ed. S. Koch.

Starishevsky, R. and Matlin, N. (1963), *Career Development: Self Concept Theory*, New York: College Entrance Examination Board.

Super, D. E. (1957), *The Psychology of Careers*, Harper & Row.

The Times (Monday, 29 June 1970), 'New York policemen take up nursing'.

CHAPTER 7

Personnel Selection

'To spend a lot of money and time choosing a machine of which the average working life is, say, ten years, and little of either on selecting men and women who may be with the firm for forty years is short-sighted, to say the least, of industry and commerce' (Sir Miles Thomas).

INTRODUCTION

Overview

We have previously stressed that techniques should be considered in relation to an overall guidance or selection procedure. We now need to consider such a selection procedure. In this chapter we will examine two studies in selection. From the first and earlier study a useful procedure is derived, and the second proposes the concept of 'synthetic validity'. We will conclude by discussing at length some of the points that emerge from such studies, especially those of criteria in selection, the relationship between selection procedures and the organization, and the place of explanation.

Theory in Selection

In approaching a selection problem and adopting a specific procedure we are necessarily assuming certain ideas, concepts, and theories. First, we must have already looked at a situation of, say, high staff turnover, and seen it as a selection problem. We might alternatively have regarded the high turnover as a problem of training or bad organization. Second, having seen a situation as one requiring a solution through selection, we immediately set about analysing the relevant jobs. We have already contended in Chapter 1 that in any scheme of job analysis is some view of what work and the human personality are all about. So in this sense also ideas and theories provide a sub-structure for a selection procedure. Finally, the techniques we use in any selection scheme, such as personality tests and interview, may also embody certain theories and views about people.

Work done over thirty years ago by the National Institute of Industrial Psychology (N.I.I.P.) still provides a useful model for selection at many levels. The study was made on the selection of Airport Manager Trainees at a large air transport organization and is reported by Rodger (1945).

Background Information
Before long-distance flights became possible it was necessary to have refuelling stations between the main airports. A new manager had responsibility for a small airport which usually would serve principally as a refuelling station. It might be sited anywhere, often in a remote and out-of-the way place. Young men, preferably single, were recruited, selected, and trained for these positions. After a successful period in such a job they would be promoted to more senior posts, in more congenial and accessible places.

Some of these new managers quitted these jobs of their own accord, and others had to be transferred. Overall turnover proved too high, and the company wished to reduce it by improving selection methods.

The Investigation
The N.I.I.P. had wanted to study at first hand what the managers actually did in their jobs; this was not possible. So they asked the company to supply detailed information on the work the managers did, the training they were given, and their conditions of employment. At the N.I.I.P.'s request personnel and finance staff who had most contact with these managers examined reports and records of their work, and correspondence with them. Then the personnel and finance people listed those better and those less satisfactory as managers, and on the basis of reports, records, and correspondence attempted to determine why. 'This manager is very good; his accounts are a model of clarity.' 'We could never

get any idea from this man's letters what actually was going on.'
'This manager was always having trouble with the local tradespeople: we eventually had to transfer him.' Reasons for failing
on the job seemed to provide particularly useful information.

An attempt was made to state the reasons for failure, or success,
in practical and specific terms, as above: 'was always having
trouble with the local tradespeople.' This seemed likely to prove
more useful than the traditional vague and almost meaningless
use of adjectives and descriptive phrases such as 'too unambitious',
'has initiative', 'needs to have leadership ability'. This comparison
of what they did or failed to do indicated certain characteristics
which differentiated between successes and failures in the trainee
manager job. There emerged seven such 'differentiating characteristics', which could be stated as causes of failure.

Causes of Failure in the Job

1. Some of those who proved unsatisfactory were apparently
unable to cope with the administrative work involved and the
making of usually minor decisions. General intelligence did
seem relevant here.

2. Some among those who failed were unable to write clear
letters and reports to headquarters.

3. Some failed to keep satisfactory accounts and records.

4. Some could not tolerate the loneliness and isolation, and
resigned.

5. Others proved unsatisfactory because they frequently dis-
regarded instructions from headquarters.

6. Others could not cope with the entertaining of distinguished
visitors, usually just for a day or so, and as a result would tend
to drink too much.

7. Some were not good at dealing with local tradespeople, and
would antagonize them.

The New Procedure

1. Job specification. Contrasting the successes and failures in
the trainee manager job led to the stipulation of differentiating
characteristics, stated as causes of failure. This constituted a
form of job specification, and provided the basis for the new
selection procedure.

2. Recruitment. Previously the advertisements had given little

information. The new advertisements were more informative, providing information now known to be relevant.

3. Recruitment. The N.I.I.P. suggested in what papers it seemed most appropriate to place the advertisement, in view of the nature of the job.

4. Application form. A form was prepared specifically for the post. For example, it incorporated items which attempted to disclose the applicant's experience of administration, of keeping accounts, of entertaining distinguished people.

5. Note to applicants. Applicants had previously received a written sheet on the trainee manager position, but this had been largely a selling exercise which referred vaguely to 'challenge and prospects'. A new note was produced, providing more facts on the job, and particularly giving information now known to be relevant and which might discourage unsuitable applicants.

6. The short-listing of written applications. The completed application forms, now containing many items known to be relevant were carefully examined, particularly with reference to the best and worst among them. The best were short-listed for interview.

Usually about two hundred people applied, and these were reduced to 36 for interview. Six had to be selected. The 36 came in groups of 8 or 9 for a selection exercise which lasted a day. A member of the transport company spoke to them about the job. During the course of the day they did a number of tests.

7. Tests. Candidates took tests of intelligence, of elementary report writing, and of simple accounting. Reference back to the causes of failure suggests that these tests attempt to reject applicants likely to be unsatisfactory for one of the first three reasons.

8. Interviews. Each applicant had two interviews, the first concerned with his past work record, the second orientated towards his ideas for the future. An interviewer would have information on the job, mainly on causes of failure, in a form he might easily refer to during interview.

9. The decisions were made, and all applicants notified.

This new procedure ran for a number of years. The outbreak of war in 1939 made any detailed follow-up impossible, but all applicants selected by the new procedure had apparently proved satisfactory.

Discussion

Many points raised by the study have been discussed previously. Failures may provide as much information and help in selection as they do in guidance, where they emerge as 'occupational misfits' (Rodger and Cavanagh, 1962). Contrasting the failures with the successes in a specific job proves particularly useful as an approach to job analysis. Rodger's differentiating of characteristics is very similar to the technique of 'critical incidents' proposed by Flanagan (1949, 1954), since his approach also attempts to collect data on success and failure in jobs. Flanagan analyses events, elements of behaviour, incidents, that are seen as critical to success or failure in a job, and he differs from Rodger only in being more detailed and specific. 'Just give me an example', says the job analyst, 'of what the man did that made you first think of promoting him.' Or the analyst asks, 'What did he actually do that caused you to move him to less important work?' In the critical-incidents technique an analyst chases bits of behaviour and specific incidents, and generalizes only on the basis of many of them. With the differentiating-characteristics approach the generalizations come more readily: 'We sacked him because nobody could ever understand his reports.' The difference between them seems only one of degree. Both aim at stating job requirements not vaguely, as in 'needs leadership qualities', but specifically in operational and preferably measurable terms, such as 'must be able to do book-keeping to such and such a level'.

Also of interest in this early selection study is the amount of information provided to applicants. With such information a certain amount of self-selection by applicants becomes possible.

A SELECTION PROCEDURE

Rodger and Cavanagh propose nine main stages for a good selection procedure (1962). We have in fact already used these nine steps in outlining the new procedure adopted at the aviation firm. We now give Rodger and Cavanagh's original account:

1. The preparation of a job-specification. . . .
2. The 'distillation', from the job-specification, of an advertisement which is concisely informative and is not unwisely reticent about difficulties and distastes commonly experienced by people in the job.

3. The publication of the advertisement through media likely to receive the attention of suitable men.

4. The preparation and dispatch of an application form (or a supplement to a standard application form) which will elicit relevant information about an enquirer's record, and which will throw some preliminary light on his chances of surmounting the common difficulties and tolerating the common distastes.*

5. The preparation and dispatch, with the application form, of a note giving information which for any reason could not be given in the advertisement.

6. The scrutiny of written applications and the listing, by a 'topping and tailing' procedure, of those worth further consideration.

7. The administration of any test (including 'situational' tests) or other devices (for example, additional questionnaires) which, because of direct or presumptive evidence of their value, are regarded as relevant.

8. The interviewing of short-listed applicants, preferably by at least two interviewers sitting separately, even if it has been decided that these (or other) interviewers should finish with a board interview of the conventional kind.

9. The notification of the decisions made about all applicants and the appropriate annotation of the application forms of unsuccessful applicants who might be worth consideration on another occasion.

A SECOND STUDY IN SELECTION

Introduction

In discussing Rodger's differentiating characteristics and Flanagan's critical incidents we suggested that the purpose of a job analysis is to derive generalizations about the job. We obtain data and synthesize them into a general statement for the specification, such as 'needs to be able to cope with being alone most of the time'. But usually in selection we confine such general statements to one job only, as that of trainee airport manager with the aviation firm or research assistant at XYZ Ltd. Obviously such a generalization might apply to a number of jobs within an organization. The many different jobs in Firm ABC may have one or more elements in common with other jobs in the firm.

* The terms 'difficulties and distastes' embody the distinction we have referred to already between ability and motivational traits, talents and temperament, aptitudes and preferences, etc.

Table 7.1 illustrates this. The seven elements listed cover all the jobs in Firm ABC. Any job in the firm can be adequately described by one or more of the seven generalizations, as with the two examples given. Causes of success or failure are common to a number of jobs (or occupations). So when we develop a 'predictor' of a given element which we can incorporate into a selection procedure, the predictor may be used across the board for the selection of any job which involves this specific element.

This is on the way to obtaining job families that would prove useful in occupational guidance and vocational counselling. We will outline Guion's study (1965) where such a generalizing and synthesizing process is suggested. In fact, Guion wished to generalize across jobs for rather different reasons, as we shall see. Guion also concerned himself essentially with tests, but the concept of 'synthetic validity', which seems to have originated with Lawshe (1952), applies to any predictive technique.

TABLE 7.1 *Job elements in a hypothetical firm*
(with two examples; adapted from Guion, 1965)

Predictor	Job element						
	1	2	3	4	5	6	7
A	×			×	×		
B		×		×			
C		×				×	
D	×						×
E			×			×	
F			×		×		×

		Job elements
Technical sales assistant		1 3 6 7
Accounts clerk		1 4 7

Selection in the Small Organization, and Synthetic Validity

In selection we usually validate a test or other predictive technique against performance in a specific job, such as computer operator. In order for the validity to have any statistical significance the numbers involved need to be reasonably large. This makes the traditional approach impossible in a small firm where the numbers in one particular job would be too small, say, six account clerks. Guion, in an important article ('Synthetic validation in a small company', 1965), suggests we can overcome this difficulty. If we find different jobs have something in common, we could use techniques to predict not performance in a specific job but on tasks or elements common to many jobs in the firm. This makes validation possible in the small firm. In the following passage from his article he makes this point, but what he says applies to any predictive technique and not to tests only:

> According to the synthetic validity idea ... jobs can be analysed into elements that are common to many dissimilar jobs. Tests can then be validated against performance in these job elements rather than against a single over-all criterion. A valid test battery can then be synthesized for any job—even a unique one—by using those tests found valid for the specific elements required by the job.

And so in Table 7.1 (adapted from Guion, 1965), the crosses indicate the two best predictors of performance on each of the seven independent job elements. In order, for example, to select employees for a job that involves elements 1 and 4, we would use predictors A, B, and D.

The Study

Guion (1965) carried out a study in an electrical wholesalers employing under fifty people. The jobs of the current employees were examined, most of them different, in an attempt to identify all the job elements that existed in the firm. The investigators identified and described seven elements, common to many jobs, and which they labelled as follows: salesmanship, creative business judgment, routine judgment, customer relations, leadership, detail work, work organization.

The firm's two most senior executives assessed and rated all existing employees on each of these seven elements. Where an individual's job did not contain a certain element, no score would be given. A subsequent examination of these ratings suggested that the seven elements originally proposed were more or less independent of each other, though a degree of overlap existed in some cases. These employees took a battery of tests, and their test scores were correlated with the executives' ratings of them. This revealed which tests predicted which job elements, and the best in each case were adopted for prediction and selection purposes.

Subsequently thirteen new staff were tested. On the basis of these correlations between tests and job elements, their test scores were used to predict their later performance. Against a later assessment of their performance by the two executives, ten out of these thirteen predictions proved correct. This was a better result than one obtained at the same time from gross overall appraisals, where only six out of thirteen predictions were correct.

In the first approach, prediction was based on an analysis of jobs into elements and a validation of tests against the separate elements. This synthesizing approach achieved a better result than did one based on validation against a single overall performance criterion. Guion's study illustrates the use of synthetic validity, and provides modest evidence for its usefulness in selection.

CRITERIA IN SELECTION

Introduction

The traditional approach of selection consists in an analysis of the job, a choice of predictive techniques suggested by the analysis, a validation of these predictors *against whatever criteria of success are adopted*, and finally a study of the correlational data to see which techniques did prove predictive. In such a procedure appropriate criteria are of paramount importance.

In selection we are primarily concerned with satisfactory performance, and so the sorts of criteria adopted have been some apparent measure of competence. These have included the assessment of an individual's work by his superiors, promotions achieved, salary levels attained, the successful completion of training, fewer accidents, a reduction in staff or labour turnover. Alternatively the job itself is the criterion, as reported in a study where the normal tasks of a policeman's job were determined (DuBois, 1966). An appraisal system which affected their merit pay was then introduced, largely on the basis of how many of these tasks a policeman actually did in a work period. Decisions on criteria are relevant, as here, to employee assessment and payment, to guidance and training, as well as to selection.

The Criteria for Criteria

Scientific selection and its techniques have proved their usefulness in many studies. However, some psychologists remain dissatisfied with the size of correlations typically found in selection studies, which though positive and significant are frequently small. Ghiselli (1955) suggests they are usually around +0·3 and +0·4. After a review of test validities in a wide variety of occupations (1966) he concludes: 'Taking all jobs as a whole, then, it can be said that by and large the maximal power of tests to predict success in training is of the order of ·50 and to predict success on the job itself is of the order of ·35.' Here, he is referring to the largest correlations that are generally found.

Recent research has been concerned with this absence of high correlations, approaching the problem through an examination of criteria. Haire, for example, says (1959): 'Only the detailed differentiation of the criterion and its eventual reconstitution seem to hold promise for raising the general level of validities.' Such an approach does not necessarily improve selection. A procedure may remain unchanged and select the same applicants. Refining the criteria might simply provide more evidence for the validity of the procedure, by raising our correlation coefficients.

What, then, are the characteristics of good criteria? DuBois (1966) suggests four; criteria should be 'pertinent, measurable, comprehensive and consistent over time'.

The first is clear enough, in that criteria should be adopted not just because they are convenient and can be measured, but primarily because they are relevant. For this reason we need to relate a decision on criteria to our job specification, since this after all attempts to determine the important and critical aspects of the job. Pertinent criteria will be concerned either with the individual, and be about his satisfactions and his personal aims, or with organizational objectives. The relationship of selection criteria to the goals of an organization is important, and will be discussed later in this chapter.

DuBois's second criterion for criteria is that they must be amenable to some sort of measurement. DuBois's third point refers to comprehensiveness, since a criterion could be relevant but not adequate, failing to cover all the dimensions of behaviour that are appropriate in the situation. Drenth (1966) suggests we might move to multi-dimensional criteria. So, for example, we would not evaluate the sales manager's secretary by the number of letters she types or her accuracy in keeping the sales accounts or her manner with customers, but by some amalgam of them all. There may be many criteria for satisfactory performance of a job in an organization, just as an organization itself can have many goals.

DuBois's fourth requirement is consistency over time, a form of criteria reliability. The significance of a criterion needs to remain the same over time, or at least we must know in what way it changes. We may validate our graduate selection against the training officer's assessment of the graduates as they end their six-month induction. We might find subsequently that his assessment bears no relationship to how they actually do on the job two years later. A study by Ghiselli and Haire (1960), attempting to validate tests used for selecting taxi-drivers, illustrates the point. Performance during the first few weeks on the job did not correlate with later competence as a taxi-driver. Therefore a test could predict performance at one point in time, but not another. We might think of predicting for a certain point in the future; in Drenth's phrase, the criterion becomes time-bound (1966). An alternative is to adopt a criterion which incorporates time and change. In the taxi-driver study, Ghiselli and Haire moved from an attempt to predict an individual's actual performance, to trying to predict the speed at which he would improve his performance. Adopting this sort of selection criterion resembles the change-over in guidance from comparing an individual with others on how well he does some job, to evaluating his performance against his own expectations and career plans (Thompson, 1965). The change is from a nomothetic to an idiographic analysis.

By refining criteria, and improving techniques, we may better the correlation coefficients that provide evidence for the validity of our selection procedures. However, other factors are relevant in determining how many of those we select prove satisfactory. The state of the labour market is one. The number of vacancies in the firm is another. Where a selection technique has been validated by statistical correlation, the better an individual's score on the technique, the greater is the probability of his success. So employing the 'best' five of twenty applicants will probably produce a lower failure rate than employing the 'best' ten from the same population, assuming all twenty differ on the relevant abilities. But a firm, seriously in need of computer operators, may still decide to engage the ten, who on the data have some reasonable possibility of success, and risk a high rate of failure, rather than risk not selecting someone who might succeed. Policy as well as technical know-how becomes involved in such a decision. And value-judgments are sometimes involved in such policy decisions. A state education department may lessen the entry requirements for higher education, knowing that though this provides more young people with a chance it may increase the failure rate among such students.

Acceptable criteria and pass standards in a selection procedure are not solely determined by technical factors. The economic situation, an organization's needs, policies, and values, become involved in such decisions.

SELECTION AND THE ORGANIZATION

The Individual and his Environment

There is an alternative explanation for the low correlations sometimes found in selection. In selection we take personality as our unit of analysis, and explain employee behaviour in terms of individual characteristics. We could adopt an opposite view, deny that personality exists, and regard differences in behaviour as the result of different environments. An employee's work and satisfaction is not a function of what is inside him, but of what goes on outside him, the supervision, incentives, organization, etc.

Alternatively we might adopt a middle position and regard behaviour as the result of an interaction between the individual's personality and what happens in the environment. Lewin's (1952) well-known model expresses this: $B = f.O \times E$. Behaviour is a function of the organism and the environment.

In selection (and guidance) we base our predictions primarily on an assessment of personality. If the interaction of personality and environment determine behaviour, and we ignore the environment, this can affect the accuracy of our predictions. In a static situation, as we might find in some unchanging machine shop or accounts department, our selection of operators and clerks could prove reliable and valid. In a changing environment, selection may prove less completely successful. Senior managers tend to operate in more fluid and changing situations, and here accurate selection becomes difficult.

The organizations for which people are selected function in economic and social systems which may be dynamic and changing. Organizations change in response to the pressures from these systems, and in response also to internal pressures from individuals and groups within the organization. Limited success in selection, manifest in a modest correlation coefficient, may frequently result because the individual interacts with a changing organization.

Selection Criteria and Organizational Goals

In selection we analyse a specific job in an organization, and then select an individual for the position. As part of this procedure we have to determine criteria for success in the job. Such selection criteria are implicitly statements about organizational goals. The policy and goals of an organization ultimately determine selection criteria in some part. An illustration of this is where candidates for a general manager post have been short-listed to two applicants. The first is an engineer, essentially production orientated, while the second is definitely a marketing man. The board of directors may choose the marketing candidate, because he seems more likely to meet certain implicit or explicit criteria they have for success in the job. The firm now has a sales-orientated general manager. The criterion adopted for selection and the selection decision it engendered may subsequently determine company goals, policy, and strategy. One hopes, in fact, that the directors had decided company goals and policy prior to the selection, and their selection criterion emanated from this decision.

Since selection criteria closely relate to organizational goals, organizations with very different sorts of objectives will have very different sorts of selection criteria. Various writers have developed classifications of organizations, where they are categorized according to such factors as the type of power exercised, the sort of goals pursued, and the sort of leaders and managers they have (see Etzioni, 1964). It might prove possible to produce similar kinds of classifications of selection (and training) criteria.

Jobs do not exist in a vacuum, but form part of an economic, social, and psychological system. A concern with the job itself, which is typical in selection, tends to ignore the organizational environment of the job. Selection criteria serve to bridge the gap between the traditional analysis of a job as an isolated, static unit, and seeing the job as part of a total organizational system, usually dynamic and changing.

EXPLANATION IN SELECTION

Non-linear Relationships in Selection

Our discussion of correlation in Chapter 3 assumes that a relationship between two sets of data is linear, that as one variable increases the other does so proportionately. Most validity studies in selection, investigating the correlations between predictive techniques and criteria, have assumed the linearity of any relationship. Kahneman and Ghiselli (1962) showed in an analysis of two hundred correlational studies that over eighty did not have linear, homoscedastic (equal-variance) relationships.

A predictive technique such as a test can correlate with the criterion over one range of scores, say, from 40 to 70, but not do so above or below that range, or at least not correlate in the same way. For example, in a selection test out of a hundred, scores from 31 to 79 might correlate with and predict competence as a computer programmer. But scores from 0 to 30 and 80 to 100 may not predict performance as a programmer in the same way, or possibly not at all. A score of 95 may mean the same probability of success as does one of 85, though the scorers of each are more likely to succeed than anyone getting below 80. On the other hand, 85 and 95 may both be completely non-predictive because no relationship with success (or failure) on the job is found with any score above 79. In both cases we are concerned with situations where a relationship between two sets of data is not linear over the whole range of scores.

In such a situation it would be inadequate for selection to use a score on the test in any simple way. We would need to break down the scores into the various predictive and non-predictive ranges. This suggests the existence of sub-groups in the total population and, as Drenth points out (1966), we return here to the concept of intervening variables.

Explaining Non-linear Relationships

When a relationship is linear we are tempted to use our data crudely, simply to say this sort of score predicts that sort of performance, without attempting any explanation of the relationship. We are tempted to operate at a pragmatic level. With non-linear relationships, and the possible existence of sub-groups, explanation becomes more necessary. Over one range of data individual scores may predict performance in a linear fashion, over another range only a general prediction is given by a group of scores (e.g. 80–100), and another group of scores (e.g. 0–30) may not predict at all. In such a situation an explanation solely in terms of observable stimulus and response, the test scores and subsequent performance, will be inadequate. It is necessary to postulate something unobserved intervening between stimulus and response. The explanation requires an intervening variable or hypothetical construct, such as we referred to in discussing Allport during Chapter 2. Table 7.2 illustrates the point, suggesting hypothetical constructs which explain non-linear relationships between typical selection items and later job performance.

We will illustrate this. The job of Table 7.2 is that of a representative at Firm XYZ, selling calculating machines and other office equipment. A test of general intelligence is employed, designed for use with people of rather above average intelligence. Most people who score between 31 and 79 succeed in this sales job. But a score below 31 or above 79 predicts nothing, neither success nor failure in the position.

TABLE 7.2 *Relationships between selection procedure and job performance* (an illustration of non-linear relationships between items in a selection procedure and satisfactory job performance explained in terms of hypothetical constructs)

Stimulus items in a selection procedure	*Hypothetical constructs* explanatory concepts	*Response* satisfactory performance on the job
—	—	—
test score 0–30 or 10 years education		no correlation
test score 31–79 or 11–14 years education	intelligence · number aptitude · social needs	positive correlation
test score 80–100 or 16 + years education		no correlation

Our explanation might be on the following lines, replete with hypothetical constructs. The sales position at Firm XYZ requires a certain level of intelligence, is essentially social, and involves a considerable amount of cognitive manipulation of numerical data. Most people scoring between 31 and 79 succeed because this is the intelligence range ideal for the job.

However, much of the difficult number work involved in the job can be handled by specialized number aptitude. Whether anyone scoring 30 or below will succeed or fail depends on what special number ability he has to compensate for his inadequate intelligence level. Down to a score of 30 intelligence is enough to cope with the job, but below this it needs to be supported by a special ability with number.

An individual scoring above 80 may succeed or fail, even though he could certainly cope with the intellectual demands of the job. The job does not require so high a level of general intelligence, and most men of this intellectual level are likely to be bored by the job and lose interest. However, if such a highly intelligent man also has strong social needs, and finds satisfaction in the dealing with people involved, this can compensate for the lack of intellectual content in the work. Motivated and interested in this way he will succeed in the job, even though his tests score is above 80.

We could explain the relationship between job performance and length of education, also suggested in Table 7.2, in a similar way. Our explanation might use other hypothetical constructs or the same ones.

In selection we have accepted the notion of individual differences, that people differ in measurable ways. The non-linearity of data suggests they also differ in the way they differ. This provides support for the anti-nomothetic bias of Allport and others, discussed in Chapter 2, which suggests that the comparison of individuals has only a limited meaning and use.

If people differ in the way they differ, it becomes useful to adopt a more individual-centred analysis. Such an individual- (or group-) centred approach approximates to a search for Allport's 'patterned individuality' (1961). It tends to be more idiographic than the traditional method of selection, resembling rather the emphasis of occupational guidance and counselling.

Whether or not an assessment should be individual-centred is part of the clinical versus statistical controversy. The clinicians assert that we should adapt and tailor our assessment procedure to the individual, sensitively reacting to him. The statisticians stress the need for objective assessment, based largely on a comparison of the individual against empirically derived norms. If the non-linear relationships of selection data suggest that people differ in the way they differ, the practitioner must attempt a synthesis. He must base his selection decisions in the empirically derived norms and relationships established by the statisticians, but he must try to understand, explain, and interpret them in terms of the individual; he must also act as a clinician. It is, of course, these tentative explanations and interpretations which provide hypotheses for the 'statisticians' subsequently to investigate and validate empirically.

Explanation and Construct Validity in Selection

Whether we favour the subjectivity of the clinician or the objectivity of the statistician, explanation is really necessary with either approach, though the latter have tended to forget this. We made this point in Chapter 2, arguing for construct rather than merely predictive validity. The discovery of non-linear relationships in selection has not introduced any need for the explanations of construct validity, but merely emphasized the point. Selection needs explanation as part of statistical, predictive validity.

If we know not only that relationships exist, but why they do, we can transfer findings from one area to another apparently different situation. Understanding the relationship between test score and competence as a representative in office equipment means we are in a better position to know whether the test might be used to select for some other position, such as computer programmer. Similarly we could suggest other predictive techniques, alternative tests, or an interview, that should give the same results. Without explanation we cannot extrapolate, interpolate, or predict in any way beyond the known data. We can only say that 'on such-and-such an occasion this was found'.

Without explanation we cannot improve on our selection. We need to know what it was about the predictive technique that gave valid results—in our example, that the test measured intelligence. If our explanation of the example is valid, we could improve selection considerably by introducing an evaluation of the candidates' number facility and possibly through interview an assessment of their social needs.

In Chapters 2, 3, and 4 we have outlined various ideas, concepts, hypothetical constructs, and theories about personality.

These are typical of the sorts of explanations or partial explanations needed for construct validation in personnel selection.

It is to be noted that the synthetic validity previously outlined constitutes, as Drenth (1966) suggests, a form of construct validity. In synthetic validity we go beyond the traditional position of generalizing within jobs, and generalize more comprehensively across apparently dissimilar jobs. For example, we might postulate that the positions of counter clerk, technical assistant, and junior salesman, in Firm XYZ all require 'a certain level of intelligence, skill in handling customers, experience of keeping routine accounts, and the ability to organize the work of two or three subordinates'. Such generalizations, which might form part of a synthetic validation, provide also construct validity, since they attempt to explain any relationship between predictive techniques and selection criteria.

Finally, if scores and assessments on various predictive techniques do correlate with the selection criteria, but the relationship is non-linear, then the correlation coefficient provides inadequate information for selection purposes. Scatter diagrams and expectancy charts would seem far more informative and helpful ways of presenting the data. Figures 3.1 to 3.5 are examples of scatter diagrams, and the following Figure 7.1 presents two sets of

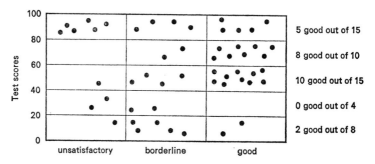

Fig. 7.1 Scatter diagram of 52 selected applicants, with their test scores plotted against a later assessment on performance criteria

selection data in non-linear relationship. Inspection of the data tabulated in this way suggests that test scores above 80 and below 20 are not predictive. Scores between these two figures are predictive, but less so in the middle range of about 40–60.

A straight inspection of the data presented in the scatter diagram of Figure 7.1 can produce an expectancy chart, such as that of Table 7.3. The probability of an applicant being rated 'good' on the performance criterion is given for various ranges of the test scores.

TABLE 7.3 *An expectancy chart for selection purposes*
(the probabilities of applicants being successful, i.e. subsequently rated 'good' on criterion, for various ranges of scores on the selection test, developed from past data)

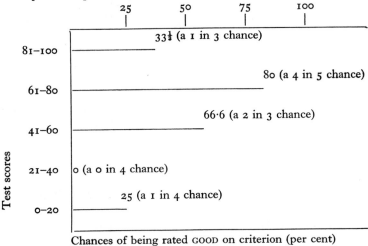

REFERENCES

Allport, G. W. (1961), *Pattern and Growth in Personality*, Holt, Rinehart & Winston.

Drenth, P. J. D. (1966), 'Some current issues in selection and placement research', in *Manpower Planning*, NATO Conference, English Universities Pre

DuBois, P. H. (1966), 'Aspects of the criterion problem in personnel research', in *Manpower Planning*, NATO Conference, English Universities Press.

Etzioni, A. (1964), *Modern Organizations*, Prentice-Hall.

Flanagan, J. C. (1949), 'Job requirements', in *Current Trends in Industrial Psychology*, University of Pittsburgh Press.

Flanagan, J. C. (1954), 'The critical incident technique', *Psychol. Bull.*, 51.

Ghiselli, E. E. (1955), 'The Measurement of Occupational Aptitude', *Univ. Calif. Publ. Psychol.*, 8.

Ghiselli, E. E. (1966), *The Validity of Occupational Aptitude Tests*, Wiley.

Ghiselli, E. E. and Haire, M. (1960), 'The validation of selection tests in the light of the dynamic character of criteria', *Pers. Psychol.*, 13.

Guion, R. M. (1965), 'Synthetic validity in a small company', *Pers. Psychol.*, 14.

Haire, M. (1959), 'Psychological problems relevant to business and industry', *Psychol. Bull.*, 56.

Kahneman, D. and Ghiselli, E. E. (1962), 'Validity and non-linear heteroscedastic models', *Pers. Psychol.*, 15.

Lawshe, C. H. (1952), 'What can industrial psychology do for small business? 2. Employee Selection', *Pers. Psychol.*, 5.

Lewin, K. (1952), *Field Theory in Social Science*, Tavistock.

Rodger, A. (1945), 'On the selection of business executives', *Labour Management*, 27.

Rodger, A. and Cavanagh, P. (1962), 'Personnel selection and vocational guidance', in *Society: Problems and Methods of Study*, ed. A. T. Welford, Routledge & Kegan Paul.

Thompson, A. S. (1965), 'The criterion problem in selection and guidance, No. 2, A Symposium', 15th International Congress of Applied Psychology, in *Occup. Psychol.*, 39, 2.

PART III

Training

CHAPTER 8

The Organization and Training

Overview

How well an individual learns his job in an organization depends on a number of factors. In the first section of this chapter we outline a framework which suggests that three organizational factors principally determine the effectiveness of training. They relate to policy, to the technology of training, and to motivation. After briefly reviewing a firm's normal channels of training we consider the first of these factors, policy, under six headings. We next consider the second factor, the actual technology of training, outlining first a simple scheme for developing a training procedure, then a more detailed scheme which specifies other important considerations. To discuss the third factor, motivation, we adopt Kelman's idea of three sorts of influence, and develop a model with which to consider different sorts of motivation and learning in the organization.

A FRAMEWORK FOR CONSIDERING THE TRAINING OF THE INDIVIDUAL IN THE ORGANIZATION

In Chapter 1 we looked at work. We now consider how people learn their work. Learning a job is invariably a social process—one learns from someone, and this usually happens in a group or organization. We may consider learning a job as an example of socialization, which we define as follows: socialization is a process by which the individual acquires knowledge, attitudes, skills, to meet the expectations of those who influence his behaviour. Wheeler (1966), following certain proposals of Brim (1960), has suggested a framework for analysing socialization in the organization. We are adapting this framework for our analysis of training as a form of socialization. Socialization suggests that the individual changes his behaviour to conform to certain expectations—the question usually is, whose expectations? Training is socialization to meet the expectations of management.

When an organization or group attempts to socialize an individual, it operates by communicating what is expected of him, by enabling him to do what is expected of him, and by making him want to do what is expected of him. Similarly for socialization to occur, the individual must be capable of seeing what is expected of him, must be capable of performing it, and must want to do it. These six variables determine the effectiveness of training or any other form of socialization. They are given in Table 8.1 under organization and individual. Table 8.1 provides a framework for considering socialization or training in an organization, in terms of the S→O→R model, using the variables we have outlined. The O or organism is here the given, dependent variable; the O is the individual whose characteristics are determined in part by the process of personnel selection. The S embraces the organization variables that may be altered to affect the socialization and training of the individual. The model is essentially one of socialization in an organization. It applies to trade union officials attempting to change employees to meet their expectations as it does to managers training employees to conform to theirs.

TABLE 8.1 *A framework for considering socialization and training in the organization*

Stimulus	Organism	Response
Organization	Individual	
Is able to provide clear, consistent expectations	Is able to see what is expected of him	
Is able to teach what is required	Is able to learn and perform what is expected of him	Learning
Is able to motivate the individual	Wants to learn and perform what is expected of him	

The first variable which is under organization in the model relates to the organization's capacity to generate clear and consistent expectations. This is primarily a matter of the development and explicit formulation of a company policy. If a policy is well-formulated in most areas, then an organization is able to state clearly and unambiguously to its employees what is expected of them. We will shortly examine this matter of company policy.

However, though the organization may provide clear expectations, the individual may fail to perceive or to react to them because of his own personal frames of reference. In most organizations, and this is particularly true of a commercial enterprise (see Fox, 1966), there frequently exists different groups with rival interests, who place different and even conflicting expectations on the individual. A production operator knows his supervisor wants him to produce more and his shop-steward wants him to produce less. He may adopt as his frame of reference either management, or the unions, or his shop-steward, or his mates in the machine-shop where he works, or a mixture of these. It is this which constitutes the first variable under the individual.

The second variable under organization is concerned with the procedures and technology of training. The organization needs to know what to teach and how to teach it, using the appropriate conditions of learning and the relevant training methods. We will examine this later in the chapter. The technology of training the individual will be developed further in later chapters, specifically with reference to the conditions of learning, to skill acquisition, and to supervisory and management training.

The second variable under Individual is a factor of ability, which we have examined in Chapter 3. Its presence in the figure serves to emphasize that a necessary condition for successful training is that the trainees should possess the abilities required. This has to be dealt with by personnel selection. Similarly the third factor under individual relates to those motivational aspects of personality we discussed in Chapter 4. Selection of individuals with appropriate drives or motivational traits is important here, but such personality factors interrelate with the organization's capacity to motivate the individual.

This last is the third variable under organization. Adapting Kelman (1961) we will suggest later in the chapter that we may usefully think of three sorts of motivation in a training situation, compliance, identification, and internalization.

We can now incorporate these points in the original framework. This is done in Table 8.2.

TABLE 8.2 *A framework for analysing training problems in an organization*

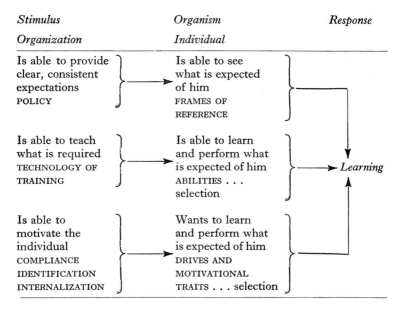

Stimulus	*Organism*	*Response*
Organization	*Individual*	
Is able to provide clear, consistent expectations POLICY	Is able to see what is expected of him FRAMES OF REFERENCE	
Is able to teach what is required TECHNOLOGY OF TRAINING	Is able to learn and perform what is expected of him ABILITIES . . . selection	*Learning*
Is able to motivate the individual COMPLIANCE IDENTIFICATION INTERNALIZATION	Wants to learn and perform what is expected of him DRIVES AND MOTIVATIONAL TRAITS . . . selection	

THE CHANNELS OF TRAINING

We will now examine training in the organization, using the model, considering policy, the technology of training, and then the motivation of the individual. We have suggested that training is socialization orientated to conform to the expectations of management. And so, suggests King (1964), 'training surely amounts to providing the conditions in which people can learn effectively' what management requires of them. King's definition immediately relates training to the learning process, and to the environment ('providing the conditions') in which learning occurs.

Learning occurs all the time; the individual employee does not wait for his manager or the training department to lay on 'effective conditions'. He might at any time be influenced by his manager, supervisor, work-mates, colleagues, or shop-steward, and learn from them. The production manager's untidiness, his way of speaking to subordinates, his carelessness with paperwork, are all communicated to the foremen under him. If the manager has influence on these foremen, and he will normally have some, they are all the time learning these behaviours from him. When this continuous and informal learning occurs between a superior and a subordinate, King (1964) refers to it as the primary learning process. This learning is, as King suggests, a function of the basic executive relationship between a superior and a subordinate.

King sees company training as occurring through three channels. The direct training of a subordinate by his superior through the primary learning process constitutes the first, and is labelled Channel A by King. Training may be delegated by the immediate manager to an individual or competent body within the organization, and King refers to this as Channel B. A company training division or personnel department is an example of Channel B. If training is delegated outside the organization, for example, to the local technical college, this would be Channel C.

Largely as a result of the work of psychologists, our knowledge of how to train the individual, in different fields and at a variety of levels, has grown considerably over recent years. What remains a crucial problem for industrial training is how to make the most effective use of such knowledge in an organization. This problem relates to the nature of organizations, to their formal and informal structures, and to the conflicting interests and power groups that normally exist within them.

This point is made by King in his distinction between a technique and a procedure. He suggests a technique may be described as 'the method by which a *person* puts an *idea* into practice'. It operates on the personal and psychological level, and refers in training to the imparting by one individual of skill or knowledge to others. It is in this area that our competence has grown so much. The problem we have referred to arises when we attempt to convert a technique into a procedure, which King describes as 'the accepted method by which *policy* is carried out in an organization'. When a technique is accepted and embodied in the practices of an organization, *as an expression of policy*, it becomes a procedure. We will subsequently examine techniques, but will immediately consider policy in an organization.

POLICY

The first variable in the model relates to the organizations' capacity to generate clear and consistent expectations. We have suggested that this is partly a matter of how company policy is developed and formulated. We will now refer to company policy as it relates to training. It is through a company policy that training techniques are converted into training procedures, and training is integrated into the organization.

Company policies, in particular company training policies and the procedures that emanate from them, may be considered under the six headings proposed by King (1964):

1. The analysis of needs. A company might base its advertising and sales policy on market research into customer demand for the firm's product. Training policy should start from an analysis of the organization's training needs.

2. The formulation of aims and principles. A company might adopt as an objective the mechanization of its accounting system. It might adopt as part of its training policy the aim of developing an adaptive and highly flexible work force.

3. The establishment of an organizational structure suitable for implementing training policy. Having determined the aims of the production department, we establish an appropriate structure for it. Similarly with training we need to have a policy on responsibility for training. If a training department is set up, it is necessary to establish policy on its authority, responsibility, and relationship to line management.

4. The determination of relevant procedures. A decision on production techniques will often involve more than the technical considerations of the engineer. The best engineering decision may fail to take account of cost and marketing factors, and of what manpower is actually available in the firm. A decision on training procedure involves technical considerations of the best methods and of the optimum conditions of learning. Such a decision, involving a choice of channels, is affected also by considerations of cost (how much money is the firm willing to spend on training?), by its convenience to production, by whether it should be broadly or narrowly based, by whether it should develop the individual as well as benefit the company, etc. All such factors, which would be relevant to the choice of procedures, involve policy decisions.

5. The selection and training of training staff. We have suggested in an earlier chapter that in a selection decision there is usually implicit a decision on policy. The managing director may select for chief production manager an engineer whose work record suggests

a keenness for mass production techniques, and reject one whose experience lies mainly in job production. In this choice there is probably involved a policy decision on future production methods. The ability of those chosen as training officers and instructors, their level of education, their specialisms, background and experience, the training they will be given, and the salaries they will receive, involve policy decisions on training in that organization, often unrecognized.

6. The establishing of review procedures. We evaluate the effectiveness of training against criteria; such criteria embody and express policy decisions on training. In fact such decisions would normally already have been made when policy was determined under 1 and 2 above. We might have decided the organization needs highly adaptable operators and junior managers able to generate new ideas, and not passively accept current practices. These become aims of training. Our review procedure could evaluate at the end of X months the foremen's account of how many jobs trained operators can satisfactorily perform, and executive reports on the creativity of trained junior managers.

THE TECHNOLOGY OF TRAINING

We have discussed the determination of policy. With policy decided, what is expected of employees by the needs of the organization becomes clearer. We will now examine how employees are trained to do what is required of them. This is the technology of training.

A Procedure for Developing a Training Procedure
A simple and useful way to consider this aspect of training, suggested by Rodger (1950), is under the three headings of what, how, and reporting. In establishing a training procedure the main technical considerations can be thought of as: (1) what needs to be taught; (2) how it should be taught; (3) ways of reporting on the training.

What. What needs to be taught is based on a study of the job. In Chapter 1 we have already discussed job analysis, but an analysis for training is usually slightly different from one for selection or grading and payment purposes. An analysis of a job for training describes its duties, activities and responsibilities, and analyses and evaluates the skills and knowledge a job occupant needs for performing them satisfactorily to a specified criterion.

Explicit in a job analysis for training is a distinction between knowledge and skill. A setter-operator on a capstan lathe knows the correct gear ratios, speeds, cutting-tool angles, for certain types of work. This is knowledge. It is essentially a knowing-about, and could be learnt at a desk away from the lathe. The same operator, learning to feed in the cutting tool, needs to know the right pressure to apply just by feel. The learner-driver needs to master the clutch in the same way. The instructors may explain and give guidance, but the driver and the machine-operator have to experience for themselves the right movements. This direct experience is the basis of a skill.

Knowledge then is knowing about, entails explanation, employs concepts like 'ratio' and 'management hierarchy', and uses symbols such as those of language and number. Skill is essentially a direct knowing, at first hand, through experience, and is non-symbolic. It is possible, in terms of hierarchical group factor theory, that the major group factor, $v:ed$, relates primarily to knowledge, and the major group factor, $k:m$, is mainly involved in skill.

In the earlier discussion of job analysis and of procedures for selection it was stressed that difficulty and failure in a job provided a useful source of information. We should determine what parts of a job people have difficulty in learning, what 'incidents' are indicative of learning difficulty or failure, and what particular tasks have caused some trainees to fail (Flanagan, 1949; Rodger and Cavanagh, 1959). Information gleaned in this way suggests what skill and knowledge is essential for a job, and provides part of the core for the *what* of a training procedure.

In an organization there are usually acceptable and unacceptable standards of performance for a job. In a job analysis, for training, guidance, or selection, it is desirable to be clear and explicit about criteria for acceptable performance. This involves both a technical decision and one of policy, though usually the policy is implicit in company procedures, methods of payment, or supervisor attitudes. The job analyst needs to make explicit what constitutes acceptable performance.

How. Having determined what should be taught, we need to decide HOW to teach it. The content of training, WHAT should be taught, partly determines how it will be taught. A group discussion would probably be an inappropriate way of training an operator in a delicate assembly skill.

We will examine the how of training in the next few chapters, but under this heading we are essentially concerned with two important considerations in developing a training procedure. Firstly, in what way can knowledge of results, guidance, practice, the sequencing and ordering of material, transfer of training, and understanding, help in the acquisition of this skill and that knowledge? Secondly, which would be an appropriate technique to use for the teaching of that skill and this knowledge—a lecture, discussion groups, case-study, projects, role-playing, business games, T-groups, the approaches of skills analysis?

Reporting. We need reports on training. We should first specify the goals of a training course—what sort of behaviour do we want of the trainee? We should stipulate the goals for various stages of training, distinguishing between long- and short-term objectives, and should stipulate also the standard of performance required after training. This last relates to the criterion of acceptable performance we have already referred to under the What of training.

Having determined goals we need reports which state how each trainee is progressing with reference to these targets. Knowledge of how he is doing usually helps the trainee. We will subsequently examine the effectiveness of such knowledge of results, but suggest here it is both motivating and informative. It may be used both to encourage the trainee in his efforts at learning, and to guide him with regard to what is right and wrong in his performance.

We need to know also what factors relate to good or poor progress. Such factors might be trainee characteristics, such as age and tested abilities, or the training methods used, or the conditions of practice, guidance, order of material, etc., or even characteristics of the trainer. Finally, if we find relationships between such factors and trainee progress, we need to know why the relationship exists. We need explanations for the success and failures of a training course. With such information and explanation we can improve the training course.

Explanation

Without an explanation of why a relationship exists between

success or failure on training and certain factors in that course, we cannot generalize. We can only say—with that type of task and these sorts of trainees, this improves learning. 'This' may refer to practising in short, spaced sessions, rather than over long periods with many breaks. It would prove much more useful if we could go on to stipulate with what other kinds of learning tasks and with what other kinds of trainees, such spacing of practice is likely to be the more effective. But without some form of explanation we cannot extrapolate in this way.

We have previously discussed predictive and construct validity at the end of Chapter 2. We suggested that guidance and selection are likely to prove more fruitful if based on useful and valid theories and concepts of personality. Similarly our decisions in training should be based on explanations of how people learn, and not just on a knowledge of relationships in certain training situations. The present state of the field makes this difficult. There is an abundance of empirical data that relates to training, but only a small amount of the developed theory seems relevant. However, a number of learning concepts are useful, such as knowledge of results and activity learning.

In the following chapters we will outline some basic theories of learning and a number of concepts. Training needs to be based on such theoretical explanations and concepts of learning. If, for example, we know why knowledge of results improves learning, we can build it into a training course, when it is relevant, in such a way as to maximize its effectiveness.

A Second Procedure for Developing a Training Procedure

Glaser (1965) analyses the development of any system for instruction into four main phases—'Instructional Goals, Entering Behavior, Instructional Procedures, and Performance Assessment'. In developing a system, whether for education or training, we must specify these. He adds also a fifth phase which runs through them all, the research necessary if the four main phases are to be improved. Among the factors that Glaser's analysis, in terms of the four phases, has served to emphasize are two we will mention here. First, a prerequisite of good training is a clear determination of the goals and objectives of that training. It may be stated in terms of what behaviour is required as a consequence of training. It should preferably be stated as an account of the overt performance that is needed of the trainee. Such an account of 'terminal behaviour' should be characterized by an attempt to reduce a complex job, such as that of the supervisor, into simpler, operationally described tasks.

Secondly, a training procedure needs to take account of the state of the trainee on entering training ('Entering Behavior'). Trainees will vary as regards the abilities, knowledge, and skill which they possess on entering training. This needs to be assessed

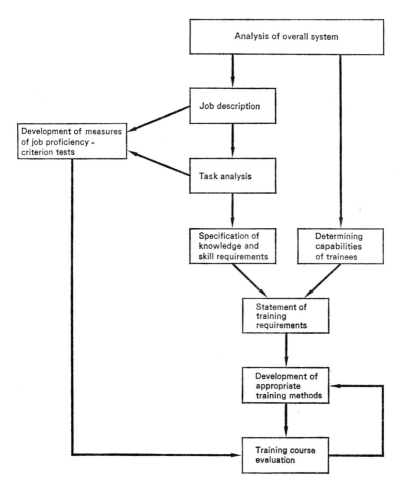

Fig. 8.1 Steps in developing a training course (Tilley, 1968)

for training, and in practice may relate training to selection procedures. In fact some of the required terminal behaviour may be already part of the behaviour repertoire of all or most trainees. It would be necessary to take account of this in determining the content of the training course.

There are more detailed procedures for setting up a training scheme than the what, how, and reporting approach, which incorporate the above and other points. We will now outline one proposed by Tilley (1968). The steps he lists for setting up a training course are given in Figure 8.1. We will go through them.

Analysis of overall system. Training is a way of increasing the efficiency of the organization and the satisfaction of the individual employee. It provides a possible solution to certain types of work problems, such as low output, large numbers of rejects in production, high labour turnover, poor morale, etc. But training is only one of a number of possible solutions. Others are selection, job re-design and ergonomics, the development of informal social relationships, introducing more effective incentives, and changing the structure of the organization. The point is, and we will examine this in the final chapter, that we need to determine what in the circumstances is the most appropriate solution to any problem.

Job description. Under this heading we start on the what of training. Tilley gives two valuable functions of good job descriptions. First, they make evident what are the important and unimportant features of a job, and ensure that training profitably concentrates on the more important of the activities in a job. Secondly, Tilley makes the point that 'by specifying objectives in terms of observable behaviour they go some way towards meeting the requirements for measurement, since objectives must be desirable if they are to be measurable'. This emphasizes the need, to which we have referred, to state terminal behaviour in terms of overt performance.

Task analysis. Above we have suggested that any account of terminal behaviour should attempt to state a complex job in terms of simpler tasks. This is the function of task analysis. Such tasks should be classified according to the sorts of training they need. In Chapter 12 we shall examine Gilbert's (1962) division of behaviours into three kinds, chains, multiple discriminations, and generalizations. Tilley adopts Gagné's (1965) sixfold classification of learned behaviour which, like Gilbert's, describes the tasks in terms of their stimulus and response characteristics. Specifying the task by the stimuli and responses that have to be learnt to perform it, suggests also how it might best be taught. At the level of supervisory and management training it seems more useful to adopt an alternative classification of tasks. Adapting Glacier concepts (Brown and Jaques, 1965), we will suggest that such tasks may be classified under the headings of peoples in roles, techniques, and programming.

Specification of knowledge and skill requirements. Though still on the 'What has to be learnt' aspect of the procedure, we can now state the performance requirements of the job in useful detail. At this stage the knowledge-skill distinction becomes helpful.

Determining capabilities of trainees. We do not train fictitious individuals who know nothing, but real, experienced people who know and can do a number of things. So the next step is simply one of investigating and determining the present skill and knowledge of trainees, by attainment tests, written and practical examinations, and other methods of assessment.

Statement of training requirements. If we subtract this last account of the present skill and knowledge of trainees from the specification of knowledge and skill requirements, we have a statement of what training is needed. In this way the content of a training course is determined, and the process of establishing the What of training is completed.

Development of appropriate training methods. Tilley's next category relates to the how of training, and what has been previously said under the how heading applies here. We might add that it is also necessary to decide under this heading which of the three channels of company training (King, 1964) is appropriate—that of the primary learning process, that of training delegated within the organization, that of training delegated to an external body.

Training course evaluation. Tilley distinguishes between education and training. In training we can specify what is relevant to satisfactory performance of the job, and stipulate the training objectives. We can establish suitable measures and tests of trainee performance against the predetermined criteria.

The objectives of education are long-term, and more difficult to specify. We shall examine this in discussing supervisory and management development.

MOTIVATION OF THE INDIVIDUAL

We must now consider the third organizational variable, the capacity of the organization to motivate the learner. For this we are adopting Kelman's proposals for considering influence (1961). Kelman suggests there are 'three processes of social influence', three different ways in which the behaviour of an individual is influenced and motivated by another person or a group. He has called them compliance, identification, and internalization. All the quotations from Kelman in the following section are from his 1961 article. In a rather different field, brainwashing and Chinese 'thought reform' illustrate attempts to influence at all three levels (Lifton, 1957).

Compliance
Kelman describes Compliance as follows: 'Compliance can be said to occur when an individual accepts influence from another person or a group because he hopes to achieve a favorable reaction from the other.' The new employee says or does what he thinks is expected of him, not because he likes it or believes it right, but because of its consequences, because it produces from others the pay-off he wants. The operator learns the assembly task, and to maximize or restrict his output, in order to obtain good pay, security, or approval, etc. He complies with whatever individual or group has the means which enable him to attain his personal goals. Sometimes rival interest groups in an organization have at their disposal the different means of rewarding him, which places the individual in a conflict situation. The operator wants to produce as much as possible because management rewards him if he does, but wishes also to restrict his output since this obtains the affection and respect of his fellow workers. Compliance is a particularly common form of motivation when the individual has no alternative

means of achieving his personal goals. An employee is more likely to comply with unpleasant management expectations in a period of unemployment than when there are many other jobs around.

If management, unions, or whatever socializing agent, motivates the individual to learn through a manipulation of rewards and punishments, that is, by compliance, then there are a number of consequences. First, it means that learning will occur, and the learnt behaviour continue, only when whoever rewards or punishes is likely to know about it. Employees might obey a 'no smoking' prohibition in a plastics factory not because of dangers to life and property, but because they would be found out and punished. If they could smoke and not be found out, they would do so. Secondly, since with compliance whatever the employee does is instrumental and motivated only by the pay-off, it continues only as long as it seems the best way to get what he wants. If his aim is a rise in pay, and good work and time-keeping fail to obtain him this, he might try to get it by becoming a trouble-maker. Thirdly, behaviour that is learnt because of compliance is usually specific to a situation. A foreman adopts a democratic supervisory style because in his firm this is generally approved of by management. If he moves to another firm with an authoritarian ethos, he is likely to comply and become more authoritarian as a supervisor.

Identification

Of his second process of social influence Kelman writes:

> Identification can be said to occur when an individual adopts behavior derived from another person or a group because this behavior is associated with a satisfying self-defining relationship to this person or group. By a self-defining relationship I mean a role relationship that forms a part of the person's self-image.

The new manager learns to behave like successful managers in the firm, because he sees himself as just such a successful manager. Kelman himself uses an occupational example:

> The more or less conscious efforts involved when an individual learns to play a desired occupational role and imitates an appropriate role model would also exemplify this process. Here, of course, the individual is much more selective in the attitudes and actions he takes over from the other person. What is at stake is not his basic sense of identity or the stability of his self-concept, but rather his more limited 'professional identity'.

Identification differs from compliance in that the 'identifying' individual really does believe the opinions and attitudes he adopts, and really approves of his new actions and behaviour.

When is the individual in the organization likely to be motivated by his attempt to establish satisfying self-defining relationships, and what are the consequences of influence through identification? First, identification is likely to occur when the employee wishes to obtain a degree of social and personal security, which he achieves by adopting a specific role of which he approves. A newly promoted chargehand might identify with the foreman's group, and see himself in terms of this group. Secondly, an employee is likely to identify when he is influenced by the attractiveness of the influencing group, not by its power as in compliance. Some time during his training the electrical apprentice may begin to like what he sees of the role of skilled electrician. He stops seeing himself as an apprentice and starts identifying with the adult electricians. Lastly, the attractiveness which leads to identification is partly a function of the alternatives the individual has. If the only other role open to the apprentice were an unskilled job on the shopfloor then he is likely to identify with the electricians. If the apprenticeship can lead to what he regards as exciting jobs in the drawing office, he is less likely to identify wholly with the electricians.

Behaviour that results from identification may change when the person no longer regards it as likely to maintain satisfying, self-defining relationships. The sorts of relationships he wants may change. If a craftsman, identifying with other craftsmen, is offered and accepts a supervisory position, he will probably begin to identify with some other group to obtain satisfying relationships in terms of his new view of himself. Behaviour, skills, attitudes, originating through a process of identification are not embedded in the personality core; they are not, in Allport's term, propriate (see Chapter 2). They relate only to a particular role, and so Jones identifying with his tough sales colleagues aggressively asserts himself at work, but at home as husband and father is the mildest of men. Of course, an individual may become attached to a particular role and regard it as part of himself. But when such a role, with its attendant behaviours, skills, attitudes, really becomes embedded in the personality core, the process has become one of internalization.

Internalization

Kelman states: 'Internalization can be said to occur when an individual accepts influence because the induced behavior is congruent with his value system.' A person adopts behaviour because it accords with his personal values. He accepts the influence of others and learns because he experiences what is taught as consonant with how he sees himself—it is propriate. The student for the ministry or priesthood may be influenced by his teachers at theological college on this level. The young medical intern, genuinely concerned to alleviate human suffering, is motivated to learn from the specialists because their knowledge relates to his concept of himself.

To what extent does this form of motivation, namely internalization, occur in a commercial organization? In Western society work may play an important part in the psychological development of the individual. Where there is choice people will tend to choose occupations that accord with how they see themselves, and the occupation they have chosen further defines and maintains this self concept. When this is so, an individual may be powerfully motivated by his experience of his work as part of what he is. Hence the remark of a manager, 'How can you work too hard, when your work is your life?'

In what situations is anyone likely to be moved to learn by internalization? A manager may be trained in a democratic style of supervision, and may firmly adopt it because it so accords with his own values. The process is one of internalization, and has occurred in this situation because the behaviour he is taught seems congruent with his value structure. Alternatively by private reading or on an external course a manager may learn of democratic approaches to supervision and wish to adopt them because they accord with his values, only to find his firm favours authoritarian supervision. He feels pressure to be authoritarian himself, because he must to keep his job (compliance), or because it is necessary if he is to maintain satisfying relationships with other managers (identification). In such a situation he will only give a shell of himself to his work—or he leaves. Similarly a manager with a highly authoritarian personality might experience democratic supervision as completely at variance with his self and his values, and go through the motions of democratic supervision, consulting staff and involving them in decisions, only because he must.

A person is likely to identify if he sees the sources of influence as attractive. Internalization is related to a belief in them; Kelman refers to their credibility. A religious novice is influenced not so much by the attractiveness of his priest-teachers as by whether they know and are likely to tell the truth. If Smith, the salesman, regards his sales manager as totally honest, he is more likely to be influenced by him at this level, and to internalize the attitudes and behaviour the sales manager has taught him.

Lastly, motivation is likely to take the form of internalization if the individual sees what he does or is taught as relevant to his basic values. If a manager comes to regard a proposed method of selection as fairer than his normal practice, and giving a fair and equal opportunity to everyone is important to him, he is more likely to be induced to adopt the new procedure.

If certain behaviour and attitudes have been acquired through a process of internalization, they will affect the individual in any situation he sees as related to those of his values they accord with. The protection of all those dear to one is normally high in the values of most people. Mr X, the safety officer at Firm Y, has over the years learnt about attitudes and ways of behaving that help to ensure the safety of employees in the factory. But they affect him also outside the plant. He is a careful driver; at home he is careful about fireguards and quick to tack down loose stair carpets; he forbids his children to have fireworks.

If the motivation for acquiring a skill or attitude has been that of internalization, under what conditions are we likely to relinquish them? Quite simply when we no longer regard the skill, attitude, or behaviour, as related to our values. A socialist works manager enthusiastically supports works councils because he sees them as a form of industrial democracy. Years later the same works manager, still socialist and democrat, no longer has any interest in works councils, since he now regards them as a charade which has nothing to do with democracy or socialism.

'Behavior adopted through internalization', says Kelman, 'is part of an internal system. It is fitted into the person's basic framework of values and is congruent with it.' The importance of honesty was inculcated into Bloggs as a child. In his teens the meticulously fair behaviour of his father in money matters was readily internalized by him. This scrupulous fairness with money is embedded in his personality core. It is characteristic of him—

as husband and father, as sales manager dealing with customers, dealing with colleagues, and as a friend and a neighbour.

A Model of Motivation and Learning in an Organization
We are proposing in Table 8.3 a scheme or model which relates the type of system operating in an organization to different sorts of motivation and learning. The organizational system is seen as affecting learning, and behaviour generally, through the nature of its motivation, and the level at which it can influence personality. By 'system' we refer here simply to units interacting to function as a whole.

In our first type of organizational system, the economic, the nature of the motivation is essentially that of compliance. The level of the individual personality involved is that of economic man whom we looked at in Chapter 2. With motivation of the nature of compliance, economic man may be trained to learn actions, but nothing more. It is often sufficient and may sometimes be appropriate to provide this form of motivation in training for perceptual motor skills. As a basis for changing an individual's attitudes and relationships in a job, and for altering the values he holds, it is inadequate.

In the second type of organizational system, the social, the nature of the motivation is that of identification. The individual personality is involved at the level of social man, whom we also briefly examined in Chapter 2. This form of motivation is normally sufficient and possibly appropriate for the acquisition of an occupational role, such as sales manager, foreman, probably even 'a company man'. Identification enables one also to learn actions.

We have labelled the third type of organizational system the 'self system', and here the nature of motivation is that of internalization. It is self-actualizing man, glimpsed in Chapter 2, who moves through this system. What he learns is value-relationships. In other words he learns to relate things in the outside world to his own values and his self. And so an individual might come to see his being a good doctor, or a first-class toolmaker, or a loyal employee of the firm, as integral to his value-system and his self. This form of motivation may affect also the learning of actions and roles, but how appropriate it is to, say, a commercial organization remains debatable.

TABLE 8.3 *An analysis of organizations according to motivation (i.e. the nature of motivation generated in the different systems and the level of personality and sorts of learning and behaviour affected by the motivation)*

Type of organizational system	Nature of motivation	Level of personality	Sorts of learning and behaviour
Economic system⟶	compliance⟶	economic man⟶	actions
Social system⟶	identification⟶	social man⟶	roles and actions
Self system⟶	internalization⟶	self-actualizing man⟶	value-relationships, roles, and actions

Real organizations are not of one or other of the three types, but may have one, two, or all three of the systems functioning in the organization at the same time. What has been outlined is given in Table 8.3, which provides a framework for analysing organizations primarily in terms of the nature of the motivation operating on the individual.

Faced with training problems, or more generally problems of motivation, we may ask in terms of the model what sorts of learning and behaviour we wish to occur. Is it at the level of actions, of roles, or of value-relationships? The model makes statements about the necessary conditions for different forms of motivation to be effective, and suggests the effects of different motivation. For example, compliance is only useful for getting someone to learn or do something if subsequently we can observe the individual, and reward or punish his behaviour as appropriate. If we wish the individual to be motivated at a deeper level, and in fact want some kind of internalization to occur, then it is important that the influencing agent be seen by the individual as attractive. These and other statements made by the model are contained in the outline we have given of Kelman's three concepts of compliance, identification, and internalization.

REFERENCES

Brim, O. G. (1960), 'Personality development as role-learning', in *Personality Development in Children*, ed. I. Iscoe and H. Stevenson, University of Texas Press.

Brown, W. and Jaques, E. (1965), 'Management teaching', in *Glacier Project Papers*, Heinemann.

Flanagan, J. C. (1949), *Critical Requirements for Research Personnel*, Pittsburgh: American Institute of Research.

Fox, A. (1966), *Industrial Sociology and Industrial Relations*, Research Papers No. 3, Royal Commission on Trade Unions and Employers' Associations, H.M.S.O.

Gagné, R. (1965), 'The analysis of instructional objectives for the design of instructions', in *Teaching Machines and Programmed Learning II*, ed. R. Glaser, Washington, D.C.: National Educational Association.

Gilbert, T. F. (1962), 'Mathetics: the technology of education', *J. Mathetics*, 1.

Glaser, R. (1965), 'Psychology and instructional technology', in *Training Research and Education*, ed. R. Glaser, Wiley.

Kelman, H. C. (1961), 'Three processes of social influence', *Public Opinion Quarterly*, 25.

King, D. (1964), *Training within the Organisation*, Tavistock.

Lifton, R. J. (1957), 'Thought reform of Chinese intellectuals', *J. of Social Issues*, Society for the Psychological Study of Social Issues, 13.

Rodger, A. (1950), 'Industrial Psychology', in *Chambers's Encyclopaedia*, Newnes.

Rodger, A. and Cavanagh, P. (1959), 'Training and professional problems', in *Electronic Engineer's Reference Book*, ed. L. E. C. Hughes, Heywood.

Secord, P. F. and Backman, C. W. (1964), *Social Psychology*, McGraw-Hill.

Tilley, K. (1968), 'A technology of training', in *Industrial Society*, ed. D. Pym, Pelican Library of Business and Management, Penguin.

Wheeler, S. (1966), 'The structure of formally organized socialization settings', in Brim, O. G. and Wheeler, S. *Socialization after Childhood*, Wiley.

CHAPTER 9

Learning Theory

In Chapter 1 we looked at employment work and at how to analyse the jobs people do. We have just examined in Chapter 8 the organizational setting within which people are trained for their employment roles. We need now specifically to study human learning, in order to attempt an understanding of the process by which the individual learns his job. Such an understanding might help us with training. If a theoretical explanation of learning is at least partially valid, it will enable us to make useful hypotheses and predictions in a training situation, which we can subsequently try out.

Definitions

What do we mean by learning and training? As we have already seen, King (1964) very simply says that 'training surely amounts to providing the conditions in which people can learn effectively'. Such a view is satisfactory for our purpose, and particularly useful generally since it forces us back to consider the learning process.

What, then, is learning? The concept is comprehensive, embracing learning to walk, to read, to remember a tune, assemble a relay, and acquire a neurotic tic. 'Change' is the common idea. We can only know that change has occurred if it manifests itself in a change of behaviour. Woodworth (1954) makes the point that 'learning is demonstrated whenever a later activity shows some after-effect of earlier activity'.

According to King (1964), 'to learn is to gain knowledge, skill, or ability'. However, this fails to indicate that acquiring an inefficient performance or the wrong answer or a bad habit is also learning. Learning shows itself as a modification of behaviour; it is only for the better or for the worse according to some external criterion. An operator's inefficient performance is usefully seen as the result not of not learning, but of learning an inefficient performance. This becomes apparent in the difference between training a completely new operator and retraining an experienced, bad operator who, we may find, has learnt the inefficient performance only too well.

We shall see learning as a process by which certain behaviour is originated or changed through interaction between the organism and the environment. Learning does not refer to modifications of behaviour which are a result of temporary states of the organism, as with drugs, nor to those which result from normal organic changes, such as in adolescence and in ageing.

How, then, do we learn? If we can suggest answers to this question, they may have relevance to industrial training. To this end we will examine a number of explanations of learning.

Overview

In this chapter we outline a number of theories which fall into two broad categories, connectionist and cognitive theories. Under the connectionist heading we consider the explanations of Thorndike, Guthrie, and Skinner; under cognitive we outline the explanations of Gestalt psychology and Tolman. After the statement of a theory we indicate generalizations and emphases which emerge from the explanation and seem relevant to training.

After each of these two main sections in the chapter we suggest highly generalized models of learning developed from connectionist and cognitive types of explanations. In subsequent chapters we attempt to use these models for considering training, adopting the connectionist approach as a framework within which to consider skills training, and the cognitive model as a basis for supervisory and management development.

Such theories have generated extensive research and experimental work, and we will refer to a number of such studies in describing them. In the following chapter we will examine further this body of empirical data under topic headings, such as practice, knowledge of results, etc.

CONNECTIONIST THEORIES

We will examine connectionist explanations of learning in terms of three major contributors, Thorndike, Guthrie, and Skinner.

E. L. Thorndike (1874-1949)

For Thorndike the basis of learning is an association of some sort between sense impressions and actions, between stimulus (S) and response (R). His major theoretical statement was the law of effect. This in its simplest form stated that the setting up and strengthening of any association and connection between a stimulus and a response depends not only on their occurring together, but also on the *effects* that follow their occurring together. These effects may be satisfying and rewarding or annoying and punishing. He attempted to define these effects objectively and more in terms of behaviour that could be observed (1913):

> By a satisfying state of affairs is meant one which the animal does nothing to avoid, often doing things which maintain or renew it. By an annoying state of affairs is meant one which the animal does nothing to preserve, often doing things which put an end to it.

Later experimental work made Thorndike modify the law of effect to suggest that reward is more important and effective than punishment in the learning situation. He retained the view that reward strengthens connections and associations, but now saw punishment as weakening them only indirectly. Punishment does not remove the response by directly eliminating its connection with the stimulus. If an organism responds to a stimulus and is punished it will attempt other responses, and eventually one of them, being correct, will be rewarded. Punishment works by forcing the organism to continue responding, till eventually it makes a right response which reward connects to the stimulus.

In Thorndike's terms, what really happens when an operator learns an industrial task like drilling, where he picks up a component, places it in a jig, brings down the drill with a certain pressure, etc.? The learning process here is seen as an establishing of a series of connections between specific stimuli and specific responses, set up by the effects of reward and punishment on the occurring together of the stimuli and responses.

Specific Emphases in Training

1. Thorndike emphasizes the relevance of an analysis at the level of the senses and the motor response mechanism of the effectors and muscles. Such an approach to the learning process in terms of determining the relevant stimuli and responses is common

to connectionist theories, and has proved very useful in training.

2. Thorndike's theory indicates the importance of practice in conditions of close stimulus-response proximity, with reward and punishment.

3. It suggests reward rather than punishment—praise Peter but don't blame Paul.

E. R. Guthrie (1886-1959) : Contiguous Conditioning

In the novel, *Howards End*, E. M. Forster gives the advice 'only connect', and this might well serve as an inscription on the work of Guthrie. For Guthrie learning depends only on a stimulus and a response occurring together. And connectionist explanations may be divided into contiguity theories, like Guthrie's, which regard this contiguity of stimulus and response as all-important, and reinforcement theories like those of Thorndike and Skinner which stress the place of reward and punishment in learning.

So in contrast to Thorndike's law of effect Guthrie proposes a law of exercise which says (1952): 'A combination of stimuli which has accompanied a movement will on its recurrence tend to be followed by that movement.' In other words, if in some situation or faced with a certain stimulus you act or respond in a specific way, then faced with that situation or stimulus again you will tend to do the same thing again. But there is a problem. Presented with a situation or stimulus the individual will do many things and make many responses, so which of them will become associated with the stimulus situation? It will be the last response, says Guthrie, which becomes connected to the stimulus.

Hill (1963) illustrates this principle with the example of someone attempting a mechanical puzzle. A man is given a mechanical puzzle and tries to solve it. He succeeds and makes the right movements which, say, separate the two pieces. Given the puzzle a second time what will he do? He will make the last response he made on the previous occasion, says Guthrie. This last response, which he will repeat, is the one which solves the puzzle. He has learnt how to do the puzzle.

But if on the first occasion he failed to grasp how the puzzle is done he would simply put it down unsolved. Next time he is handed the puzzle he repeats his last act in the previous situation, and puts down the puzzle again, unsolved. Seemingly one has learnt to solve the puzzle and the other has not. For Guthrie both have learnt different things, by the same process of contiguous conditioning.

An experiment by Guthrie and Horton (1946) illustrates this and a second aspect of the law of exercise. A cat is placed in a box with food on the outside. In the centre of the box stands a pole which, when the cat touches it, opens the door and enables the cat to get out to the food. On its first few occasions in the box the cat moves randomly about until it eventually strikes the pole and is released. After a few times the cat will go straight to the pole when placed in the box, press against it, and get out.

But in some cats a considerable amount of stereotyped behaviour is observed. If a cat gets out the first time by striking the pole with its head, it will tend on subsequent occasions to use its head again. If originally it opened the door by backing into the pole the cat tends subsequently to repeat this. We have here modest confirmation for Guthrie's contention that the learner repeats the last, and here identical, response.

The experiment lends support also to Guthrie's view that reward is not essential in learning, since sometimes the cat merely sniffed the food and walked away. Guthrie argues that this final, successful act is learned not because it is successful and leads to reward. It is learned, he contends, just because it is the final act, and in succeeding or failing changes the situation—the cat is now out of the cage, the man puts down the metal puzzle unsolved. And so we acquire last acts, responses which change the situation, regardless of whether they are efficient or inefficient. We learn not by reward but by doing. By and large, what we do is what we learn.

Specific Emphases in Training

1. Like Thorndike, Guthrie was concerned with analysing learning in terms of stimulus-response connections. It is probably in such a view that the skills analysis approach to training, concerned with studying work performance in terms of relevant stimuli and responses, has its origins.

2. If, as Guthrie suggests, an individual learns what he does, the trainee should not be given the chance to perform incorrectly or this is what he will learn. One objective of training should, therefore, be to minimize the possibility of making errors. This stresses the importance of GUIDANCE, of showing the trainee the

correct way from the start and making him practise it this way only.

3. If what we do is what we learn, the inefficient operator has not failed to learn, but has learnt an inefficient performance, probably only too well. If we attempt to teach him a better method he has first to unlearn or overlearn his inefficient way.

The Anti-Theory of B. F. Skinner

Skinner remains probably the best known of contemporary thinkers in the connectionist tradition. Not a theorist, he is a thinker who in fact eschews theory. Rather he is concerned with statements of the relationship between stimulus and response, environment and behaviour, and with an analysis of the effect that differences in reinforcement have on behaviour. Skinner is like Thorndike in emphasizing the importance of reinforcement in learning. He has attempted to develop a body of knowledge relevant to changing and moulding behaviour, and related to this is the important part he played in the early development of pro-grammed instruction. Many of his views on how behaviour may be shaped through manipulating the environment are embodied in the technique of programmed instruction.

Programmed learning is a form of operant conditioning. This is central to Skinner's work but before outlining what it entails we will briefly refer to the Pavlovian model of classical conditioning. Here some innate reflex exists, such as meat causing a dog to salivate. A neutral stimulus, which has no effect on the dog, such as the sound of a bell, is paired with the first stimulus, meat. Eventually the dog will salivate at the sound of the bell. Through the process of learning the meat acts as a reinforcement. It continues to do so, and if the dog ceases to receive the meat at the sound of the bell, it will eventually cease to salivate when the bell rings. Figure 9.1 outlines the process.

Skinner has concerned himself not with classical conditioning, as just described, but with perfecting the technique of operant or

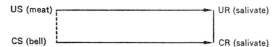

Fig. 9.1 Model of classical conditioning. US is unconditioned stimulus; UR is unconditioned response; CS is conditioned stimulus; CR is conditioned response

instrumental conditioning. This often uses the sort of box employed in the Guthrie and Horton experiment, now usually
referred to as a Skinner box. Skinner has, for example, done much
of his work with rats in such a box or cage, with a lever inside it
which when the rat presses or knocks releases a pellet of food into
the box. As with Guthrie's cat, the rat eventually knocks the lever and
obtains the food. The period of time between its being placed in the
box and its striking the lever becomes shorter and shorter, till
eventually the rat goes directly to the lever. This type of learning
does not depend directly on the presence of innate reflexes.
Figure 9.2 illustrates the process.

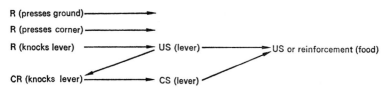

Fig. 9.2 Model of operant or instrumental conditioning

A Skinnerian account of learning and behaviour emerges from
Figure 9.2. Skinner postulates an active organism impinged on by
internal and external stimuli, such as the smell of the ground, the
sight of the corner, the feel of the lever for the rat. The organism
all the time emits responses to the stimuli, and so the rat presses,
knocks, etc. Some of the responses are followed by reinforcement,
as when the rat strikes the lever, and the law of effect operates.
Reinforcement subsequent on some emitted response makes that
behaviour more likely to occur again. Learning has occurred.

Shaping and Reinforcement. Skinner has done a considerable
amount of work on animal training, basing his approach on the
principles of operant conditioning. He refers to it as shaping.
Skinner shapes the behaviour of animals by reinforcing only the
relevant and appropriate responses that the animal makes. The
animal emits a variety of behaviours, and by rewarding some and
punishing or ignoring others the experimenter gradually brings
the pattern of the animal's responses to approximate to what he
wants.

With the rat in the Skinner box there is no problem, as it will
eventually strike the lever by chance and this can be suitably

reinforced. But adopting so casual an approach with more complex behaviour is less likely to be successful. It would not be a sound strategy to place a monkey at a typewriter, wait till it does type that sonnet of Shakespeare, and then give it a lump of sugar. It is more realistic to break down a complex operation into responses that are likely, or can be made to occur, and can then be rewarded. And so if Skinner wishes to train a pigeon to play a form of table tennis (it might be fairer to say ping-pong), as indeed he has done, he will gradually build up the complex operation by reinforcing bit after bit of the behaviour as they occur.

The primary school teacher who, according to report, gave a sweet for every correct answer was applying the principle of reinforcement, albeit crudely. Programmed learning is a more sophisticated application of shaping. The point is that an apparently complex performance can be broken down into elements that are sufficiently simple to ensure that the learner will get them right. These correct responses can be reinforced by rewards at the right time—by suitably scheduled reinforcement.

In an experiment, Greenspoon (1955) instructed each of his human subjects 'to say singly all the words, exclusive of sentences, phrases and numbers, that he could think of for 50 minutes'. While a subject was responding the experimenter said 'mmm-hmm' every time the subject gave a plural form. The results indicated that 'mmm-hmm' increased the frequency of the individual's plural responses. When the experimenter stopped his 'mmm-hmm', the frequency of plural responses declined. Presumably 'mmm-hmm' registered a form of approval, and acted as a reinforcement. Subjects who had seen the relationship between the noise and plural forms were excluded from the data. The results are chastening for teachers who are aware of their own use of an 'mmm-hmm' or similar in seminars and tutorials! But it serves to illustrate the role reinforcement may play in the shaping of behaviour.

Though reward or positive reinforcement is the key to Skinner's shaping of behaviour, punishment is another matter, and is seen by Skinner as a poor method of controlling behaviour. There are better ways of eliminating an inappropriate response. A rat may have been trained to press a lever for food, and the experimenter now wishes to make the rat stop pressing the lever. If he gave the rat an electric shock every time it touched the lever, the animal would stop soon enough. The rat would not have unlearnt the lever pressing, but would merely be inhibiting its response. However, if the experimenter were to cease rewarding the rat with food for pressing the lever, it would go on doing so only for a certain time, and then eventually stop. The learnt response will become extinguished.

The importance of reinforcement is illustrated in work with autistic children, based on Skinnerian principles (see *The Times*, 24 November 1967). The behaviour therapist teaches autistic children to speak a few words with scarcely any use made of punishment. For example, the therapist shows the child a cup, says 'cup', and goes on and on mouthing and repeating the word till the child says it or something on the right lines, then rewards the child with a sweet or praise. It is important to reinforce the correct response and only the correct response, so the therapist must make it clear to the child what response is being rewarded. If he shows the cup, and the child makes a bad response and says 'c' or 'sh', but then says 'cup' properly, the therapist does not reward. Had he done so the child is rewarded for responding 'sh, cup' to the stimulus. So after such a mixed response the therapist gives the stimulus again, the sight of the cup and the sound of the word, gets only the right response, then rewards it.

Schedules of Reinforcement. Skinner has stressed as one of the major factors in learning the pattern according to which reinforcement is given, and he has done much work in this field (Ferster and Skinner, 1957). He makes a number of distinctions in classifying patterns of reinforcement, the first being that between the continuous and the intermittent. Continuous reinforcement is simple enough since every correct response is reinforced. The autistic child is given praise or a sweet every time he does the right thing. Intermittent reinforcement is more complex since only some of the correct responses are reinforced. So with intermittent scheduling the question arises which of the correct responses should be reinforced in order to make learning occur most effectively.

The second distinction arises between making reinforcement intermittent on a time or number basis. The trainer or teacher might reinforce every sixth, or tenth, etc., *correct* response. This is a ratio schedule, and here the number of reinforcements the learner receives depends on the frequency or rate of his correct responses. But the trainer may decide to reinforce the learner not more than once every five minutes, and so gives a reinforcement to the first correct response to occur after the five minutes is up. This is interval scheduling.

Both these two categories are subdivided by a further distinction between fixed and variable schedules. With fixed schedules reinforcement is tied to a definite time or number, whereas with variable schedules it varies around a predetermined average. This now gives four types of intermittent reinforcement: fixed ratio, fixed interval, variable ratio, variable interval, as follows.

Fixed ratio: here the trainer ALWAYS reinforces, say, the fifth, or tenth, etc., correct response. It is analogous (though it might be misleading to push the analogy) to piecework.

Fixed interval: the trainer ALWAYS reinforces the first correct response after, say, two minutes, ten minutes, etc. The attaching of the reward to a fixed interval of time means that time payment such as a weekly wage is a form of such scheduling, though it would be unusual to withhold the payment till the employee's first correct behaviour after the week ends.

Variable ratio: here the trainer will reinforce the tenth correct response, then the second, then the sixth, etc., but the variation is around an average. For example, the trainer may have previously decided to reinforce *on average* every fifth correct response. Fruit-machines and 'one-armed bandits' operate basically on this principle.

Variable interval: the trainer will reinforce the first correct response after, say, two minutes, ten minutes, five minutes, etc. But again the variation of interval is to constitute an average of a certain time. This is like waiting for a bus.

With animals, ratio schedules normally give higher rates of responding than do interval schedules. We have already pointed out that piecework systems are analogous to ratio scheduling, and that payment by the hour or week or month is a kind of fixed interval schedule.

Both kinds of fixed schedules produce a drop in response immediately after reinforcement. With fixed schedules the animal already has experience of the length of time that must lapse or the number of correct responses that must be made before reinforcement will be received again. With variable ratios such a drop in the rate of response does not occur after reinforcement. Here it is in the animal or individual's experience that the time or number of correct responses occurring between one reinforcement and another is unpredictable, and so one reinforcement may be immediately followed by another. We might speculate on the possibility of accounting for compulsive gambling in terms of an individual's experience, possibly in childhood, of variable schedules of reinforcement.

Some of the relevant experimental work provides evidence for the effectiveness of variable ratio scheduling with animals. Such scheduling produces a steady and rapid rate of response, and normally the animal will continue responding for the longest time without reward after this type of scheduling. As Hill points out (1963):

> It is possible, in fact, to get animals to work for food reinforcement on ratios so high that they are actually operating at a biological loss: the energy expended in operating the manipulandum is greater than that obtained from the occasional food reward, so that the animal can literally work itself to death.

As we have said, fruit machines function on the basis of variable ratio scheduling, and we need only observe people operating the machines to appreciate their powerful hold on behaviour.

Finally, returning to the original distinction, evidence suggests that extinction occurs earlier after continuous reinforcement than it does following intermittent schedules. By this is meant that when the trainer stops providing reinforcement, the animal that has learnt the response under intermittent schedules of reinforcement continues responding for a longer time than does the animal trained by continuous schedules.

Specific Emphases in Training. Emerging from the work of Skinner has come an approach to teaching and training developed by T. F. Gilbert, and termed mathetics (Gilbert, 1962). We will examine this in a subsequent chapter, but we may usefully here refer to a specific point of Gilbert's concerning reinforcement. When human beings learn, esteem, pay, promotion, have their place as reinforcing agents. But often it is more useful in the teaching and training situation to regard mastery of the learning task as the prime reinforcemnt. The individual's reinforcement for learning is the achievement he experiences when he masters the task.

1. Skinner sees the organism as essentially active in the environment, emitting behaviour. Any aspect or bit of that behaviour may be (fortuitously) reinforced by the environment. The job of the trainer is to ensure by correct organization, structuring, programming, in the training department, that the right bit of behaviour is reinforced. This means he needs to be clear as to what the right bits of behaviour are. The trainer must start with a precise statement of desired terminal behaviour. He must also ensure that the appropriate stimulus, the right bit of behaviour, and the reinforcement (mastery?), are connected in the individual's experience. Programmed instruction attempts to do all this.

2. Skinner's views on reinforcement may be summarized:

(a) He reaffirms Thorndike's earlier contention, that positive reinforcement is to be preferred to punishment. Since positive reinforcement is so important we need to break down the learning task, as in programmed instruction, to ensure that the individual will make responses that are correct and so may be reinforced positively.

(b) The timing of reinforcement is crucial, and by and large the sooner it is given after the correct response the better. Again in programmed instruction the correct response is followed, in Skinner's terms, by immediate reinforcement. As we shall see, this parallels what the trainer does when he provides the trainee with knowledge of his results.

(c) Skinner has also provided data on the effects of different schedules of reinforcement on learning, and derived general laws. At present their relevance and applicability to training is not clear, except in the field of programmed learning.

A CONNECTIONIST MODEL FOR SKILLS TRAINING

We will now outline a generalized model which derives from connectionist explanations of learning (Thyne, 1966). Though primarily concerned with learning and teaching in the classroom, Thyne's proposals may prove useful as a framework within which to consider training for perceptual-motor skills. All subsequent extracts are from his 1966 text.

Thyne points out that 'to learn is to adopt a new response to a situation'. The trainee enters the training department ignorant of how to assemble a certain relay. He leaves the department for the production shop having learnt to produce fifteen components an hour. On the shop floor he restricts his output to conform to the group norm, and turns out only ten an hour. On both occasions he has learnt to produce a new response to a situation, first fifteen components an hour and then ten. The teacher (or trainer) has, therefore, says Thyne, 'to see to it that a new response is made to some specified kind of situation, and so he must decide exactly what form of response he wants and what kind of situation has to elicit it'.

From such a view of learning, Thyne suggests, we can deduce what are the essential requirements for learning to occur. They are the cue, the force, the prompt, and the reinforcement.

Cue

The cue is that which releases or triggers off the response. The individual through the appropriate rewarding of his actions learns to respond not to the total environment or stimulus situation that impinges on him, but only to those stimuli which are the occasion of reward. These relevant stimuli are the cues. The operator needs to learn cues which tell him when he should increase or reduce his pressure on the component.

We suggest that an ideal world would have learning situations which had the cue as the only stimulus. An inspector in a woollen mill must learn to ignore colours of the wool, sizes, irregularities which are part of the pattern, and respond only to a specific type of irregularity. In the real world by varying the conditions of learning a task, the one element they have in common becomes the cue. In an inspection task the cue is the irregularity of a particular stimulus; in an operator task, it is the regularity of a particular stimulus. This is what Thyne refers to as the requirement of cue (1966): 'In any instance of learning, there must be a series of situations sharing, and sharing only, the cue of that instance.'

Force

For learning to occur a situation must in the first place be able to elicit some response from the individual. The capacity of the environment, stimulus, cue, simply to elicit any response at all from the environment is its force. Force makes a response occur. The concept of force is useful since it encourages the trainer to think of providing an environment which does produce some response from the learner.

For learning to occur it is not enough that any part of the environment can elicit behaviour. The requirement of force asserts that it must be the cue that can produce some response. Thus Thyne, 'the cue must have force'.

Prompt

It is still not enough for the cue to be able to produce some response from the learner. For learning to have occurred the cue must be able to obtain a specific response, this one rather than that one. The cue must come to determine what response the trainee makes, and this necessitates the presence of a prompt in the learning situation. The prompt fixes the character and form of the individual's behaviour which the cue elicits. The prompt is in the nature of a criterion. This leads to the requirement of the prompt (Thyne, 1966): 'In any instance of learning, a prompt must appear in one or more of the successive situations.' In the training department, as in the classroom, the instructor needs to find good prompts which ensure the learner gives the appropriate response to the cue. Visual and other aids, guidance methods, knowledge of results, are some of the ways of providing suitable prompts.

Frequently in industry we can solve a work problem by building the prompt into the work situation. It may be important on certain jobs for a machinist not to feed in the cutting tool beyond a certain dimension. In training the instructor might place a stop on the machine so that the trainee just cannot move the cutting tool beyond the relevant point. Alternatively we can incorporate the prompt into the work situation, and provide the machinist with the stop to fit on his machine every time he is on those jobs. Here we are solving the problem not by training, but through job design and ergonomics.

Reinforcement

The correct response or appropriate form of behaviour will tend to occur as long as the prompt is present. But while the prompt remains necessary, adequate learning has not occurred. Something is needed to tie the correct response to the cue, and this is the function of the reinforcer. Whatever connects the correct response to the cue is a reinforcement. This is a broad concept of reinforcement and says nothing about its nature. Thus the requirement of reinforcement (Thyne, 1966) states: 'In any instance of learning, the specified form of response must be tied to the cue.' We are back to the law of effect.

COGNITIVE THEORIES

We will examine the cognitive explanations of learning proposed by the Gestalt psychologists and by Tolman, and from them attempt to outline a framework for management and supervisory training which incorporates also the more recent writings of Miller, Galanter, and Pribram (1960).

Learning in Gestalt Psychology

In German *Gestalt* is pattern or form. Gestalt psychology postulates that the individual organism tends to perceive and react to phenomena in terms of significant and meaningful wholes. Previously in Chapter 2 we discussed the Gestalt or holistic approach to personality which regards a reduction of personality to separate elements as almost a *reductio ad absurdum*. So here, learning is not seen as the addition of discrete units, but as an attempt by the organism to impose meaning and structure on the data of its experience.

We do not see Figure 9.3 as four lines more or less at right angles, and nearly touching. We usually perceive a square. The organism strives to structure meaningfully its experience.

Wertheimer's Phi phenomenon is another example of an attempt

Fig. 9.3 Four straight lines, more or less at right angles, and nearly touching—or a square?

after meaning, and is illustrated in certain types of advertisement. Electric light-bulbs are placed to form the word BOOM. When it is dark, the current is run so that first the letter B lights up, is extinguished, but as it goes out O lights up, as this goes out the next O lights up, and as this is extinguished the M lights up and then goes out. But the observer does not see it as we have just described it, as four adjacent letters consecutively going on and off. The observer perceives movement. He sees one light moving across the word. In Gestalt language the individual is striving to structure what he perceives in a meaningful way.

The Gestalt analysis of the learning process is in terms of the change in the individual's perception of the situation. Learning may be regarded as the individual's restructuring of his perception of a situation, and when learning has occurred, what previously was perceived one way is now seen in a different (and more useful) way. Learning is the changing of one Gestalt for another.

When the individual's perception of a problem is suddenly structured in a new and more useful way he usually experiences a feeling of insight. This is the 'Ah! Now I've got it' sensation that may accompany the grasping of a geometrical proof, or which the learner-driver feels when he masters the relationship between the accelerator and clutch in starting the car.

Kohler's classic study (1925) with apes illustrates the point. In one group of experiments the ape was placed in a cage. On the outside was fruit, which the animal could see clearly, and on the inside was left a stick with which the animal might reach out for the fruit through the bars of the cage, and pull it in. There were variations on this, such as where two short sticks were provided which had first to be fitted together. In another group of experiments fruit, usually a bunch of bananas, was hung from the ceiling, too high for the ape to reach. Boxes were left around, and the animal had to learn to stack the boxes on top of each other to enable him to get the bananas.

The apes sometimes handled both sticks and boxes for some time before they found a solution. Kohler saw this as a process of growing in awareness of the potentialities of the environment, and not as an example of the trial-and-error behaviour beloved by the connectionist theorists. Kohler says that such trial-and-error behaviour was rare, and that the learning of a solution, when it occurred, occurred suddenly. The ape had new perceptual structures for old. When the solution was seen the animal subsequently remembered it, which is what we might expect if learning is thought of as the grasping of new perceptual structures.

Such insights seem often to consist of a new awareness of relationships, frequently about means and ends. Sticks become not just playthings, but tools for raking in bananas with, and boxes are now for stacking up and getting on, as a means for reaching the fruit. Kohler noted that if the boxes were stood widely apart an ape often failed to learn the solution of stacking them on each other. It was as if the sensory data were spread over too wide a perceptual field to enable the animal to restructure the information into a solution.

G. H. Bower, in a paper at the 1969 International Congress of Psychology, referred to research at Stanford University where subjects had to learn and remember nonsense syllables such as 'deb' and 'det'. He suggested that people did not in the experiments try to learn them as nonsense syllables, but rather attempted to make them meaningful first. They would attempt to learn and remember 'deb' by thinking of it as 'debt', and 'det' as 'death'. We have here again this striving after meaning in the learning situation.

Specific Emphases in Training. Gestalt psychology suggests that the learning process consists of a perceptual restructuring of the situation into a more meaningful and insightful form. Such learning is highly resistant to forgetting. In training the instructor must structure the environment to ensure that the trainee is able to perceive and grasp the relevant relationships. The point is illustrated by the failure of the apes to solve the problem when the boxes were widely separated.

Tolman's Purposive Behaviourism

E. C. Tolman (1886–1959) proposed his views originally in *Purposive Behaviour in Animals and Men* (1932), and developed them in subsequent publications. His work is more readily seen in perspective if we regard it as in part a reaction against connectionist theory. Tolman insisted that behaviour, particularly human behaviour, is characterized by purpose, by a striving after goals. Any explanation of learning and behaviour should attempt to incorporate this apparent purposiveness. Tolman was, however, seeking a theory which also retained the objectivity of the connectionist approach. Any such explanation of learning and behaviour must be grounded in the observation of external stimuli and external, measurable responses by the organism. Tolman was attempting an approach of 'purposive behaviourism'.

Purposive behaviourism is concerned then with explaining learning in terms of the effects of external stimuli on observable behaviour, and with the way behaviour is changed through the organism's experience of the environment. This is the behaviourism. But, contended Tolman, behaviour is not adequately described simply in terms of responses to stimuli; on the contrary it contains an active search for goals which give unity and significance to the discrete elements of behaviour. Tolman suggests that the individual learns not movements (S-R connections), but meanings (signs or cues and what they signify). This is the purposiveness. Hence for these and other reasons which will become apparent, Tolman's approach has been described also as sign-learning theory, as sign-Gestalt theory, and as expectancy theory.

He referred to connectionist explanations as the 'telephone-switchboard school', because for them learning seemed merely the acquisition of various connections between stimuli and responses. An adequate explanation of learning and behaviour must, in Tolman's view, take account of the attitudes, aims, aspirations, and goals of the individual. Purposiveness, like the Gestalt idea of striving after meaning, stresses that the organism is an active agent in learning and behaviour.

The essential feature of this account of the individual as an active agent was the introduction of the intervening variable. Between the observed stimulus and the observed response something happens that we cannot see. Tolman postulated an intervening and mediating process because, he said, we cannot really account for the organism's response, and for the complexity of behaviour generally, in terms solely of the characteristics of the stimulus and the reinforcement. Allport said the same when he introduced the concept of trait into his analysis of personality. The main intervening variable proposed by Tolman was that of cognitions.

For Tolman the organism through its experience of stimulus, behaviour, and possibly rewards, does not simply learn S-R connections; it acquires cognitions. These cognitions are about the significance and meaning of the various stimuli and signs in the environment. A cognition may be about which path leads to which place; about what a colour means, as at traffic lights; about the significance of certain shapes or signs, such as a road sign; about what data meaningfully go together, like the boxes and the fruit with Kohler's apes. For Tolman cognitions in learning are of the order that 'responding in this way to that stimulus will lead to this'. Learning is a process of acquiring cognitions that are usually about relationships.

Tolman argues that reward is not essential in learning, but it does serve to heighten the meaning of a stimulus, and to bring out its relationships. 'If I respond to that in such a way, this will happen' is heightened by the presence of reward, and becomes 'if I respond to that in such a way, I will receive this reward'.

Later (1949) Tolman suggested that different types of learning existed, one of them being a process of acquisition of cognitions about the way the world is structured. These cognitions develop through experience, and are of the nature of cognitive maps about the environment.

From Tolman's explanation of learning a number of predictions were made which did not seem to emerge readily from connectionist theory. We will briefly examine here those that relate to latent learning and reward expectancy.

Latent Learning. This is learning that is hidden or not manifested because it is irrelevant to the circumstances in which it occurs. When I visited a friend he took me out on a pub crawl. If almost incidentally but as a result of that walk I now know my way around his neighbourhood, then latent learning has occurred.

If latent learning exists, it means learning occurs in situations where it is irrelevant and so unrewarded. This would support Tolman's contention that reward as such is not essential for learning. Latent learning would suggest that Tolman is also right in saying that we learn not s-r connections and movements, but meanings and cognitions about relationships. We acquire these all the time, store them, and then use them in appropriate circumstances.

An experiment by Buxton illustrates the point (1940). Rats were placed on a number of different occasions into a large maze where there was no food or reward of any sort. After a period they were taken out, usually from different parts of the maze, so that they did not come to associate 'being taken out' with any particular part of the maze. After this preparatory period of the experiment the rats were tested. They were deprived of food, fed for a short time at the goal box in the maze, and then placed at the start of the maze. About half of them ran straight to the food in the goal box without making a single mistake. Their performance was far superior to that of the rats in the control group who had no previous experience of the maze, and so provides evidence for the existence of latent learning.

Reward Expectancy. If, as Tolman suggests, we learn meanings, then we learn to expect specific things. In acquiring a cognition of a relationship, we learn to expect that this will lead to that. The concept of expectations would be out of place in most connectionist models which refer more simply to the correct responses to the appropriate stimuli being rewarded by reinforcement and need reduction. The question is, therefore, does the organism have specific expectations in learning regarding, say, reward, or is it just a matter of the correct behaviour being reinforced?

Tinklepaugh (1932) trained monkeys to find bananas under certain containers. He substituted a lettuce, which is a less preferred food. The monkey finding the lettuce showed surprise, disappointment, and continued its search—presumably for the bananas. The monkey, like Dickens's Pip, had 'expectations'.

More recently the concept of feedback has helped us understand expectancy better. We can acquire through learning a feedback system. A driver has to, if he is to keep his car on the correct side of the road. A piece of behaviour is monitored, and its effects noted and compared against an internal criterion. If there is a discrepancy, further behaviour occurs to correct it, and then the test is made again. When there is no discrepancy, the organism can continue on to its next action. The feedback cycle is shown in the diagram of Figure 9.4, from Miller, Galanter, and Pribram's book, *Plans and the Structure of Behaviour* (1960). They call the feedback cycle the TOTE unit, which functions as follows:

Test—if there is a discrepancy, then
Operate.
Test again—if there is no discrepancy, then
Exit.

If reward can be a need-reducing system, as in some connectionist theories, it can also be an expectancy-meeting system. This is really what Tolman was saying.

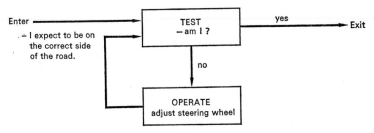

Fig. 9.4 A driver's behaviour in keeping his car on the correct side of the road, as a TOTE model (adapted from Miller, Galanter, and Pribram, 1960)

Specific Emphases in Training. These follow from purposive behaviourism:

1. If behaviour is essentially goal-directed, training must take into account the trainee's goals. A foreman may join a supervisory training course with his own specific objectives—he wants to know how to obtain higher output from the operators. The trainer might build his course around the foreman's goals, or he might start with an attempt to change them, but he will achieve very little if he ignores the fact that they exist.

2. The trainer should structure the learning situation so that relationships between stimulus, response, and goal are emphasized. He should stress for the learner the meaning and significance of relevant aspects of stimuli and behaviour. Styles of supervision, for example, need to be related to operator behaviour, and to the objectives of the company and the supervisor.

3. The trainer needs to take into account the totality of the learning situation. Trainees react not to stimuli in isolation, but to the total pattern of relationships in a situation. This suggests that whether or not a task is broken down into elements for the purposes of training, it is important for the trainee to be able to perceive the task as a complete structure. The totality of the learning situation is relevant also in other ways. There is some evidence, for example, that older people will often learn better in isolation than in a situation where others are present.

PROPOSALS FOR A COGNITIVE MODEL OF MANAGEMENT AND SUPERVISORY EDUCATION AND TRAINING

Schemes and Strategies

According to cognitive theories the effect of the stimulus is determined by internal cognitions and cognitive maps. Bartlett's 'schema' is a similar concept, referring 'to an active organization of past reactions, or of past experiences, which must always be supposed to be operating in any well-adapted organic response' (1932). More recently Miller, Galanter, and Pribram adopted the term image (1960): 'The Image is all the accumulated, organized knowledge that the organism has about itself and its world.' We will use the everyday word 'scheme' to refer to this intervening variable typically found in cognitive explanations.

When the individual adopts a scheme, say, of the sort of summer holiday he wants, he still has to make plans to implement it. Miller, Galanter, and Pribram suggest that cognitive theorists failed to account for the implementation of the scheme. Tolman's critics had jibed that he left the rat sitting in the maze lost in thought. To account for the way in which the scheme is put into effect, these authors propose the concept of the plan (1960): 'A Plan is any hierarchical process in the organism that can control the order in which a sequence of operations is to be performed.' The implementation of my scheme for a summer holiday or for solving a problem at work is mediated through a plan. 'Tactics and strategies' are similar concepts, and in the following discussion we will adopt the term of 'strategy'.

Schemes and Strategies as a Basis for Management and Supervisory Training

We can analyse behaviour in terms of a scheme and a strategy to implement that scheme. Faced with a problem the manager needs to be able both to see the solution and to implement it. The distinction is real enough, and is sometimes dramatically illustrated in academic men who can see solutions clearly but are quite unable to give effect to them. We propose, therefore, seven requirements in management training.

1. Training must take account of the trainee's goals, both short-term and long-term. We have previously outlined this point as the first 'Specific Emphasis' in our discussion of Tolman.

2. The trainee must learn schemes in training. This is a requirement of information. The manager can learn to see low output as
an outcome of bad selection. Most management training fulfils this
requirement, and any inadequacy is usually that of providing
too few alternative schemes; low output can be an outcome of
bad selection, bad organization, poor morale, etc.

3. The trainee must acquire skill in cognitively manipulating
such schemes. Management and supervisory training often fail to
fulfil this requirement of practice with knowledge of results. On
a two-week course at technical college a foreman is taught in
lecture to see low output as a result of poor selection, training,
morale, organization, etc. But he scarcely benefits from the course
because never during the two weeks is he provided with an
opportunity to practise thinking for himself in these terms.
Seminars, role play, case studies, provide situations in which he
can practise thinking in terms of such schemes.

4. The trainee must acquire readiness to adopt alternative
schemes. There is little point in giving information and practice
to a manager if he is so insecure and preoccupied with his own
personal anxieties that he cannot even see or accept new schemes.
For the paranoid manager 'Communist shop stewards' is the most
satisfactory explanation of low output. A readiness to consider
alternative schemes, and not to resort invariably to old solutions,
seems partly a function of self-awareness, and personal security
and confidence, which if a manager does not already have he needs
to acquire. Supervisory and management training often ignore
this, but should attempt to develop the manager in this way. The
T-group is the technique most obviously orientated to such
training.

5. The trainee must learn strategies to implement schemes. A
foreman may finish a training programme aware of the inadequacy
of his supervisory style or his machine loading, and having learnt
alternative and better schemes. But at no stage in training was he
taught in detail ways and means, strategies, for implementing
these new schemes.

6. The trainee must acquire skill with strategies for implementing schemes. 'Too theoretical' or 'not practical enough' is a
frequent criticism supervisors and managers make of a training
course. They have learnt what to do but not how to do it. Training
should provide opportunity for acquiring confidence and skill

with the relevant methods, techniques, strategies. It is sufficient to tell an individual the direction to a place, since he already knows how to walk. But, for example, just to teach a foreman what democratic supervision is (a scheme), may not be enough. If adopting a democratic supervisory style requires new behaviour of the foreman, he needs the opportunity to practise the new behaviour.

7. The trainee must develop a capacity to construct schemes and strategies. This relates particularly to learning to cope with change, and is an educational process. We will return to this in Chapter 12.

REFERENCES

Bartlett, F. C. (1932), *Remembering: an Experimental and Social Study*, Cambridge University Press.

Bower, G. H. (1969), 'Elaborative strategies during associative learning', paper given at International Congress of Psychology, London.

Buxton, C. E. (1940), 'Latent learning and the goal gradient hypothesis', *Contrib. Psychol. Theory*, 2, No. 6.

Ferster, C. B. and Skinner, B. F. (1957), *Schedules of Reinforcement*, Appleton-Century-Crofts.

Gilbert, T. F. (1962), 'Mathetics: the technology of education', *J. Mathetics*, 1, 7–73.

Greenspoon, J. (1955), 'The reinforcing effect of two spoken sounds on the frequency of two responses', *Amer. J. Psychol.*, 68, 409–16.

Guthrie, E. R. (1952), *The Psychology of Learning*, Harper.

Guthrie, E. R. and Horton, G. P. (1946), *Cats in a Puzzle Box*, Rinehart.

Hill, W. F. (1963), *Learning*, Methuen.

King, D. (1964), *Training within the Organisation*, Tavistock.

Kohler, W. (1925), *The Mentality of Apes*, Harcourt Brace.

Miller, G. A., Galanter, E. and Pribram, K. H. (1960), *Plans and Structure of Behavior*, Henry Holt.

The Times, (Friday, 24 November 1967), 'Rewards and punishments'.

Thorndike, E. L. (1913), *The Psychology of Learning*, New York: Teachers' College.

Thyne, J. M. (1966), *The Psychology of Learning and Techniques of Teaching*, University of London Press.

Tinklepaugh, O. L. (1932), 'Multiple delayed reaction with chimpanzees and monkeys', *J. comp. Psychol.*, 13, 207–43.

Tolman, E. C. (1932), *Purposive Behavior in Animals and Men*, Appleton-Century.

Tolman, E. C. (1949), 'There is more than one kind of learning', *Psychol. Rev.*, 56, 144–55.

Woodworth, R. S. and Schlosberg, H. (1954), *Experimental Psychology*, Henry Holt (p. 530).

CHAPTER 10

Factors in Learning

Overview

We suggested in Chapter 8 that to establish a training procedure we must determine the what, how, and reporting of training (Rodger, 1950). This chapter examines the how. We are concerned here with Tilley's 'Development of appropriate training methods' (1968), or in terms of the Glaser model (1962), with 'Instructional Procedures'. We are examining research data and ideas about learning, grouped around concepts which seem relevant to training. The concepts are knowledge of results, guidance, practice, sequence and order of material, motivation, transfer of training, and understanding.

The experimental work is well-documented, and published in the standard experimental psychology textbooks and in studies such as those of Holding (1965) and Annett (1969). We have already referred to a number of experiments in the discussion of learning theory. This chapter is primarily concerned with suggesting the dimensions and concepts to consider in developing training methods, using experimental work mainly to indicate the theoretical significance of the concepts, and to illustrate their practical relevance.

KNOWLEDGE OF RESULTS

Introduction

If a machine operator feeds in the cutting tool too fast, there will probably be a smell of burning or the tool will break. If a manager speaks very aggressively to a typist, she might leave, become hostile or react in some other overt way. The operator and the manager are receiving knowledge of results which they might use as a basis for altering their behaviour in the future. Knowledge of results has considerable importance for training, from the acquisition of perceptual-motor skills to the learning of appropriate management behaviour. Raphael (1962) in a study of communications found that junior and middle managers complained frequently of a lack of 'knowledge of how they are doing as individuals'.

Bartlett (1947) has expressed the importance of knowledge of results in almost epigrammatic form: 'The old saying that practice makes perfect is not true. But it is true to say that it is practice, the results of which are known, which makes perfect.' The statement says something about both knowledge of results and practice.

Some Studies

The first study, by Thorndike (1927), was called by him 'The law of effect', and as we shall see the title has its significance. Two groups of subjects, all blindfolded, drew lines on paper over several days. They had to draw lines of 3, 4, 5, or 6 inches, as instructed, and the errors were recorded. Neither group was obtaining the normal visual knowledge of results. But one group was given this verbally, as the experimenter said 'right' or 'wrong' if the line that had just been completed was or was not within a quarter of an inch of the correct length. The accuracy of the group with no knowledge of results grew steadily worse. Whereas the group which received verbal knowledge of results became considerably more accurate.

Trowbridge and Cason (1932) later repeated this experiment in a more developed form, with the addition of another blindfold group, which was given verbal knowledge of results in more detail. They were not just told 'right' or 'wrong', as was one other group in the experiment; they were given detail on their performance, such as 'five-eighths of an inch too long'. This last group improved even more than did the group with just the 'right-wrong' information.

Why does knowledge of results improve learning? As might be guessed from the title of Thorndike's article, he regarded its effect as being primarily motivational. The trainee does a task, and is then told how this compares with a standard. We can see here that knowledge of results might be rewarding or punishing according to how well he has done, and regarding it in this way as reinforcement would be a typically connectionist explanation. Alternatively knowledge of results may improve learning through the information it provides to the learner. In Tolman's terms, it enables the learner to acquire cognitions. This is a cognitive type of explanation.

Lindahl (1945) describes a study concerned mainly with using an analysis of the operator's movements as a basis for developing training. A machine operator had to cut small tungsten discs. The machine was operated manually and with the use of one foot, and the task necessitated correct speeds, form, rhythm, and pressure from the operator. The old method of training was basically 'exposure' or sitting-by-Fred; a new operator learned the job as best he could from the supervisor and the other operators. New (and old) operators had most difficulty with the foot movement on the pedal. Correct control of the pedal was essential, and incorrect pressure on the pedal caused damage to the tungsten discs and broke the cutting wheel.

The experimenters selected good, experienced operators, and recorded their foot movement on paper tape. From this paper tape record the trainers developed the standard pattern of a correct foot movement on the pedal (see Figure 10.1a, b). Figure 10.1b shows that the operator starts with an upward movement of the

Fig 10.1a Standard pattern of the foot movement on pedal of a good, experienced operator, in the disc-cutting cycle (from Lindahl, 1945).

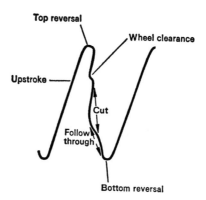

Fig. 10.1b Enlargement of standard pattern of a good, experienced operator's foot movement for one disc-cutting cycle (from Lindahl, 1945)

foot that releases the pedal. He stops momentarily, begins to exert slight pressure, moving the pedal down, holding it again as the wheel clears. He then exerts a steadily increasing pressure for the actual cut, reducing the pressure for the follow-through, and then releases the pedal to start the operation again.

For training, large instructional posters were made, showing correct foot movements (as in Figures 10.1a and b) and common incorrect movements. The types of damage that resulted from wrong foot movements on the pedal were indicated. During training the foot-movement patterns of individual operators were recorded from time to time on the paper tape. The trainer could then compare with an operator his own foot movement against the standard pattern, and analyse the differences with him. The operator was being provided with very useful knowledge of results in an area of crucial importance to the job and known to be particularly difficult for the learner.

This provision of a visual aid to learning, and its use specifically as knowledge of results, was effective in a number of ways. Training time was reduced, in that higher output figures were reached in a shorter time. Wheel breakages by trainees dropped, and became lower by the end of training than those of experienced operators. Experienced operators improved after being retrained in this new way.

So far we have looked at manual or motor tasks, but a study by Smith and Knight (1959) suggest the usefulness of knowledge of results in a different area of learning. A number of managers participating in a development programme met daily to review and comment on each other's progress. They openly discussed their own and other people's leadership performance and contribution to the group. These managers appeared to develop more in problem-solving facility and to attain more insight into their own leadership roles than did those managers who did not take part in such feedback or knowledge-of-results sessions.

Knowledge of Results as a Prompt

In the previous chapter we indicated that Thyne lists a prompt as an essential requirement of learning. The prompt helps determine the nature and form of the response the individual makes; it ensures he does this rather than that. Knowledge of results is one form of prompt. We may refer here to a distinction made by

Holding (1965). On the one hand there is the prompt provided by knowledge of results which is actually part of the task to be learnt. This is intrinsic knowledge of results. Alternatively there is the prompt for the learner from knowledge of results which are extraneous and not intrinsic to the task, but are provided by the trainer to aid the trainee. This is artificial knowledge of results.

Where intrinsic knowledge of results exists the trainer's task is to maximize its prompt function for the learner. He does this by directing the learner's attention to its relevant aspects. The instructor makes the driller respond to the burning when his pressure is too great, or to the cues of a well-produced component or a badly drilled one.

The prompt which artificial knowledge of results gives the learner is probably useful only if it directs his attention to cues that will always be present in the situation, that are intrinsic to the task. An example from Seymour (1954) illustrates this. Operators had to handle pottery before firing, taking care to hold it firmly, but not too firmly since this would cause fractures or cracks. What seems to have been the essential element to be learnt is the correct feel of pressure in the fingers and arm. We refer here to the kinaesthetic sense which 'provides information about the position of our limbs and the pressures which we are exerting with them . . . Information is derived from deeper-seated nerve endings in muscles, tendons and joints' (Seymour, 1966). Seymour used dummy insulators with spring-loaded sides which responded to different pressures in handling. If the operator held it just right the springs made contact with a micro-switch and caused a white light to flash. If the operator's grip was too firm this caused another switch to turn on a red light.

The red and white lights provide the operator with extrinsic knowledge of results. They will undoubtedly improve his performance while they are present, as any prompt ergonomically built into a situation should. Whether these prompts have aided learning will be manifested only when they are removed. They will aid learning only if through them the operator learns to respond to those prompts intrinsic to the task, such as here the feel of pressure in fingers and hands in gripping the pottery.

Conclusion

How does this awareness of the results of what we do affect our learning? Is it through reward and reinforcement, a characteristic connectionist position, embodied in Thorndike's law of effect? If this is so, then all Skinner's work on the scheduling of reinforcement is relevant to the timing of knowledge of results. Or does knowledge of results affect learning primarily through its informational content, basically a cognitive position? This view is embodied in Tolman's assertion that reward functions essentially through its heightening the perception of relationships in a situation, that is, it maximizes the learner's awareness of information.

The question is extensively discussed by Annett (1969), who sees knowledge of results most usefully conceived of in terms of a feedback system. For Annett, 'Knowledge of results is regarded as information about the outcome of a test carried out on the environment'. But it is to be noted that learning may occur without the trainee himself actually carrying out the test. Annett states:

> The essential implication of experimental results in guidance and prompting is that in many situations the subject can either make a response in order, for example, to find out which of two possibilities is 'right', or he can be told the outcome without having to make a response.

GUIDANCE

Introduction

We may, then, see knowledge of results as sometimes provided even in the absence of an overt response from the learner. Annett says in the above quotation that 'he can be told the outcome without having to make a response'. This provision of information in advance, of knowledge *before* results, is usually referred to as guidance. Guidance provides information before the learner overtly responds to a stimulus and in this way reduces the likelihood of an incorrect response occurring.

Guidance may take a number of forms but is essentially a prompt before the event. The trainer may simply say 'when you are rotating at this speed, feed in the tool very slowly', or 'hold the file flatter when you work on this sort of metal'. Here the guidance is verbal. The trainer may supply supplementary information to guide the learner in visual form, as was done in the Lindahl study referred to under knowledge of results. The correct foot movement was visually displayed on a poster to guide the responses of the trainee. Or guidance may be mechanical where the trainer by physically restricting the movements of the trainee forces him to make a correct response. The apprentice instructor, for example, may place his hand next to the apprentice's on the drill lever and force him to engage the bit with the component at the appropriate speed and pressure.

Some Studies

Kaess and Zeaman (1960) gave subjects thirty different questions. The subjects were presented with alternative answers, printed on a sheet of paper, and using a keyboard they punched or attempted to punch the answer they thought correct. If the subject's answer was correct the punch pierced the paper. If he answered wrongly, the action of the punch was blocked, and it simply struck the metal backing and failed to make a hole in the paper.

The learning period consisted of one run through the thirty questions, but with different conditions for a number of groups. The conditions of the different groups of subjects on the learning trail were varied in terms of the number of alternative solutions presented. They answered using the punch, but were allowed to continue answering the same question till they eventually punched the correct answer. Conditions for the one learning trial were:

Group 1 presented with five alternative answers to choose from.
Group 2   ,,   ,, four   ,,   ,,   ,,   ,,   ,,
Group 3   ,,   ,, three ,,   ,,   ,,   ,,   ,,
Group 4   ,,   ,, two   ,,   ,,   ,,   ,,   ,,
Group 5   ,,   ,, one   ,,   ,,   ,,   ,,   ,,

Group 5 is of particular interest here, since in being presented with only the correct answer it is the group which is essentially learning under conditions of guidance. The groups are increasingly, from 5 to 1, learning by their mistakes; they are learning from information presented after they have made an overt response. Group 5 is receiving guidance since it is prompted as to the correct answer before it actually responds.

This learning period was followed by four testing trials which all groups did under the same conditions of being presented with five possible answers. The best results were in reverse order to the above list; group 5 made the least number of errors, and group 1 committed the most. The fewer the alternatives made available to the trainees in the learning period, the better was their subsequent performance.

An analysis of the data reveals that people tend to repeat their errors; they actually learn the mistakes they make. This seems in line with Guthrie's contention that we learn what we do.

An experiment by Holding and Macrae (1964) illustrates the usefulness of mechanical guidance. Subjects had to learn to move a knob exactly four inches along a rod, while blindfold. The subjects did twenty test attempts, then nine training trials under different conditions according to the group they were in, and finally twenty more test attempts. The experimenters measured learning in terms of the difference in the number of errors for each subject between the first twenty attempts and the second twenty.

The six groups of subjects had different training during the nine training trials:

Group C   (control group) received no training in the form of guidance or feedback during the nine trials.

Group CG received guidance in the form of forced response in all nine trials. A door-spring pulled the hand along decelerating to a stop at the four inches.

Group DG recieved distributed guidance on the nine trials. Forced-response guidance of the sort just described was alternated with normal practice.

Group RG received restricted guidance for the nine trials. A stop screwed on to the rod at four inches ensured that the subject moved it just that length.

Group RW was told simply 'right' or 'wrong'.

Group KR was provided with more informative knowledge of results, being told the amount and the direction of the error.

Figure 10.2 presents the results, and indicates that the best conditions for learning, as evidenced in improved performance, were in descending order as follows—RG, KR, RW, DG, CG, C. All conditions of guidance effect considerable improvements, but the superiority of both forms of knowledge of results over the forced-response type of guidance is interesting. Holding remarks also on the unexpectedness of the overall superiority here of the restricted-guidance conditions of practice. This might be explained in terms of a memory of where the stop had been, when the test attempts were resumed.

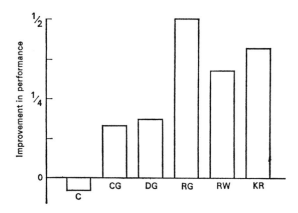

Fig. 10.2 Improvement in performance under six different conditions of learning, principally comparing knowledge of results with different kinds of guidance. See text. From Holding and Macrae (1964)

Conclusion

An early experiment by Ludgate (1924) on maze learning suggests that people make the best use of guidance if they are given the opportunity to explore the maze for themselves first, on a trial and error basis. A similar finding was that of von Wright (1957) in a study of a maze-tracking task. He found that showing visually the wrong alleys as well as the right path speeded up learning and reduced the number of errors.

Providing the learner in this way with a knowledge of the incorrect alternatives, while clearly detailing the correct response, is referred to by Holding as multiple guidance. The advantages of multiple guidance, though the evidence is slight, are accountable in terms of a sign-Gestalt explanation of learning. Tolman did not see the individual as learning the right connections and movements, but as acquiring a knowledge of relationships. Information on both correct and incorrect cues and responses would augment this knowledge of the relevant relationships and so help learning.

On the one hand it seems that knowing about alternatives will improve learning (Ludgate, von Wright, Tolman), and on the other hand that if the individual actually makes these alternative (*and wrong*) responses he will tend to acquire them (Kaess and Zeaman, Guthrie). Following Holding, we would suggest that the ideal is possibly to provide the learner with a knowledge of all alternatives by enabling him to perceive them, but to ensure the correct responses are the ones he actually carries out.

Annett's statement on knowledge of results is again relevant here: 'Knowledge of results is regarded as information about the outcome of a test carried out on the environment.' Guidance similarly can be seen as the prompt to the learner provided by the information from such a test on the environment, but a test made by an individual other than the learner. In guidance the learner can, in Annett's words, 'be told the outcome without having to make a response'. The trainer provides this information to the learner before he responds or while he does so. Such an account of guidance is in line with cognitive thinking.

A connectionist formulation would explain guidance in other terms. For Thorndike and Skinner the appropriate response must be connected with the correct cue by reinforcement, particularly positive reinforcement. Guidance ensures the learner tends to make only the right responses to the right cues which can then be positively rewarded. It does this by, as it were, high-lighting the stimulus.

Similarly Guthrie's law of exercise might account for the effectiveness of guidance. For Guthrie those stimuli and responses associate, bond, and connect which have simply been contiguous, which have merely come together in time. Guidance ensures that the right stimulus does come together with the right response. What we do is what we learn, contends Guthrie. With guidance we tend to do, and so learn, the right behaviour.

PRACTICE

Introduction
That 'practice makes perfect' is, like many such adages, a half-truth. It is only practice under certain conditions which 'makes perfect', or at least improves performance. Practice with knowledge of results is one such condition. Others are practice under guidance, and practice with suitable aids to learning. Knowledge of results, guidance, aids to learning, are sufficiently important to be dealt with under separate headings, but all three are essentially concerned with stipulations about the conditions of practice.

We will consider practice under three headings, each of which we can see in terms of a question. First, during his practice sessions should the trainee aim for speed or accuracy? As we shall see, the answer to this relates to a decision on whether the trainee should practise the whole task even in the early sessions or just bits of it at a time. This is the whole-versus-part controversy. Secondly, how should we schedule the practice sessions? Should the trainee practise over extended periods, or should the training sessions be short, numerous, and separated by rest pauses? Should practice be massed or distributed? Thirdly, how important is it to involve the trainee actively in practice—or is his passive acquiescence enough?

Speed and Accuracy: Whole and Part

If the trainee learning any complex task tries to work fast, he will probably make mistakes. If, however, he aims at accuracy and at avoiding mistakes, he is likely to work slowly. The trainer seems often to be faced with a problem here, of whether to make the trainee speed- or accuracy-minded.

If the trainee works fast but inaccurately, he may never complete the task correctly but in fact learn the wrong responses by doing them. The objection to practising the task correctly but slowly and then speeding up is slightly more subtle. It is possible that a perceptual-motor task done at two different speeds is for the operator two different tasks. When the operator does task A slowly he will probably rely heavily on visual ones. When he does the same task at speed he will almost certainly be relying more on information from his kinaesthetic sense. In other words in moving from a slow to a fast performance of a task the operator may in part be having to relearn the task.

Many observers have noted that in graphs of trainees' performance during practice, there is often a form of plateau, indicating a period of no improvement. Figure 10.3 indicates a typical plateau. Motivational factors such as lack of interest may be relevant. Other explanations have been the need for an unproductive period of mental reorganization in learning, a sort of Gestalt experienced as insight, and followed by sudden improvement.

But another explanation inherent in what we have suggested is part of the speed-versus-accuracy dilemma. If a task done slowly (task A_s) involves a different skill from the same task done fast (task A_f), then speeding up during practice entails relearning for

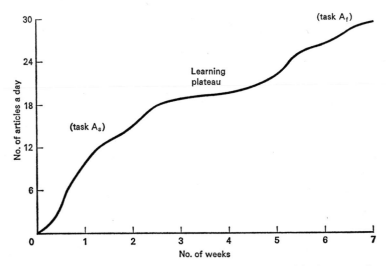

Fig. 10.3 A typical learning curve of trainees practising a complex perceptual-motor task, such as certain kinds of stitching involved in clothing production, with a plateau in the curve

the operator. The performance plateau on the learning curve possibly occurs as the operator moves from practising task A_s to practising task A_f.

One solution to this practical problem for the trainer of speed or accuracy is simply to avoid it. Seymour (1954, 1966) and others have developed the idea of reducing the job into parts which are simple enough for the trainee to learn at speed and without making errors. The acquisition of the skilled performance of a task then becomes a process of learning parts of it correctly and at speed, and building up these parts into the whole task. We will return to this in Chapter 12, but we can note here that the controversy shifts to that of part versus whole, the value of a reductionist as opposed to a Gestalt type of analysis.

The advantages of whole or part conditions of practice are discussed in the psychology text books, and again by Holding (1965) and Seymour (1954, 1966). Many factors are relevant to the discussion, such as the nature of the task, its complexity, and whether symbolic or non-symbolic learning is involved. But the reductionist approach has proved its value as a basis for skills training. The main problem it poses is, naturally, that of connecting the parts, and this we will examine in our discussion of skills training.

Massed versus Distributed Practice

Should the trainee practise hard over long periods until he has mastered the task? Or alternatively should his practice sessions be broken up into short periods by intervals for rest and other activities? If one adopts this second approach, that of distributed practice, rather than the first procedure, massed practice, then how long should these practice sessions be?

Clay (1964), examining the bulk of recent research in this area, suggests that in most cases distributed practice proves superior. A typical result, for example, is that reported by McGehee (1949) where the time for training spinners in textile mills was reduced by 30 per cent when trainees practised under a distributed schedule. However, much of this research on the scheduling of practice has been done with training for motor skill, and the findings with more cognitive and symbolic learning are not so conclusive.

One explanation for the frequent superiority of distributed over massed practice with perceptual-motor tasks is commonly given. Practice causes fatigue, boredom, and 'reactive inhibition' in the learner. Whereas massed trials produce a build-up of such inhibitory factors, the spacing and distribution of trials enable them to dissipate.

However, if we put the individual's retention of a partially learned skill or knowledge on a graph, the 'curve of forgetting' we plot typically has a certain shape. It usually drops sharply at first, and then flattens out, as in Figure 10.4. In other words, the maximum amount of forgetting or loss of skill occurs im-

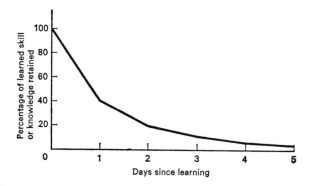

Fig. 10.4 A common shape for the 'curve of forgetting', indicating that maximum loss occurs during the period immediately after learning

mediately after learning. After this the rate at which one loses knowledge and skill reduces considerably. This suggests then that in spacing and distributing practice, the intervals between practice sessions should not be too long. In general then with skill acquisition, distributed practice with short intervals between trials is likely to be most effective, though the length of sessions and intervals needs to be determined for a particular situation.

Activity Learning

'Why', said the Dodo, 'the best way to explain it is to do it' (Lewis Carroll, *Alice in Wonderland*).

Activity learning is normally treated as a separate category; here we are considering it as practice of a certain type. It usually consists of a series of progressively more difficult tasks, with a minimum of demonstration and verbal instruction from the trainer (see Belbin, 1958). Activity learning is essentially concerned with actively involving the trainee in the learning process during 'practice' sessions. In more conventional methods the trainee has to practise operations that have already been explained to him. Part of the activity in activity learning is for the trainee to find out for himself how the task is actually done. This is the reason why he is given progressively more difficult tasks. Using the knowledge and skill he has acquired in tasks A and B he can work out for himself and then perform task C. It is similar to the counselling idea that the knowledge and skill which really influence the individual are what he has learnt for himself (see Chapter 6).

Belbin (1958) found the activity approach particularly useful with older trainees, proving more successful than a traditional memorization of instructions method. But in her Post Office study (Belbin, 1964) it appeared that the activity method is useful for the older worker only to the extent that it really does keep him mentally active. The presentation of progressively more difficult tasks as an approach to activity learning may often involve the trainee in obvious physical activity while at the same time allowing him to remain intellectually passive or inactive. But the activity method remains as yet a relatively unexplored field of training.

Conclusion

'A combination of stimuli which has accompanied a movement will on its recurrence tend to be followed by that movement' (Guthrie, 1952). The mere occurrence together of a stimulus and a response, suggests Guthrie, creates a bond between them. If in certain circumstances you do something, then the next time you are in those or similar circumstances you will tend to do that something again. What you do is what you learn, and the tendency of trainees to repeat their errors lends some support to Guthrie's contention. This law of exercise lays emphasis upon the importance of practice.

But the environment within which 'exercise' occurs, the conditions of practice, are also important. The trainee's goals in learning need to be taken into account. 'Reward' also has some relevance, either because it provides reinforcement or because it communicates information to the learner. Practice with knowledge of results is invariably more effective than practice with no knowledge of results. Knowing how he has done either motivates the trainee more, or again functions as an additional provision of information.

In the acquisition of skills some form of distributed scheduling of practice normally improves learning more than does a massing together of the practice trials. Similarly, practising the operations of a manual task at speed is likely to prove more effective than practising them slowly at first and then speeding up. The cognitive involvement of the trainee, even in the practice of a manual skill, is a new approach to practice which is likely to prove useful, especially with older trainees.

SEQUENCE AND ORDER OF MATERIAL

In any training situation we cannot learn everything at once. So whether the trainee is an operator, an apprentice, or a manager, the trainer has to decide on a sequence and order of presentation of material. And often what appears the common-sense order of presentation is not necessarily the best. The logic of a training programme may not coincide with a 'psychologic' of learning. Gilbert's proposal for a 'retrogression through the basic exercise model' (1962) illustrates the point. He suggests that in a task consisting of a series of operations or sub-tasks, it is the last operation or sub-task we should learn first, then the last but one, then the last but two, etc. Gilbert's proposal, which we will examine in more detail in Chapter 12, emerges from the Skinnerian position on the importance of the immediacy of reinforcement. The connectionist viewpoint would also emphasize an order and sequence in the presentation of learning material which would facilitate the setting up of the correct s–r connections, and minimize the possibility of the incorrect bonds and associations being established.

Learning material needs to be presented to the learner in structured and manageable sizes. Kohler's apes were only able to solve certain problems when the boxes were sufficiently close together. 'Structured and manageable sizes' is a Gestalt type of concept, whereby the total job is perceived as consisting of wholes that will be experienced by the learner as meaningful.

Relevant at the level of supervisory and management training is work from the social psychological field on attitude change. The 'law of primacy' raises the question of whether the first or early communications influence the individual's thinking, his attitudes, and his behaviour, more than do later and more recent communications. The evidence is confused, suggesting that a number of factors need to be taken into account.

What does emerge as an effective order for presenting material in the field of attitude change is one where the communicator first arouses a need, and then presents information which should satisfy it. This approach is common in marketing where an advertisement first suggests the advantages for a woman of being slim, and then explains how the advertiser's product will help her become slim. Cohen (1957) in a study on the order of presentation of material attempted to test this view, stating the hypothesis as follows: 'A communication situation in which information assumed to satisfy aroused needs is placed after need arousal will bring more acceptance of that information than a situation in which the information is placed before need arousal.' Students were given information on student-assessment practices calculated to cause some anxiety about the possibility of stiffer assessment procedures (presentation A). The same students were given information which would obviate or resolve any such anxiety (presentation B). With one group of students presentation A preceded presentation B; with another group presentation B preceded presentation A. The results supported the hypothesis—the information reducing anxiety was better grasped and retained when it was presented subsequent to the information that generated anxiety. There were some exceptions, such as students who structured and made sense of the information as they received it. For them the order of presentation was irrelevant.

Material should also be organized and presented in an order and sequence which is calculated to promote an understanding of underlying principles. This is likely to maximize the transfer of learning to other situations.

MOTIVATION

Trainees have goals. People learn with objectives in view. These goals and objectives may be as specific as being able to mend a fuse or master a theory, or more general such as earning a living or personal development. An undergraduate's sole concern in his study may be with passing his degree, getting 'the little bit of paper'. If the syllabus is such (God forbid!) that sheer rote memorizing provides the surest way of passing, then exhorting him to 'develop his critical faculties' and 'become more analytical' will achieve very little.

If, as Tolman suggested, human behaviour and learning is essentially purposive, a training programme must realistically take account of the learner's goals. When the trainee is only concerned with moving off the trainees' low rate of pay on to production and higher earnings, he will not work at those parts of the training course he sees as irrelevant to the subsequent performance for which he will be paid. Trainees will learn according to the relevance of training to their goals, their own personal goals or those they have provisionally adopted from the organization. A study of retraining (McGehee and Livingstone, 1952) makes this point. Operators whose production figures were characterized by high wastage rates were retrained to aim specifically at lower wastage, and not, for the time being, to concern themselves with maintaining high output. In fact, the operators, orientated towards lower wastage, were able to reduce wastage without any drop in their level of output.

Training must take account, therefore, of the fact that trainees have goals. If the trainer regards a trainee's goals as unsatisfactory or inadequate he may try to persuade the trainee to change them. More realistically this will need to be preceded by organizational change which gives value to these new goals or to other means of attaining the original ones. In firm x managers are promoted only on the basis of their technical performance, and supervisory competence is ignored. To the extent that a manager wishes to be promoted, to that extent he will be interested only in training that furthers his technical knowledge. In order to make the manager more interested in developing supervisory competence, it would be necessary first to make supervision a basis for promotion. Similarly with our undergraduate above, if his finals now became a test of analytic and critical ability he would no longer be content with learning by rote.

An alternative to analysing the motivation of the trainee in terms of goals is to adopt a connectionist approach, and employ such concepts as drive, reward, force, and reinforcement. But when the law of effect, drive-reduction, schedules of reinforcement, and similar ideas are considered in terms of rewards such as food, water, sex, pain-avoidance, etc., their use is limited and more appropriate to the training of rats, pigeons, and possibly autistic children. Such concepts seem more useful in industrial training if we think in terms of a drive or need to achieve 'mastery' of the task (Gilbert, 1962). The trainee, generally orientated in training to achieving certain goals, strives specifically for the immediate mastery of a learning task. The laws and principles of reinforcement, such as Skinner's schedules (see Chapter 9), may be applicable to such a drive for mastery, and to the drive-reducing or rewarding properties of the achievement of mastery.

Alternatively it may be useful for training (and teaching) to think, as in Thyne's model, in terms of force rather than drive. Force is that which makes a response occur. The trainer is concerned with providing for the learner an environment that has force; it will cause behaviour to occur. By means of the prompt the trainer ensures that eventually the appropriate behaviour or response occurs, which then may be rewarded and reinforced.

TRANSFER OF TRAINING

Transfer of training refers to the effect of learning and behaviour acquired in one situation on subsequent learning and performance in another situation. It has an obvious relevance in the industrial and commercial field. Will an operator who has worked many years on machine x benefit from this previous experience when he is transferred to machine y, or will it put him at a disadvantage? Will considerable management experience in production planning help an individual if he moves to a senior marketing position?

This transfer of the effect of learning and training to a subsequent job may either help or hinder. If it helps, if the manager's years in planning benefit his marketing work, we refer to the transfer as positive. If it hinders, if the operator's training on machine x interferes with his learning to operate machine y, the transfer is negative.

In an experiment by Gagné and Foster (1949), subjects first practised on only a part of the total skill they had subsequently to acquire. Above a certain minimum level of practice, there was positive transfer from practising part of the total task to acquisition of the total skill. Extensive practise on the component of the whole task frequently resulted in trainees starting training for the total skill at a performance level which showed they had already completed half the necessary learning.

An earlier study (Cox, 1934) illustrates a different approach. He was primarily concerned with examining the differences in the transfer effects of what he termed practice and training. Practice consisted of the mere repetition of a task at speed; training constituted an explanation of the general principles involved in the operations, and instruction together with formal exercises in a suitable work method. As might be expected, trainees who had training did better on the subsequent learning task of assembling a lamp holder than did those who had practice. The training produced more transfer than the practice.

Cox's study illustrates positive transfer which results from the comprehension of principles in one situation that are relevant in a subsequent situation. Positive transfer occurs because one has grasped a meaning, understood the significance of certain stimuli, perceived a relationship, that are applicable subsequently. On the other hand when an individual subsequently applies such a principle or general rule quite inappropriately, because of inadequate information or bad judgment, negative transfer of training has occurred. If we explain all or some transfer of training in terms of 'transfer through learning general rules or principles', we are essentially adopting a cognitive view.

The Gagné and Foster study, and results of a similar nature, can be explained in connectionist terms. The learner is acquiring identical elements or s–r bonds. Transfer of training is likely to occur where there exist elements or s–r bonds common to the original and subsequent situations. If in both situations the correct operator response to s_1 is R_1, then positive transfer results. On machine x the operator moved the lever A to the right; with machine y he does exactly the same with a similar lever. But if s_1 occurs in both situations, and is followed by R_1 in the first and by R_2 in the second, then negative transfer is more likely to result. On machine y the operator must now move the lever to the left. A connectionist approach can, therefore, account for positive and negative transfer in terms of identical or apparently identical s–r bonds that are common to two situations.

There is a third view of transfer of training (see Bass and Vaughan, 1966). In the experiment referred to Cox found that his 'training' group besides doing better on the specific assembly task, somehow became more trainable. The group members had improved their potential for learning. He says of this 'training', as we have described it above, that 'the skill thus developed . . . tends to transfer to other operations over a fairly wide range of manual activity'.

A similar finding emerges from a study by Harlow (1949). He conducted a number of experiments involving discrimination and choice with monkeys and young children. If they respond to the correct cue they are rewarded with food or toys. The experimenter continues to reward them for responding to the appropriate cue (say, box with a certain shape) until that series of tasks ends, and a new series with different objects and cues begins, when the children, or the monkeys, must learn which is the new correct cue. Naturally, each time they eventually find out the relevant cue. But over a period the time they require to do so becomes progressively shorter. They appear to learn not only the solution to the current task—which cue?—but to acquire ways of approaching every problem. They learn strategies and procedures for determining the right cues. They eventually solve the problems more quickly because they learn how to learn.

What we have here, suggests Harlow, is a learning set, some

sort of preparatory adjustment or readiness to react in a certain way. An individual's acquired learning set may consist of a readiness to adopt a specific approach to a problem and a willingness to attend to certain cues and not others. The individual now has cognitions about the nature of the cues, just as Harlow's monkeys found that usually the nature of the object and not its position was relevant (Harlow, 1950). A readiness to abandon swiftly fruitless lines of enquiry might be another characteristic of a specific learning set. We might say that in acquiring learning sets the individual is, in the language of Tolman, learning expectancies.

We might regard education as a process for the formation of learning sets. The teacher does supply ready-made answers, but attempts also to provide procedures for solving problems, strategies, and guides on what to look for in problem situations (expectancies). But since even the nature of the problem may change, the individual must also learn to develop for himself new problem-solving methods and new ways of seeking solutions. So education teaches the individual to learn how to learn; it attempts to teach for transfer (Hovland, 1951) to the greatest possible number of subsequent situations.

There is evidence that the ability to recall information, which we would regard as operating in most intellectual activity, does not decline through middle age among people who initially had a high level of the ability (Raven, 1948). Raven's data suggest that this capacity to recall information does decline over the same period of time among those who started with a lower level of the ability. The first group of people will probably have had more stimulating jobs and life styles than the second, since there is a relationship between intellectual ability and occupational and social stratification. If we regard intelligence as in part the capacity to learn and retain new information, then the data illustrate that this needs to be exercised and developed, like any other skill. People, having learnt to learn and retain new information in childhood and at school, enter occupations and adopt life styles which in the case of some maintain this capacity, and with others allow it to atrophy. This has implications for the growing problem of the training and retraining of the older worker.

We have suggested three types of transfer. Bass and Vaughan (1966) describe them in terms of identical elements, training through principles, and learning to learn. If we attempt to train for transfer, the three ideas will partly determine the form of the training scheme. First, the teaching and content of syllabus must direct the learner's attention to *identical elements* common to the old and new situations. Second, the teaching and syllabus must emphasize the applicability of any general *principles*. Third, they must attempt to develop the trainee's *learning capacity*.

The last is a more long-term consideration. We will discuss this further under management training.

The three ideas also provide criteria for the choice of training techniques and methods, though much research remains to be done in this area. What techniques facilitate transfer in what situations needs to be examined. Does a case study, representing specific situations, help the trainee to identify and transfer identical elements, but fail to teach him principles that transfer? If this were so the case study would need to be supplemented by some attempt, such as a lecture, to educe general principles. In fact, in a study by Szekely (1950) which we will shortly outline, a practical lesson gave greater transfer than did a formal lecture.

UNDERSTANDING

Training needs a specific objective. We should be able to state the behaviour repertoire we want. In these terms the trainer teaches for understanding and a grasp of principles only if this helps the trainee do what is required. But, as we have just discussed, comprehension may help in less obvious ways than by simply determining whether he can perform narrowly and precisely defined tasks. Training for understanding, besides providing additional interest for the learner, may develop the individual intellectually more than does mere instruction in procedures. It is partially synonymous with training through principles and learning to learn. It may also, as we have suggested, maximize the transfer of learning to other situations.

Maier (1965) stresses the activeness of the cognitive process involved in comprehension and understanding: 'Understanding is always an active rather than a passive process since the person must impose organization on the sensations supplied to his senses.' With the term 'organization' we return to concepts of schemas, cognitive maps, and images (Bartlett, 1932; Tolman, 1949; Miller, Galanter, and Pribram, 1960).

In an experiment by Szekely (1950) two groups of students were instructed in the principle of the moment of inertia. The first group received a formal lecture on the subject. The second group had a more practical lesson as part of which they all attempted to predict the behaviour of a twisting pendulum. A few days later all the students were given the following problem: 'Two spheres are identical in size, exterior appearance, and weight. But one is a solid ball of light metal; the other is a hollow ball of heavy metal. Could you tell them apart by rolling them?' Transfer of learning was better from the more practical lesson than from the formal lecture. The study usefully counters our expectation that a lecture will always maximize transfer since it is able to generalize and discuss principles. The practical approach may have been more successful because the active involvement of the learner facilitated understanding which in turn increased transfer.

Understanding, comprehension of learning content, the grasp of principles, are essentially active processes; they involve discovery by the learner. One may conceive of them in connectionist terms as a process of stimulus generalization. Or alternatively we may see them as the acquisition of relevant Gestalts, cognitions about meanings and relationships, cognitive maps, or images. Either way the essentially active nature of the process is relevant to choosing appropriate techniques to aid the learner to acquire understanding. An active learning situation such as a seminar discussion or case study might often prove more effective than, say, a lecture where the learner tends to assume a more passive role. Ideally we might facilitate understanding by supplementing the active learning of seminar, case study, and practical exercises, with a formal account of the transferable features of a learning situation, such as is possible in a lecture.

CONCLUSION

We have briefly discussed a number of concepts relevant to the learning process, such as guidance and knowledge of results. Over the years many material aids to learning have been developed, from blackboard and chalk to teaching machines. There are visual aids which function by clearly demonstrating the learning task, which is what Nellie tried to do for the girls who sat next to her. Other aids attempt to help the early stages of learning by magnifying the cues, usually visually. One interesting and promising new development is that of the algorithm (Lewis, Horabin, and Gane, 1967). These authors describe it as 'an orderly sequence of instructions for solving a problem'. Usually an algorithm consists of a series of instructions to the user about what he must do in order to achieve a goal or perform a task. The instructions are usually presented in the form of a simple visual chart or diagram (see Lewis, Horabin, and Gane, 1967). It has a number of uses and could be developed as another aid to learning.

Such material techniques and aids to learning help the training process in a number of ways. Some amplify the information; some increase motivation; some lay out a plan or guide for the trainee; some help the trainer to assess the trainee's progress. Training functions through a process of psychological programming which we can consider in terms of the concepts of guidance, knowledge of results, practice, the structuring of learning material, motivation, understanding, and transfer of training, all of which we have considered in the chapter.

REFERENCES

Annett, J. (1969), *Feedback and Human Behaviour*, Penguin.

Bartlett, F. C. (1932), *Remembering: an Experimental and Social Study*, Cambridge University Press.

Bartlett, F. C. (1947), 'The Measurement of Human Skill', *Brit. Med. J.*, 1, reprinted in *Occup. Psychol.*, (1948), 22.

Bass, B. M. and Vaughan, J. A. (1966), *Training in Industry: The Management of Learning*, Tavistock.

Belbin, E. (1958), 'Methods of training older workers', *Ergonomics*, 1, 207–21.

Belbin, E. (1964), 'Training the Adult Worker, Problems of Progress', in *Industry Series No. 15*, Department of Scientific and Industrial Research.

Clay, H. M. (1964), *Research in Relation to Operator Training*, Department of Scientific and Industrial Research.

Cohen, A. R. (1957), 'Need for cognition and order of communication as determinants of opinion change', in *Order of Presentation in Persuasion*, ed. C. I. Hovland, Yale University Press.

Cox, J. W. (1934), *Manual Skill*, Cambridge University Press.

Gagné, R. M. and Foster, H. (1949), 'Transfer of training from practice on components in a motor skill', *J. exp. Psychol.*, 39, 47–68.

Gilbert, T. F. (1962), 'Mathetics: the technology of education', *J. Mathetics*, 1.

Glaser, R. (1962), 'Psychology and Instructional Technology', in *Training Research and Education*, ed. R. Glaser, Wiley.

Guthrie, E. R. (1952), *The Psychology of Learning*, Harper.

Harlow, H. F. (1949), 'The formation of learning sets', *Psychol. Rev.*, 56, 51–65.

Harlow, H. F. (1950), 'Analysis of discrimination learning by monkeys', *J. exp. Psychol.*, 40, 26–39.

Holding, D. H. (1965), *Principles of Training*, Pergamon.

Holding, D. H. and Macrae, A. W. (1964), 'Guidance, restriction and knowledge of results', *Ergonomics*, 7, 289–95.

Hovland, C. I. (1951), 'Human learning and retention', chapter 17 in *Handbook of Experimental Psychology*, ed. S. S. Stevens, Wiley.

Kaess, W. and Zeaman, D. (1960), 'Positive and negative knowledge of results on a Pressey-type punchboard', *J. exp. Psychol.*, 60, 12–17.

Lewis, B. N., Horabin, I. S. and Gane, C. P. (1967), *Flow Charts, Logical Trees and Algorithms for Rules and Regulations*, C.A.S. Occasional Papers No. 2, H.M.S.O.

Lindahl, L. G. (1945), 'Movement analysis as an industrial training method', *J. app. Psychol.*, 29, 6, reprinted in *Readings in Experimental Industrial Psychology*, ed. M. L. Blum, 1952.

Ludgate, K. E. (1924), 'The effect of manual guidance upon maze learning', *Psychol. Mon.*, 33, 148.

Maier, N. R. F. (1965), *Psychology in Industry*, Harrap.

McGehee, W. (1949), 'Training reduction through distributed practice', in *Current Trends in Industrial Psychology*, University of Pittsburgh Press.

McGehee, W. and Livingstone, D. H. (1952), 'Training reduces material waste', *Pers. Psychol.*, 5.

Miller, G. A., Galanter, E. and Pribram, K. H. (1960), *Plans and the Structure of Behavior*, Holt.

Raphael, W. (1962), 'Employers' and workers' attitudes towards communications', in *Attitudes and Methods of Communication and Consultation between Employers and Workers at Individual Firm Level*, O.E.C.D.

Raven, J. C. (1948), 'The Comparative Assessment of Intellectual Ability', *Brit. J. Psychol.*, 39.

Rodger, A. (1950), 'Industrial Psychology', in *Chambers's Encyclopaedia*, Newnes.

Seymour, W. D. (1954), *Industrial Training for Manual Operations*, Pitman.

Seymour, W. D. (1966), *Industrial Skills*, Pitman.

Smith, E. E. and Knight, S. S. (1959), 'Effects of feedback on insight and problem-solving efficiency in training groups', *J. appl. Psychol.*, 43, 209–11.

Szekely, L. (1950), 'Productive processes in learning and thinking', *Acta Psychol.*, 7, 388–407.

Thorndike, E. L. (1927), 'The law of effect', *Amer. J. Psychol.*, 39, 212–22.

Tilley, K. (1968), 'A technology of training', in *Industrial Society*, ed. D. Pym, Penguin.

Tolman, E. C. (1949), 'There is more than one kind of learning', *Psychol. Rev.*, 56, 144–55.

Trowbridge, M. A. and Cason, H. (1932), 'An experimental study of Thorndike's theory of learning', *J. gen. Psychol.*, 7, 245–60.

von Wright, J. M. (1957), 'A note on the role of guidance in learning', *Brit. J. Psychol.*, 48, 133–7.

CHAPTER 11

Induction

Overview

In the introduction to this chapter we outline the components of a normal induction course and say what is usually regarded as its purpose. We then return to the idea of training as a form of socialization and to our earlier model of levels of motivation in the firm. The concept of group helps with the analysis of induction, and we suggest that the primary group has a key function in the identification and internalization processes which are so important to induction.

We relate induction as a socialization process to certain concepts of morale, and find the primary group again emerges as a key agent in induction. We suggest that in the large firm management's influence on the employee is affected by the employee's position in the firm's hierarchy and by his group membership. This applies to the attempt to influence the individual in induction. Finally we state that influence should be a two-way process in a firm, the organization influencing and being influenced by the employee. In induction the organization should prepare the employee to influence and change the organization.

INTRODUCTION

Many firms provide some form of induction for new employees. Induction courses usually consist of the following sorts of activities: a talk on the company, its products and services, history, plans, and organizational structure with an account of the senior personnel; a conducted tour of the firm; and a second talk, on company personnel policies as implemented in the firm's rules and regulations, wage and salary structure, training and promotion opportunities, holidays, sickness benefits, and pension scheme.

The personnel management textbooks give the purposes of

induction as 'to help new entrants to fit into the company's daily life and understand their part in it' (Moxon, 1951), and 'to assist the organization in assimilating the person who has accepted a job offer and to assist the individual in adjusting to the organization' (French, 1964). Staff and labour turnover tend to be highest among employees who have been with a firm for only a short period, such as under six months. Since good induction provides one method for attempting to increase a new employee's interest and involvement in the firm, it can play an important part in reducing turnover.

INDUCTION, SOCIALIZATION, AND THE GROUP

We have previously described training as socialization to the expectations of management. Induction training is a specific example of this socialization. We also suggested in Chapter 8 we could see training as motivated at three levels in the organization. Similarly we can think of induction as motivated at the levels of compliance, identification, or internalization. The employee may be motivated by pay-offs, in which case the talks, tours, lectures affect only his actions. He may wish to identify with the organization and his future colleagues, which means induction would affect both his actions and his roles. Or possibly what he sees and hears so accords with his self that he internalizes, and in induction learns value-relationships as well as actions and roles.

Induction is a continuing process, relevant not merely to an employee's first few months at a firm, but to his whole length of stay. The extended socialization of an individual in induction training may move him through two or all three of the motivational levels. Students at medical school may behave correctly at first for fear of discharge, but do so later on in their training because they have begun to see themselves as doctors. Finally they internalize the values that relate to this behaviour.

Woodcock (1969) argued the importance of groups in induction. But we must distinguish between primary and secondary groups, adopting Cooley's account of the first: 'By primary groups I mean those characterized by intimate face-to-face association and cooperation . . . they are fundamental in forming the social nature and ideals of the individual.' Primary groups are personal, even intimate, and involve feelings. They tend to be small. Secondary groups are usually large, such as 'those persons dwelling within the boundaries of the city of Manchester', or the two thousand employees of Company XYZ Ltd. Secondary group relationships are impersonal, formal, and often have a contractual basis. People living in the same Manchester street, or a foreman and operator at XYZ Ltd, may relate to each other in this way. But naturally their relationships can become more personal, involve their feelings to a greater extent, and develop into primary group relationships. There will be many primary groups within Manchester and XYZ Ltd. Groups can be placed on a continuum from those which are essentially primary to those which are completely secondary, with groups that are a primary-secondary mixture in the middle.

The concern with pay-offs and overt behaviour of compliance motivation is characteristic of the rational, calculative secondary group. The operator can be made to obey safety regulations if we can observe him at the relevant time and punish him when he breaks them. The primary group with its satisfying social relationships is essential to identification. If we want a new maintenance fitter to identify with the maintenance department, the department should be a primary group. The primary group also plays a part in identification, though primary group relationships are not sufficient to make the individual internalize. Internalization is less dependent on immediate external factors. The superintendent, newly promoted from the shop floor, enjoys close friendly relationships with his new manager colleagues. This makes him more understanding of their political conservatism, but leaves unaffected his commitment to socialism. Table 11.1 illustrates how groups relate to the three levels of influence in induction training.

TABLE 11.1 *Relationship of primary and secondary groups to three levels of influence*
(For identification to occur, a primary group must exist; a primary group may facilitate the process of internalization, but is not sufficient to cause it)

	Groups	
	primary	secondary
Levels of influence in induction	identification internalization	compliance

Since the existence of a primary group is relevant to identification and internalization, we need to know what causes a secondary group to become primary. First, a nucleus of six or seven people will normally become a primary group when interaction between them is permitted. But the mere opportunity for interaction is insufficient to develop in the larger group, such as a factory of a hundred people or a big office or machine shop, the more informal and spontaneous relationships of the primary group. If the large group is to become primary, extensive social interaction really must occur so that people come to know most others, either directly or by knowing people who know people, by a social chain reaction (Sprott, 1958). Good communication in the machine shop will facilitate its development into a primary group. A factory of a hundred employees functioning as one administrative unit, with characteristic procedures which give it identity for its personnel, will tend to develop into a primary group. Whether group members come and go, or are permanent, is obviously relevant. If the manager of a large office can keep staff turnover low, primary group relationships among staff are more likely to emerge.

INDUCTION, SOCIALIZATION, AND MORALE

If we regard induction not as a three-week or three-month affair, but as a more extended process of socialization, we can usefully see it as an attempt to inculcate aims morale, that is, 'identification with the group goal' (Holmes, 1968). Such identification may exist in the individual prior to his entering an organization, as when a young man enters a religious order. In industry and commerce such morale is rare, since an individual is unlikely to identify with a firm before he is actually an employee. More typically an individual interested in sales work applies for a position in a sales department, and having worked there for a period eventually identifies with the goals of the firm and the sales department. The identification with goals arises only as a consequence of being a member of an organization. Holmes terms this organizational aims morale.

We should know how organizational aims morale is caused, since after all it is this sort of morale, and not vocational, that can be developed within the commercial firm. First, both sorts are examples of what Holmes terms aims morale, which he distinguishes from progress morale. Progress morale 'refers to the state of feeling that allows the individual . . . "to work and live hopefully", performing his task with "enthusiasm" ' (Holmes, 1968). This state of feeling may be experienced individually, as when making good progress with one's studies, or can be a group experience, as in the involvement of a happy, successful research team. The group experience of progress morale is relevant to how organizational aims morale is caused. Holmes contends 'that organizational aims morale arises out of successful group progress morale—that dedication to a group cause will arise out of a common striving for that cause'. A chemist, offered jobs in plastics, plating, or a safety engineering firm, takes the third position since the firm is situated nearer where he lives. At the firm he develops foam and other possible compounds for fire-fighting. As a member of its research team he works with interest, hope, enthusiasm, and some measure of achievement. From this successful group-progress morale emerges an organizational aims morale, his commitment to the firm's research goals of producing efficient chemical compounds for fire extinction.

Induction, seen as a long-term socialization process, is essentially concerned at the level of identification and internalization with developing the employees' organizational aims morale. We are suggesting that this sort of morale arises from involvement in successful group action. This indicates again the importance of the primary group, here in the formation of morale.

INDUCTION, SOCIALIZATION, AND THE NATURE OF MANAGEMENT INFLUENCE

A view of senior management as affecting and influencing employee behaviour directly and at first hand is an over-simplification for the big organization. Such a view of management influence, presented schematically in Figure 11.1, applies only in the very small organization of, say, under thirty or so personnel.

A more realistic model for the large organization would indicate that certain conditions intervene between senior management and the individual employee. We will outline two of them. First, as we have already stated, the individual is usually a member of a group, and he responds to communication, influence, pressure, as a group member. Secondly, the employee has a specific position and role in the hierarchical structure of the organization.

First, what effect does the individual's membership of a group have on any communication or attempt to influence him from management or some other influencing agent, such as a trade union? Secord and Backman point out that the group can inhibit and interfere with the effect of the communication and influence, or may supplement and reinforce their effect. For example, the foremen's group provides support for the ideas, views, attitudes, currently held by members, and so acts to resist new proposals and

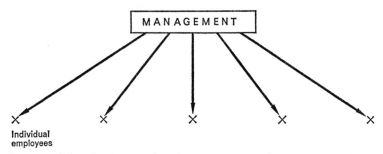

Fig. 11.1 The simplest model of management influence on employees (the xs)

suggestions from, say, the work study department. The structure of the group can also act as a filter, rejecting ideas and communications unacceptable to members. A group can make communication ineffective when the members support each other in their doubts about the reliability of the source, as shop stewards might do with information from management. The group, in fact, tends by itself to reject anything new which might change the present situation, and to favour a *status quo*. A definite strategy is required if the group is to function as an agent in change. Group discussion, alterations in the external environment, and various approaches to group decision-making, must be used to encourage acceptance in the group of communication and influence from outside.

A second important factor mediating between senior management and the individual employee is his specific position and related role in the organization hierarchy. There is usually more than one social system in any commercial organization (Fox, 1966), and each has its own values, norms, and frames of reference. Persuasive communications may be consonant with the values, norms, and frames of reference of one social system in the organization, such as management's, and dissonant with those of another social system in the same concern, such as that of the manual workers. In which case the information and persuasive communication moving from one social system to another is likely to be rejected by the recipient social system if they are dissonant with its norms and values. So the individual's position in the social systems becomes relevant, and this is in part a function of his position in the formal organization hierarchy. The senior manager, the foreman, the production operator, the clerk, are all likely to have positions within different social systems in the same factory. Within such a concern certain positions, linking one social system with another, become of key importance in any attempt by management, unions, or any pressure group, to influence others. In industry the foreman, production manager, and shop steward, are examples of such key positions.

Our original model of how employee behaviour is influenced proves much too simple for the big concern. Management's attempts, as in induction, to influence an employee are mediated

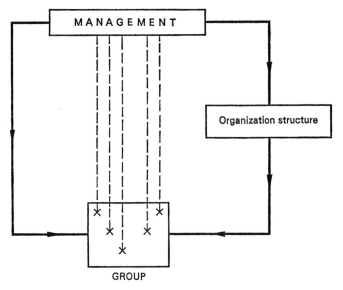

Fig. 11.2 A more complex model of management influence on employee behaviour, which suggests that the influence is mediated by organizational and group structure; x is an individual employee

by his group membership and by his position in the organization, as indicated schematically in Figure 11.2. For example, management introduces a new type of lighting into the machine shop. In this firm the foremen are part of the management social system, since their pay-off comes from management, since they identify with them to some extent, and since they even internalize some management values. Consequently men in foremen positions see the new lighting as a sincere management move to improve working conditions. The operators see the action very differently from their different position in the organization hierarchy, regarding it as an attempt by management to get more output for the same wages bill. But, because of group influences, there are differences of opinion among men in the same organizational positions. The drillers at one end of the machine shop have an aggressive, anti-management leader who sees the action as attempted management exploitation, and influences the others to see it this way. Another group in the shop contains a number of 'faithful old servants' of the firm, and they influence the rest of their group to regard the new lighting as indicative of a genuine management concern for working conditions.

In viewing induction as a process of socialization to management's norms, mediated through the group and by the individual's organizational position, there is a danger of seeing the model as a process of influence in one direction only. But notionally the model is one of interaction and influence in two directions. The employee brings to the organization his economic needs, his attitudes and values, his concept of self; in other words, he enters the organization with a personality. If his personality accords with the organization's expectations, he attempts to behave as is expected of him. We have been examining this. If, however, these expectations are wholly or partly unacceptable to his personality, and the organization fails to change him, he can do one of two things. He can leave. Alternatively he might attempt to change the organization in the direction of his own expectations, norms, and personal values. This would be difficult, but in a sense is necessary. How else are organizations to change? To say they will change in response to external pressure provides only a partial answer since, as a dinosaur would confirm, this still leaves the organization or organism with the problem of how to change. Organizations are adapted and changed by the individuals within them.

We will examine this again under management education, but the point stands that the model is at least notionally one of influence in two directions, and in practice induction training should emphasize this. Induction, and management education also, should partly socialize the individual to the organization as it is, should emphasize that its present state is probably provisional and temporary, and should make the individual aware of the possibility of changing the organization, and even prepare him for this.

REFERENCES

Cooley, C. H. (1909), *Social Organization*, Scribner.

Fox, A. (1966), *Industrial Sociology and Industrial Relations*, Research Paper No. 3, Royal Commission on Trade Unions and Employers' Associations,

French, W. (1964), *The Personnel Management Process*, Houghton Mifflin.

Holmes, R. (1968), 'The Nature of Morale', in *Industrial Society*, ed. D. Pym, Penguin.

Moxon, G. R. (1951), *Functions of a Personnel Department*, Institute of Personnel Management.

Secord, P. F. and Backman, C. W. (1964), *Social Psychology*, McGraw-Hill.

Sprott, W. J. H. (1958), *Human Groups*, Penguin.

Woodcock, F. (1969), 'A Discussion of the Problems of Employee Induction and Internal Promotion within a Work Organisation', unpublished B.A. Business Studies (C.N.A.A.) essay, Enfield College of Technology.

CHAPTER 12

Supervisory and Management Training and Development

Overview

In the introduction to this chapter we consider the supervisor's and manager's job, and suggest categories within which we can describe their work. A distinction is made between managers and supervisors. We outline different levels of management and supervision, and suggest characteristics of the levels and their typical training problems. We conclude the introduction by relating management and supervisory training to the framework for analysing training problems in an organization, proposed in Chapter 8.

We then consider three different 'approaches to supervisory training', indicating the theoretical basis of each. Since the first approach is now outmoded we next examine in more detail the second, the common-skills approach, and outline a common-skills training programme. We argue that the general usefulness of the approach is limited, since such skills are not common to all supervisory jobs. We suggest the sort of situations where a common-skills approach has a contribution to make in supervisory training.

The next section outlines the third approach to training supervisors, one based on an analysis of specific supervisory positions. For our outline we rely considerably on Meade and Greig's account (1966), structuring the approach within Tilley's framework (1968), which we stated in Chapter 8.

We consider management training and development in terms of two aspects of the manager's job. We suggest that the static aspect needs the same approach as that of supervisory training. The second aspect of the manager's job requires an ability to cope with change, and management development facilitates this through what is essentially an educational process. We argue that many methods and techniques, which the manager needs to be trained in, can be taught in such a way as to educate and develop him also to cope with change.

In the section on methods we give a brief account of the lecture, seminar, case study, project, T-group, and role-playing. We conclude with an attempt to evaluate these six methods in connectionist and cognitive terms.

INTRODUCTION

As soon as we discuss supervisory and management training, we are forced to consider what we are training for. What work do supervisors and managers do? The answer is that it varies. So we have to see if there are any categories in which we can usefully classify the variety of different tasks they do. Those suggested by Brown and Jaques (1965) seem particularly useful.

However we categorize the operations of employment work, and Brown and Jaques suggest developing, producing, and selling, we can think, as they do, in terms of three main dimensions for any such activity. These are as follows:

People in Roles. Within this dimension we can consider tasks of recruiting, selecting, and training people for those jobs for which the supervisor or manager has responsibility. Developing an appropriate departmental structure, promotion, pay, and other 'personnel-type' activities come within this dimension.

Techniques. This category embraces the technical considerations that are part of any supervisory or management job. It includes decisions on products, production methods, materials, standards, etc.

Programming. A supervisory or management job entails planning and scheduling, whether it is of the development, manufacture, or sales of goods. Machine-loading and allocating work to meet production deadlines are examples of tasks under this heading.

Brown and Jaques see the accounting task as relevant to all three operations and to their three main dimensions.

It is these three dimensions that we are primarily concerned with here, and significantly Hacon (1961) refers to three sorts of qualities or abilities a manager needs, 'personal qualities, technical expertise of differing sorts and perhaps some organizing ability'. His categories seem more or less identical with those of Brown and Jaques. Jobs of supervisors and managers may vary from situation to situation, but for the purposes of training we may consider and compare these differing jobs under the headings of people in roles, techniques, programming, and normally also accounting.

The supervisor and manager work through people, and frequently the people-in-roles aspect of their job is emphasized. Jaques (1964), for example, describes the manager as follows:

> An individual occupying a role with managerial authority over subordinates; namely, the authority to veto the appointment of subordinates not acceptable to him, to assign work to subordinates, to decide their performance assessment relative to each other, and to dismiss them from his own command if they are not acceptable to him.

However, such a definition embraces all management, from the first-line supervisor to the managing director. For training it is useful to distinguish between different levels of management, since each level may need a different sort of training.

Following Thurley and Hamblin (1963) we can distinguish between the manager and supervisor, if we see the purpose of management as essentially one of control. These authors state:

> This control can be exercised in two ways: first, by administrative methods, i.e. at a distance; and secondly, by actual 'overseeing', inspection and direction in the area of operations. A 'supervisor' (as distinct from a purely administrative manager) is someone who exercises control by the latter method.

This is a useful idea, and is relevant in manufacturing as well as outside the production sphere. A man in charge of a small shop whose job is to oversee the work of the sales assistants is a supervisor. A head office man controlling a chain of such shops by administrative procedures is a manager.

Hacon (1961) suggests that when an organization has reached a certain stage of growth there are usually three levels of management:

> Firstly, there are those whose main concern is general management, overall direction and policy formation; secondly, those specialist managers who as middle managers serve as the indispensable link between general managers and the third level, the first-line supervisors.

In industry one commonly refers to junior managers, by which are meant those just above first-line supervision and whose control is largely through administrative procedures. Such managers would be categorized with the specialist managers.

Figure 12.1 presents a diagram of supervisory and management levels based on Hacon (1961). Specialist technological management is used in a broad sense, and refers here to 'technologies' such as engineering, plastics, accounting, planning, personnel. It implies the requirement of specialized knowledge in one of the three Glacier (Brown and Jaques) dimensions, people in roles, techniques, programming, or in accounting.

The figure lists characteristics of the different management levels as continuums. The more senior the position, the more is it concerned with the formation of company policy rather than its implementation. Related to this is the greater length of the time-span of discretion at senior positions in the hierarchy—see Jaques (1961). The senior manager functions at the borders of the organization, making decisions that take account of changes in the external environment, where economic, technological, political, and market conditions are often in a state of flux. These changes in the environment usually impinge more on the senior manager, and we will subsequently argue the relevance of this to management training. Similarly the senior position seems to involve knowledge rather than skill, which also has repercussions on training programmes.

The figure immediately suggests that certain types of training problems will normally exist. The supervisor is usually a skilled, technically competent man, promoted from the shop floor. Therefore, in Glacier terms his performance as regards techniques is probably satisfactory on promotion. The immediate need of the newly appointed supervisor is likely to be for training in the people-in-roles and programming aspects of his job.

If supervision is recruited and trained in this way, most super-

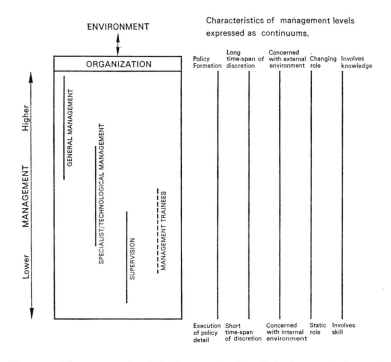

Fig. 12.1 Management levels in the organization, their characteristics, and their relationship to the environment

visors are unlikely to have the ability or technical knowledge to become specialist, technological managers. The problem arises, therefore, of where such managers are to be obtained, and management trainee schemes originate partly as an attempt to provide a source for this level of management.

How should these management trainees be trained for the positions they will fill in specialist management? Should they be prepared through experience which is highly specialized and functional, as when an engineer is immediately taught the techniques and procedures of the production line he will eventually be concerned with? Or alternatively should the trainee be rotated through several departments to provide him with broad and general experience? Should the training be theoretical or practical?

Effectiveness at the level of specialist, technological management will depend largely on competence in one field, such as marketing or engineering. But general managers, who come from this specialist level, require competence over a broad area, and may need to base decisions on information from several fields, such as personnel, engineering, marketing, and accounting.

Answers to these problems of supervisory and management development and training involve policy decisions. Our framework for the analysis of training in the organization, given as Table 8.2, lists such policy decisions as a factor in organizational training. The framework of the table lists the technology of training as its second organizational variable, which is principally what the rest of this chapter will examine with regard to supervisory and management training.

Motivation is the framework's third variable. Managers and supervisors may be motivated at any of the three levels outlined. We would suggest that they need to learn both roles and actions, and for this the motivational process of identification is most relevant.

APPROACHES TO SUPERVISORY TRAINING

In their Industrial Training Service pamphlet on supervisory training, Meade and Greig (1966) provide historical categories for supervisory training. They suggest it has passed through three phases: (1) supervisors are born not made; (2) supervisors can be trained; (3) training must be based on an analysis of the job.

The first view seems a form of the Great Man theory of leadership. As Cooper and McGaugh (1963) put it,

> In general, the 'great man' theory holds that particular individuals are natively endowed with characteristics that cause them to stand out from the many and permit them to guide, direct, and lead the majority. . . . The select few are natively endowed with qualities that make their leadership possible.

Such an over-simple view probably originates in the sort of thinking that led also to faculty psychology. Leadership behaviour, like any other, could be explained in terms of a number of faculties an individual has.

If we see the situation in this way, supervision does not give rise to any training problem. The task becomes that of selection, and we have simply to choose the right man and provide him with appropriate job experience. He is then able to cope with a supervisor's job, not just with one specific job but with any supervisory position. At the management level a similar view has been frequently held. Organizations have dealt with management succession by recruiting young men of the right background, usually with an executive or professional father, and who have been to the 'right' university—though this last does in part imply the need for suitable 'training'. These young men, 'natively endowed with qualities', have been held to be equipped as managers 'to guide, direct, and lead the majority'.

The extreme position of great man theory is now abandoned by most social scientists. Stogdill, in a survey of leadership studies (1948), did find that a leader often differed in a number of ways from an average member of the specific group he led. But Gibb, in a later review of the literature (1954), concluded that no pattern of personality traits had been found to be typical of all or many leaders.

The second view, that supervisors can be trained, does not assume any extreme great man theory. Such training attempts to be comprehensive and all-purpose, and prepares the supervisor for any supervisory job. In this inheres its basic assumption, that one supervisory job is much like another, and so an individual can be trained for any one of them by developing certain common skills.

Such a view partly originates in the work of Mayo and others at Hawthorne, and in the human relations school, referred to in Chapter 1, that emerged from their thinking. The human relations approach emphasizes the importance of informal relationships, of the employees' involvement in the working group, and of their participation in decision-making. With such a system the supervisor becomes an important link in this social network, and needs to be trained for his key-role in developing satisfactory human relationships. The supervisor needs to acquire these social skills common to all supervisory positions.

Such common-skills training can suitably be given to supervisors anywhere, within the firm or outside at the local technical college or on the premises of consultants. We will subsequently outline a typical common-skills programme, but such an approach to supervisory training has been criticized as being partially ineffective. Its shortcomings relate to the fact that its basic assumption is to a large extent invalid.

The basic assumption of the common-skills approach is that supervisory jobs do not differ significantly from one situation to another. But they do. Woodward (1958) provides evidence that supervisory jobs differ in the size and nature of the work group supervised (that is, in people in roles), the extent of the technical content involved in the job (that is, in techniques), and the amount of administration it entails (that is, in programming). Woodward saw these job differences as resulting mainly from differences in the firm's production technology. So, for example, a supervisor in a mass production plant has a very different job from that of a supervisor in an oil refinery.

Thurley and Hamblin (1963) also found that supervisory jobs differed. A supervisor's tasks and activities were determined not only by the type of technology, but were also affected by his own particular approach to his job. It would seem that no one particular type of personality is required for supervision.

Emerging from this, therefore, is the third approach to supervisory training, which suggests that the training needs to be based on an analysis of the specific job. A supervisory position in a particular situation may require a certain type of individual to fill the post; it will definitely require a certain, specific training.

Such a view of the supervisor's job is similar to the times theory which sees leadership as a function of a particular social situation. The leader is the man who satisfies certain needs at a certain *time*. The times theory, say Cooper and McGaugh (1963), 'agrees that humans are not all alike—that there are individual differences, and that the unique characteristics of a given person may at a given time meet the needs of a given group most adequately'.

Supervisory training should be specific to a given supervisor's job, and should be determined by the needs of that supervisor in that job. Training, therefore, should be based in the organization, and largely done in the firm, by the firm.

COMMON-SKILLS SUPERVISORY TRAINING

We will outline a supervisory training course typical of the second phase. This sort of 'common-skills' programme is concerned only with people in roles, and does not train in techniques and programming. The approach, influenced by the human relations school, emphasizes the importance of a satisfying social system for employees at the work-place. The supervisor has some responsibility for integrating the individual in the organization, for maintaining satisfactory personal relationships in the office or factory, and for developing in employees the right attitudes to work. This important responsibility is seen as present in all supervisory positions. Such a human relations supervisory training programme is primarily concerned with teaching the supervisor how to provide employee satisfaction, and to influence individual and group behaviour.

The following is the outline of such a training programme, adapted from Maier (1952, Chapter 2).

A Human Relations Training Programme

Democratic Leadership. The whole idea of different leadership styles would be examined, and the differences in the 'tells, sells, consults, joins' sorts of approaches to supervision would need to be evaluated (Likert, 1961 and 1967). The value of commonly adopting a more democratic approach should be discussed.

Causation in Behaviour. The emphasis here is on teaching supervisors to see behaviour as caused by an interaction of the person and the environment. Poor work or absenteeism is not simply the result of something bad in the employee which needs to be corrected by punishment. Each is the result of some interaction between the employee and his environment which needs to be analysed as a problem, and solved.

Individual Differences among People. People differ; these differences can be measured; they should be considered when we select and place people in jobs; the performance of employees is determined by training, and by their differences in motivation and ability.

Nature of Attitudes. Supervisors should become familiar with 'attitudes' as a way of thinking about the outlook and frames of reference of employees. An attitude is a useful unit for understanding behaviour. Supervisors need to become more aware of how the attitudes and frames of reference of their men frequently differ significantly from those of management. A supervisor might view his people-in-roles function in terms of his attempting to develop more favourable attitudes in his men—to management, to high output, to good time-keeping, etc.

Frustration and its Effect on Behaviour and Attitudes. This is a consideration of a specific, important example of causation in behaviour. Maier suggests that the supervisor should learn the characteristic differences between motivated problem-solving behaviour and frustrated behaviour. The first sort of behaviour is variable and goal-orientated, while the second, according to Maier, is aggressive, regressive, fixated, or resigned.

Morale and Group Structure. Here one might usefully discuss what morale is and its relevance to behaviour at work. The role of the supervisor in developing morale through good supervision and employee-involvement could be stressed. We would need to examine also the importance of relationships in the work group for good morale and satisfactory work performance.

Motivation. The supervisor could consider what motivates the individual. One then considers what incentives in the work situation can motivate the individual—praise, punishment, money, job satisfaction, status, different styles of supervision, group pressures, involvement and participation in decision-making, etc.

Fatigue and Boredom. Rest pauses, informal chats, music, hourly quotas, job enlargement, and job rotation might be considered. It would be suggested that these and similar features of an organization are most usefully considered not as management concessions to the employees' idleness and craving for change, but as rational attempts, based on a knowledge of behaviour, to increase employee output and satisfaction through reducing fatigue and boredom.

Employee Contacts, Interviewing and Counselling. Maier suggests that supervisors need to become more aware of how informal, everyday contacts with employees may be used constructively—to become familiar with their attitudes, to motivate them, etc. This applies also to formal interviews which might occur for some explicit purpose, such as merit rating. Similarly supervisors might learn about simple, supportive counselling for employees who are troublesome or have personal problems.

Common-Skills Training and Effective Job Performance

The principal objection to common-skills training arises from the evidence that the skills which supervisors require are not common; they may differ considerably, particularly from one technology to another. But we have already argued in Chapter 6 the usefulness in personnel selection of the concept of synthetic validity. A variety of different jobs may be analysed into tasks many of which are common to some or all of these jobs. A selection technique known to be predictive of performance on a certain task can be used as part of the selection procedure for all jobs that contain that task. The idea is applicable in supervisory, and other, training situations.

In discussing the third approach to supervisory training we will suggest that the analysis of supervisory jobs in an organization will often reveal many common job elements and tasks. When job analysis identifies common areas in a number of supervisory positions, the common-skills approach seems appropriate as a basis for a training programme—in those areas. This would refer not only to the people-in-roles dimension of the job, which Maier's human relations syllabus attempts to cover, but to techniques and programming also, where they are found to be common to a number of the organization's supervisory positions.

The common-skills approach frequently faces another difficulty, that of helping the supervisor implement back on the job the things he has learnt in training. This is a transfer-of-training problem. The supervisor needs to experience his training as related to his day-to-day job. This may be difficult if the training is given in general terms, which seems a danger with a common-skills approach. It becomes particularly difficult when the training is given outside his department, at the local technical college. This sort of training has frequently been done away from the supervisor's firm.

The supervisor can experience his training as meaningfully related to his job only if it agrees with his day-to-day experience on the job. If, on a course, he is taught a more democratic leadership style, but back on the job his own manager remains authoritarian, the training will achieve very little. As King says (1964), 'for company training to be successful, it must grow out of the primary executive relationship between superior and subordinate'. This is always a problem, but is particularly so when training is not firmly based on the supervisor's own specific situation, of which the manager's attitudes and the norms of the organization are part. The third approach to training provides no simple or ready-made solutions to this problem; it merely ensures the problem is faced.

SUPERVISORY TRAINING BASED ON JOB ANALYSIS

The approach of 'supervisors are born not made' is a child of the great man theory; the common-skills approach derives from the Hawthorne idea of the supervisor as a social engineer. That supervisory training should be based on an analysis of a specific job is related to a form of the times theory of leadership. A department with a certain technology, with a rigid or flexible organization structure, with bureaucratic or loosely defined administrative procedures, employing certain categories of labour, pursuing certain goals, may need specific roles to be carried out by its supervisors. Times theory suggests just that. Anyone, in the right place at the right time, whose personality is compatible with the demands of the role, might come forth and satisfactorily fill a leadership position. 'The particular needs of the group may, of course, be met best at a given time by an individual who possesses particular qualities' (Cooper and McGaugh, 1963).

In the work situation, the supervisor is selected, preferably because he possesses those 'particular qualities', abilities, traits, interests, values, needs, which are compatible with the demands of a specific supervisory position and related role. He will need training in order to cope satisfactorily with the demands of this particular supervisory position.

In the following outline of this third approach to supervisory training we are considerably influenced by the Ministry of Labour publication (Meade and Greig, 1966). Our analysis is, however, structured in terms of Tilley's model (1968), given as Figure 8.1 above. It will become apparent that this analytic approach does not stipulate, as the common-skills approach does, what the content of a supervisory training course should be. It cannot, since the content depends on the specific jobs, which differ. The analytic approach can only outline a procedure for determining the content of a supervisory training course.

Analysis of the Overall System

A supervisor may be inefficient, and dissatisfied in his job, for a number of reasons. He may be in the wrong job, in which case it is a problem of placement, to be solved by guidance and selection. But a particularly important cause of ineffective performance with supervisors, and possibly also among managers, is that of structural or organizational dysfunction.

Organizational Solutions to Supervisory Problems

According to Parsons (1954), 'a process or set of conditions . . . is dysfunctional in that it detracts from the integration, effectiveness etc. of the system'. The foreman is unpleasantly aggressive with his operators, not because he does not know how to supervise; he just has too much work to do and this places some strain on him. The office manager has disciplinary problems; possibly he was never given the necessary authority for his responsibilities (see Jaques's definition of a manager (1964), quoted on p. 288 above). The production superintendent is criticized, by the works manager for failing to meet targets on the standard lines, by Export Sales because he does not always push their special jobs to the front of the queue, by Personnel because he responds to shop-floor disputes too slowly, and by Planning because he is remiss with his paper work. Training will hardly help him.

Such ineffective performance can be seen as caused by different expectations made of the supervisor or superintendent, which compete, conflict, are unclear, and therefore become dysfunctional. This is usefully conceptualized as role strain. A role is what one does in carrying out one's social position. We can think of a role in terms of expectations placed on the position, here the work position of a specific supervisor.

Role strain refers to 'difficulty in conforming to role expectations' (Secord and Backman, 1964). We will outline some of the factors which cause role strain in the social system of an organization or a whole society (see Secord and Backman, 1964, Chapter 15).

1. Expectations may not be clear. The foreman is instructed to take more interest in the men, but is not told what this means in terms of his behaviour.

2. A lack of consensus exists among those who place expectations on the role occupants. According to policy at a certain company supervisory staff are part of management, but lunch in a different room, and are kept at a social distance by many managers.

3. There are conflicting expectations on a role. The foreman feels his operators like to see him as a friend and almost one of them; but management regard him as the 'first line' of management, and definitely on their side.

4. There are competing expectations within a role. Given a job with technical, administrative and personnel duties, the foreman may not be provided with any indication of what his priorities should be.

How then is role strain to be resolved? It is essentially a problem of a malfunctioning organization, and therefore to be solved by modifying the organization's structure.

1. Make expectations clear. This is probably not a training or just a communications problem, but one of getting a policy decision and of then explicitly formulating expectations.

2. Get agreement among the 'expecters'. Again this is partly an organizational task which probably first needs a policy decision. The typical 'personnel procedures and practices' handbook has a function of reducing such role strain. Thus: 'When a chargehand is promoted to foreman he becomes monthly staff and may use the B Lunch Room.'

3. and 4. Resolve the problem of conflicting and competing expectations; this involves two sorts of decisions. First, what is required of the foreman, the expectations of his particular role, need to be determined. Second, the order of importance of these expectations must be decided, so that when he is short of time he knows what are the essentials of his job, and what can be left or at least postponed.

Job Description and Task Analysis

The main purpose of a job description and of a task analysis, for supervisory as for most other training, is to determine WHAT, in terms of knowledge and skill, the supervisor needs to know for a particular supervisory position. Description and analysis help resolve any differences about WHAT the supervisor is supposed to do. Normally we cannot determine whether an ineffective supervisor needs to be trained or whether, in fact, his job and the organization need to be restructured, until the job description and task analysis are complete. Frequently when the problem is really organizational, one of role strain, training is given and achieves very little. The job description serves also to specify its requirements, for purposes of selecting supervisors.

What form should this description and analysis take? The Glacier dimensions are satisfactory for classifying the information, and hardly differ from those proposed by Meade and Greig (1966):

Technical (Glacier's technical)—concerned with designs, products, machines, materials, production methods, etc.

Administrative (Glacier's programming)—planning, scheduling, machine-loading, making out requisitions, completing reports, etc.

Social (Glacier's people in roles)—selecting, overseeing, motivating, disciplining, etc. This area is what the typical human relations programme, such as we outlined on pp. 294-6, attempts to teach.

In completing an analysis and description of a supervisor's job the emphasis, as always, should be on recording behaviour, and on providing an account of what the supervisor is to do. Attempting to record what the supervisor 'is to do' will frequently provide different data which suggest the existence of organizational problems. One set of data is what the supervisor says he does. A second is what he in fact does do. A third is what his manager says he does. The fourth, and possibly most important, is what he really ought to be doing to meet the organization's needs. This last again relates supervisory training to organizational structure.

It is essential, in making the job description and task analysis, that the supervisor's immediate manager be involved since, as we have already suggested, 'for company training to be successful, it must grow out of the primary executive relationship between superior and subordinate' (King, 1964). If the supervisor is taught what is at variance with the way his manager thinks and behaves, the training will achieve very little. If what the manager thinks and does is wrong, he needs training.

Information for the description and analysis is collected by the usual methods; by watching the supervisor, by talking to him, by talking to his immediate manager and to those managers and specialists he comes into contact with, by getting the supervisor to record what he does through the day.

Specification of Knowledge and Skill Requirements

The job analyst will have specified the activities and responsibilities of the supervisor under the three headings of people in roles, techniques, and programming. The statement of activities or duties is similar to that of many other jobs and could be incorporated into a job description card such as is given in Table 1.2 on p. 22. However, a statement of a supervisor's responsibilities would need to be more extended, clearer, and more precise, than that of, say, an operator's job. The supervisor's responsibility for personnel, their safety, discipline, selection, etc., his responsibility for materials, machines, etc., for meeting production schedules, etc., need to be explicitly stated. The activities involved in carrying out these responsibilities have to be described.

From this account of activities and responsibilities, given under the three headings, the analyst can develop a specification of the knowledge and skill requirements of the particular job. Preferably this should be stated in terms of the terminal behaviour required of supervisors.

Determining the Capabilities of Trainees

The analyst has looked at the job of a supervisor or of a number of supervisors in a certain factory. He must now appraise the men in the jobs and the trainee supervisors. This appraisal of the knowledge and skill of existing and trainee supervisors is a continuing process.

We have described what knowledge and skill is required in terms of desired terminal behaviour. So we can appraise a supervisor in terms of his present performance, of what he actually does. As we have argued with selection (see Chapter 7), we might more usefully describe the individual operationally in terms of what he can and cannot do, rather than by a list of vague adjectives or descriptive phrases, such as 'weak on administration', 'has problems with discipline'. We are interested in effective performance, not in how it is achieved. So we appraise an existing or a potential supervisor in terms of his actual performance, against previously established criteria of effective job performance.

We have suggested in Chapters 1 and 8 that 'difficulty' or 'what one can't do' are key concepts in job analysis. So a first stage in appraising and identifying the training needs of a supervisor or group of supervisors is to agree with them on what areas of their jobs cause them most difficulty.

Meade and Greig (1966) suggest that such training needs to be expressed in terms of objectives for supervisors. Having determined by a sort of 'critical incidents' approach the specific shortcomings and weaknesses of an individual, we can convert them into positive goals and objectives for him to achieve.

Statement of Training Requirements
From the specified requirements of the particular supervisory job we subtract our appraisal of what the supervisor already knows. This gives a statement of training requirements. If we have in the way suggested examined weaknesses and converted them to targets, then the first general statement of requirements might be in a form as follows: (1) to reduce absenteeism by 5 per cent over the next six months (people in roles); (2) to reduce by 10 per cent scrap produced on capstans over the next six months, by better machine setting (techniques); (3) to reduce by better planning and machine-loading the time machines are not used by 5 per cent, over the next six months (programming).

Development of Appropriate Training Methods
From the statement of training requirements three different sorts of training courses might be developed:

1. Common training for existing supervisors with the same training needs. Where such identical training needs exist, some form of common-skills training seems possible.

2. Similarly, common training for potential supervisors. Here again a training programme may adopt a common skills approach.

3. Individual training for a particular supervisor with a specific training need.

Here, concerned with the HOW of supervisory training, it is necessary to decide which of the three channels of company training (King, 1964) is to be used. King's Channel A refers to training on the job, the primary learning process, whereby the supervisor learns formally and informally in the interaction with his own manager. At least the manager may now train his subordinate supervisors from the vantage point of a statement of their training requirements, given in terms of positive objectives. In the same way formal internal courses, King's Channel B, can be based on such a statement of specific training requirements.

When this precisely defined training need cannot be met in the organization, external courses, King's Channel C, will be used. They will obviously tend to be more useful where common training is needed for several supervisors with similar training needs. However, external training still needs to be seen in terms of the original statement of training requirements for a supervisor or several supervisors. In this way external training can be related to training inside the firm and to the work of the individual supervisor, and so attempt to overcome the difficulty of transferring the learning from the outside situation to the actual on-the-job situation.

Next, in order to establish a specific training procedure, we must determine what sort of conditions and training situations are necessary for learning to occur. We refer here to decisions concerning practice, knowledge of results, understanding, and similar factors we have discussed in Chapter 10.

A final consideration would be of techniques and training methods to be adopted, such as lecture, case study, seminar, etc. We will consider these in the final section of the chapter, since most methods are relevant both to supervisory and management training and development.

Training Course Evaluation

Regardless of the channels through which training is done, it has to be evaluated. If, as Meade and Greig (1966) suggest, supervisory training has been based (1) on a specification of the actual behaviour required of a supervisor, in terms of positive objectives to be achieved, and (2) on an appraisal of the supervisor's present job performance, in terms of those same objectives, then we already have a basis for evaluating the effectiveness of the training,

A specific requirement of training for supervisor Smith has been to enable him to 'reduce absenteeism by 5 per cent over the next six months'. Has he done so?

MANAGEMENT TRAINING AND DEVELOPMENT

Introduction

Organizations exist in an environment. There are many aspects of this environment: there is the economic situation, the state of the market, the climate of industrial relations, government policies, technological developments, etc. In our discussion of Figure 1 of this chapter we suggested that the more senior the manager, the nearer he is to the environment external to the organization. This concept of nearness to the environment or to the boundary of the organization is important. The environment in its economic, technological, and other aspects, is normally a changing one. It is difficult to predict, and the manager's control over it is limited.

We are suggesting it may be useful to see the manager's job as made up of two roles, (1) the within-the-organization, inward-looking role, and (2) the at-the-border of the organization, looking-out-at-the-environment role. The first tends to be static, and the second tends to be dynamic and changing.

Training for Role 1

To the extent that Role 1 is static, everything we have said about supervisory training applies. Training the manager for Role 1 must be based on an analysis of what he actually does in this part of his job, on an appraisal of the manager's performance, and on the training requirements stated as specific objectives. This is essentially training, and we classify it as management training.

Here, as with supervisors, the importance of appropriate organizational structures needs to be stressed. The ineffective performance of a manager functioning within the firm, in his more static role, may often be as much an organizational problem, which we have discussed as role strain, as a training one.

Role 2

But the dynamic aspect of the manager's job presents a different problem. The well-being of the organization depends on how well the manager performs Role 2. It relates first to how effectively the manager can predict or control the external, changing environment. It relates secondly to how well the manager can adapt the organization to meet the demands of the changing environment. Top management is immediately and directly concerned with the external environment. Middle, technological management's experience of the environment is only at second-hand since at this level the effects of outside change have been cushioned by policy decisions. Middle management is immediately concerned only with the shifting 'environment' of the organization above, changing to cope with changes in the environment.

The supervisor is obviously remote from the environment as regards the techniques and programming areas of his job. He seems very close to the environment in his people-in-roles, personnel aspect, since he directly supervises the men on the shop floor, who in their attitudes, values, frames of reference, embody the external environment, particularly that of industrial relations. But the supervisor, though physically close to the men, is in reality remote from the industrial relations environment they represent, since he normally has no part in policy or in many decisions that affect them. These are the responsibility of more senior management. The foreman simply follows laid-down procedures with regard to the men. Hence situations arise, which to the outsider may seem absurd, where an executive as senior as a personnel director is involved in, say, the discharge of an operator for consistently going to lunch too early or for refusing to do certain types of work.

The manager then in his Role 2 has to predict or control the behaviour of the environment, and must adapt the organization to meet its changing demands. In other words, the manager has to be able to cope with change, change which cannot be predicted in detail. If it is impossible to foresee change in any detail, we cannot wholly deal with it by organizational means; we cannot put together an organization that can cope with any possible change in the environment. Any suggestion that this is possible seems to arise fallaciously from talking of organizations as if they were living, adaptive organisms, and then believing they really are.

Management Development
The problem can only be solved by having at the borders of the organization individuals capable of coping with this changing

environment in an unpredictable future. We can only deal with it through management development—the preparation of individuals to cope with change.

In other words the problem of preparation for handling change seems amenable only to a psychological solution, not to a sociological or structural one. We might be able to prepare, develop, and educate the individual so that he can cope with most of the unknown and unforeseeable. We cannot structure organizations so that they can cope with most kinds of problems of adaptation.

However, we need to structure organizations so that management roles are loosely enough defined to enable the manager to behave flexibly when necessary. And this is related to an organization's aims, since the task of adapting to a changing environment may be made easier if an organization's goals are not fixed and may be modified. The commercial firm is always restricted by having to achieve one particular goal, that of making a profit, if it is to survive.

The preparation of a manager for his Role 2 would be different from the sort of training we have discussed, since there is no specific job analysis to write or terminal behaviour to specify. So training for Role 2, which we will refer to as management development, seems more usefully conceived of as an educational process. It would be foolhardy to attempt a definition of education, but we are referring here to a process of individual, personal growth. This view of management education or development implies a Maslow-type concept of self-actualization, which is rather different from thinking in terms of a specification of job roles and a moulding of individuals to fit them.

Training and Development
We distinguish then between training and developing the manager. Training seems characterized by short-term objectives, and by objectives and goals that can be specified, possibly in terms of required behaviour. The content and syllabus of training is simple (compared with that of education), and consists of behaviour skills and knowledge. Among the more obvious features of management development which distinguish it from what we mean by training, are its long-term objectives, and the lack of specificity of these goals and objectives. We may regard it as a preparation to cope with change, but cannot specify this in terms of the actual be-

haviour required. Its content is complex, and is orientated to the acquisition of cognitive skills in conceptualization and analysis.

The education and development of the individual impinges on the core of personality more than does training. In schools, universities, polytechnics, industrial and commercial organizations, education and development may affect not only the individual's actions and roles, but his self. This is to suggest, in terms of Table 8.2, that management development will sometimes function at the level of the self system.

This makes it all the more important to stress that influence is in either direction. If the manager were selected and trained to fill an already existing role, and to assimilate completely the attitudes and approach of the firm, then innovation, new ideas and improvements, originating as they must from individuals, could not occur. Management development cannot be about training individuals to fit present organizational positions and structures. It must be concerned with the personal development of individuals so that, when necessary, they can change and improve those positions, structures, and organizations. Influence between the individual and the organization needs to be a two-way process. Management development attempts to educate individuals capable of influencing the organization.

We have already suggested that ineffective management behaviour in Role 1 is essentially a task of management training, and all that was said of supervisory training applies. A procedure such as that outlined in the Tilley model (1968) may be fruitfully adopted. We will now briefly consider management development for Role 2 in terms of what, how, and reporting.

First, as a prerequisite we must recruit and select people who are educated and bring with them a capacity to cope with change, because in an organization it is difficult, and expensive, to start right from the beginning. But the process is continuous, and how do we realistically continue it in the firm?

There is a sense in which the stuff and content of education, WHAT is taught, are irrelevant. We can develop an individual and teach him to think clearly and critically through studying a play of Shakespeare, the second law of thermodynamics, or the techniques of estimating. Provided the content is reasonably complex, the way it is taught determines how educative and developing the experience is for the learner. A teacher may examine the causes of the industrial revolution in a way that develops the student's capacity for analysis and criticism; alternatively he may give the student a list of ten causes and tell him to remember them.

What we are suggesting is that we can have management education, the development of individuals, occurring in the process of imparting management training. This will happen only if the training is given in a sufficiently critical and analytical way. In Table 12.1 are listed under the Glacier headings a number of skills and areas of knowledge a manager may need to acquire. The mere acquisition of them could be done as a training process. But any one of them could also be used to provide an educative experience. We might take 'work measurement', evaluate it as a technique, critically discuss its applications, attempt to see what

TABLE 12.1 *Examples of skills and areas of knowledge relevant to management training and development* (*Glacier headings*)

People in Roles	Techniques	Programming	Accounting
leadership	method study	work measurement	costing
organizations	inspection	estimating	budgetary
interviewing	metal fatigue	production planning	control
methods of payment	design	operational research	

ideas about human behaviour are behind it, investigate these ideas, see if they relate to any ideology, etc. Similarly any one of the topics, given as examples in Table 12.1, might be taught in an educative and individually extending and developing way. It seems more realistic for management development to occur while managers are acquiring knowledge and skills relevant to their work, than through studying Hamlet.

In Table 12.1, therefore, are examples of topics that might constitute part of the WHAT of management development. We are suggesting that HOW they are taught, critically, analytically, in depth, is crucial to management development. Other than through examination, with all its limitations, there seems at present no obvious approach to short-term reporting and evaluation of management education and development.

METHODS

We will first provide an account of a number of methods used in supervisory and management training and development. These will be the lecture, seminar, case study, project, T-group, and role-playing. How do such techniques work? It is ironic that a teaching technique, such as a lecture, widely adopted by a theoretically orientated profession, has rarely been analysed in terms of a theoretical explanation of why it succeeds—or fails. Presumably any explanation of why a teaching or training technique works is related to a theory about how people learn. We will subsequently discuss briefly these six teaching methods in terms of essential requirements of learning from a connectionist and a cognitive viewpoint.

Lecture

Someone knowledgeable rises and speaks; the audience listen and absorb what he says. An alternative view suggests that information is transmitted from the notes of the lecturer to those of the listeners, without ever passing through the minds of either. Assuming the first is true, then one can say the lecture does transmit a lot of information in a short time. Though for many reading is a faster process, and teaches more than a lecture in an equivalent amount of time, a skilled teacher can over a series of lectures raise or lower the intellectual pitch to suit the level of his audience, which a book cannot do. The lecture is, of course, economic in that it enables one man to teach or train a large number at the same time.

The lecture does concentrate largely on one sense, hearing, since the audience only has to listen, though this can be supplemented by visual aids and handouts. In the lecture the audience are overtly passive which may reduce their receptivity, and may in particular provide difficulty for adults. If, as Guthrie suggests, what you do is what you learn, the lecture is unlikely to be useful for training in behaviour skills. It is more likely to be useful for transmitting abstract knowledge, though even here the response formally required of the listener is not understanding but note-taking.

Seminar

We refer under this heading to seminars, tutorials, or *any form of discussion group*. Characteristically the trainer remains a central figure. In some situations he is perceived as being the source of all knowledge, while the student must learn. In others the student is seen as having a contribution to make, and this last seems a more realistic position in the teaching and training of adults. In a discussion of, say, leadership or inspection methods with managers, inevitably some will have experience or insight which the trainer lacks.

Students may talk and participate actively, so they have the motivation that arises from participation and involvement. Seminars and discussion groups seem particularly suited to managers and supervisors since they spend much of their work time talking to other people. The student has no control in the lecture over what the teaching is about. In a seminar students can exert influence, and can sometimes steer discussion in the direction of their own interests and experienced needs, though this does depend on the trainer's approach.

Some research (Lewin, 1958) suggests that attitudes are more likely to change in the group situation of the seminar, than in that of the lecture. The seminar remains like the lecture a matter of, in Hamlet's phrase, 'Words, words, words', and in the same way seems useful for transmitting information and knowledge. But in the interplay of discussion it is possible for the participants to develop also some intellectual diagnostic skill.

Case Study
A problem of some sort, usually written into documents, is presented to students. It may, for example, be an industrial relations or marketing problem, and the documents provide an account of the background to the situation, relevant facts and figures, and possibly comments by the individuals mainly concerned. Alloys Ltd., which begins the final chapter of this book, is an example of a case study.

In the case study it is the problem rather than the trainer which is the source of learning. The problem creates a structure within which learning may occur through participation in discussion and analysis. To suggest the problem is the sole source of learning assumes that the trainer adopts a completely non-directive role, which is hardly ever the case. A leader in a case study will often feel that not to intervene and indicate more fruitful lines of enquiry is only to waste time. The lecture, seminar, and case study, differ only in degree on the extent to which the trainer directs and controls the situation.

The starting-point of the case study, a representation of a real-life situation, and its problem bias, does motivate highly certain trainees, such as managers and vocationally orientated students. It usually makes the trainee aware that there is normally more than one possible solution to most problems. The case study teaches skill rather than knowledge; it seems essentially suited to developing in trainees intellectual skills of analysis and diagnosis.

Project

In a project a student investigates a problem which is usually, though not always, of his own choosing. We see it as different from a case study in its requirement of some practical work by him. A case study remains at the level of 'words, words, words', in that apart from discussion it only needs a report to be written, and possibly some data checked or obtained from the literature. The project normally involves the student in doing something. It may, for example, involve research to obtain certain data at the laboratory bench, or interviewing for a study of a firm's high labour turnover. Projects may be done on an individual or group basis.

The project seems to provide the same sort of learning situation as the case study. Both make the trainee participate actively in solving real or realistic problems, but with the project participation involves also action and practical work.

The trainer may use the project in two different ways. He can emphasize the final product, and get the trainee to produce a good piece of work which might almost serve as a management report. Alternatively he may see the project as an educational process, and have the trainee learn by exploring many ideas and techniques. With this approach the trainee will probably make mistakes, produce a report he could hardly hand to his senior manager, but may benefit by a stimulating and creative learning experience.

In a project, as with a case study, the attempt of the trainee himself to solve a problem provides the direct and immediate source of learning. The project is also like the case study in being highly motivating, in enabling the trainee to see alternative approaches to a problem, and it would seem to develop the same sort of intellectual skills.

T-Groups

The origins of T-groups are in the work and theory of group social psychology, and T-group training requires a book rather than a few paragraphs (see Schein and Bennis, 1965).

Normally they are groups of up to a dozen people who meet frequently. On a training course they might meet for two or three hours a day over a period of a fortnight. Their main purpose is to study their own behaviour, and through doing so to sensitize the participants to the effects of their behaviour on others. Thus Robert Burns prayed:

> O wad some Pow'r the giftie gie us
> To see oursels as others see us!

During the course of the sessions responsibility, say, for what to discuss, moves from the trainer to the members of the group. Usually discussion turns not on any original subject matter but on personal feelings and reactions to others in the group. This frank revealing of feelings, and the support, understanding, insights, received from others, can facilitate self-awareness and self-development. The individual receives feedback about his effect on others in an atmosphere of confidence and support. It is the psychoanalytic situation writ small, since the presence of more than just the analyst and client means the experience is usually less intense and deep than that of analysis.

In providing the individual with personal insight, and by sensitizing him to the effects of his own behaviour on others, T-groups can develop a social competence and an openness to influence from others which seems a requirement in most management roles. However, in discussing supervisory training we suggested that when the training that is given does not accord with the spirit or accepted practices of the organization, there is a problem. Similarly, as Furlong (1969) suggests, 'a manager will only exhibit sustained behavioural change after a T-group if the organization encourages and places value on that behaviour'. Furlong points out that T-groups attempt to develop many responses, attitudes, values, which are alien to the sort of behaviour required by the procedures and structures of many organizations. When this is the case the T-group is unlikely to win out; back in the firm the individual will change his behaviour to conform to what it expects of him—or leave.

Role-Playing

Role-playing for training resembles the psycho-drama used as a form of therapy in mental health. Trainees act hypothetical situations, in assigned roles, improvising their behaviour. Even for training there are two sorts of role-playing, the first being some form of skill practice. Acting as a chairman in a group discussion might simply provide useful experience in the chairing of meetings. Similarly two men might act the parts of an operator and his foreman so that the second might practise under supervision how to reprimand in a helpful and encouraging way.

The second sort of role-playing is rather different. Here the emphasis is on acting a realistic situation, possibly where a problem or conflict exists, primarily to provide the participants with insight. A typical 'drama' might involve a personnel officer, a foreman, an operator the foreman wishes to discharge, and the man's shop steward. In taking one of these parts an individual may become more sensitive to a viewpoint which previously was alien to him. Insight can sometimes be increased by having an individual act a role which normally would be alien to him. In the example just given a real-life foreman might take the part of the operator who is to be discharged, and a real personnel officer might act the shop steward.

The role-play attempts directly to develop insight, and in doing this to develop indirectly the individual's skill in analysing situations. The role-play entails not just discussion but action also, usually in fact acting on a decision. It may, therefore, provide practice not only in the analysis which leads to decision-making, but in the decision-making itself.

A Connectionist Evaluation of Methods

We will briefly discuss these training and development methods in terms of Thyne's four requirements of learning, cue, force, prompt, and reinforcement (Thyne, 1966), which we outlined in Chapter 9.

A trainer might lecture on styles of supervision. A lecture can provide cues in that the speaker is able to convey to his audience what are the significant features which characterize, say, democratic supervision. Force, the capacity to elicit a response, seems present in the lecture only in the sense that the trainee can be made to be present, to look as if he were listening, and possibly to take notes. However, in this situation the trainee can see the characterizing features of the cue, of democratic supervision, and understand. Clearly a lecture can provide prompts which determine that the response, understanding, is correct. But such prompts would need to take a standardized form, such as visual aids, since the trainee's response is not overt (unless he looks puzzled) and so the lecturer cannot modify his prompts according to the trainee's present progress. Similarly the lecture is unable to provide suitable reinforcement, Thyne's fourth requirement for learning. What needs to be reinforced is the understanding and comprehension. But the lecturer cannot see and so reinforce these; he can only see the note-taking. Even if there were something appropriate to reinforce, the lecturer does not have the machinery for providing reinforcement.

The seminar would seem to score better than the lecture on a number of these counts. In a seminar on, say, styles of supervision the trainer is able to supply the cue, by indicating the characterizing features of democratic supervision. Force also is possible in a seminar since the trainer can ask the students to comment or give an opinion. The trainer may also prompt, by suggesting, giving information, or structuring questions, in such a way that the right answer is forthcoming. Since the trainee's understanding, or lack of it, is apparent in his verbal responses, the trainer can modify and adapt his prompts according to the progress of the trainee. With praise or simply by stating that what a trainee says is right, the trainer can provide reinforcement.

The cue is not provided in the case study, since its purpose is for trainees to discover for themselves the relevant cue. Faced with an account of high labour turnover, an overworked foreman, and industrial conflict at Firm XYZ, students may learn that bad organization can be seen as the cause of Firm XYZ's situation; that is the cue. A case study has force in that, as we have suggested, it causes trainees to become involved, and to make some response. The individual receives prompts in the direction of right responses and correct solutions from the trainer, from the structure of the case study material, and from other trainees participating in the exercise. Reinforcement is provided by the trainee obtaining what he experiences as a good solution. This is supplemented by the trainer's comments on the proposed solution, usually given at the end of a case study exercise.

The project, like the case study, has the identification of cue as its objective. A student examines high labour turnover at a firm to find its cause, or attempts to determine the best method of training older workers in an assembly task. The force, apart from external constraints, is that of interest and involvement in a task the trainee may have chosen for himself, which causes him to work in some way on the project. Prompts are provided by the project supervisor and by relevant literature. Particularly important are prompts emanating from success or failure. For example, if one method of training older workers gives better results than another, this serves as a prompt to the right sort of response and solution. Success would provide a reinforcement, as do the trainer's comments. It is the trainee's own responses, his own ideas and contributions, not just his understanding of someone else's, that are being reinforced. This is important.

It seems useful with T-groups to see cues in terms of personal behaviour. The trainee must become aware of characterizing features of certain categories of his own behaviour, particularly with reference to the effect they have on other people. The force to respond in a T-group arises from the personal and emotional involvement it generates. The prompts are essentially provided by other participants' reactions and comments on one's own behaviour. Positive reinforcement in a T-group seems long-term; because one has learnt the cues it is possible to function better and more satisfyingly in social relationships, and this is reinforcing. However, learning in a T-group can be hindered or prevented by the reinforcement in the short-term of not learning. If a participant rejects the comments and statements made about his behaviour, he is rewarded by his being able to maintain his old ideas about himself, which at least provided a *modus operandi*.

We will confine our discussion of role-playing to that of the insight-providing, not the skill-practice type. Again it is the discovery of the cue which is the objective of the method, cues being viewpoints of particular roles. The extent to which the role-playing has force and can elicit response from the participants will vary, and depends on their personalities, on how interesting the role-play material is, and on the skill of the trainer. The prompts towards the right insights and viewpoints will also come from the trainer, the case material, and from other participants. Their success will depend in part on the extent to which these and other factors help the individual identify with his role. Reinforcement is given by the trainer, by other participants, by the satisfaction provided by one's skill in interplay, by the satisfaction of acquiring insight into the viewpoint of a role.

A Cognitive Evaluation of Methods

Elaborating on cognitive explanations we have suggested seven requirements if effective learning is to occur in management and supervisory training. They are:

1. Training must take account of the trainee's goals, both short-term and long-term.
2. The trainee must learn schemes in training.
3. The trainee must acquire skill in cognitively manipulating such schemes.
4. The trainee must acquire a readiness to adopt alternative schemes.
5. The trainee must learn strategies to implement schemes.
6. The trainee must acquire skill with strategies for implementing schemes.
7. The trainee must develop a capacity to construct schemes and strategies.

In discussing techniques we will assume a trainee always has long-term goals, related to what he sees as the reason for his training. Here we will concern ourselves only with short-term goals.

A lecture would seem to provide short-term goals only if it treats the subject in the way the trainee sees as relating to his needs. A retail supervisor, deeply interested in selling techniques, might hear a lecture on customer motivation and fail to relate it to what he wants from training, which is more effective approaches to customers. A lecture can teach schemes, but is unable to provide the opportunity for practice in cognitively manipulating such schemes. Similarly a lecture cannot develop in trainees any personality characteristics that make them more ready to adopt alternative schemes. A lecture might develop cognitive skill with strategy but not the behaviour skill. It seems unlikely that the lecture fosters any ability to construct new schemes and strategies. Its strength is essentially in conveying information.

The seminar may give a student an opportunity to turn discussion to his own interests, and through social interaction and influence may involve him in the interests of others. To this extent it can provide a trainee with goals. The seminar can teach schemes; it enables the trainee to manipulate cognitively such schemes. The social nature of the seminar may affect this readiness for alternative approaches, but probably only peripherally. The seminar can teach strategies, can foster skill in handling their cognitive elements but obviously not their behavioural aspects. It seems likely that the cut and thrust of seminar discussion can develop an ability in the trainee to develop schemes and strategies for himself.

The case study does seem able to provide the trainee with an immediate goal, that of achieving a satisfactory analysis and solution. To do so the trainee has to learn schemes, which he must appropriately manipulate and employ for the analysis and solution of the problem. As with the seminar, the involvement and social nature of the case-study method might peripherally affect the personality, and bring on greater readiness to adopt alternative schemes. Whether trainees learn strategies to implement skills depends on whether the action or 'What needs to be done' aspect of the case study is dealt with. A trainer can certainly use such studies for examining action and appropriate strategies, though often case studies are used only for an analysis of a situation and for discussing its general implications. In the same way a study can provide opportunity for acquiring cognitive skill with strategies, not behaviour skills. To the extent that the case study extends the individual intellectually in discussing real-life problems, it should develop in him the ability to construct new schemes and strategies.

Since the basis of a project usually is a problem, often of the student's choosing, it does immediately provide the trainee with a short-term, limited objective. He has the goal of finding a solution. In attempting to do this, he will learn of schemes, through reading, and through discussing the problem with his project supervisor, other students, and if the problem is from life, with those actually involved. The trainee acquires skill in manipulating schemes as he actively seeks solutions. A project develops a willingness to try alternatives only to the extent to which it gives the student confidence. Through a project he will learn of strategies, but only if the project is practical and calls for action will it develop skill with such strategies. Finally, the project should help the trainee to cope with new problems, since this is in effect what he does in the project.

The T-group, like psychoanalysis, seems not to provide the trainee immediately with a short-term goal he can experience. If he remains with a group long enough and becomes involved, goals may emerge. In the T-group the trainee learns nothing of schemes explicitly, nor does he acquire skill in cognitively manipulating schemes. It is on the fourth requirement of learning that the T-group scores since it is largely concerned with the self-development of the individual. Growth in self-awareness and in personal confidence would seem likely to foster flexibility and a readiness to try alternative ways of looking at problems. The trainee will learn nothing of alternative strategies in T-groups, such as how to reduce labour turnover. But to the extent to which it develops a social competence the T-group develops skill in the behaviour that might be needed to implement a strategy, so that the manager, for example, knows better how to talk and relate to supervisors and men in his attempt to reduce staff turnover. Finally the T-group is unlikely to develop any capacity to construct new schemes and strategies; its strength is essentially in developing in the individual a less defensive attitude and an openness to anything new.

A role-play of an industrial or commercial situation, to find the causes of a dispute or explanations of why customers buy, does present the manager and supervisor with immediate goals. Through the insight such role-play gives, the trainees do learn schemes, and in acting roles they may become more adept in dealing with such ideas. It is difficult to know whether trainees become more ready to adopt alternative schemes through role-playing. It seems unlikely they would learn new strategies, but they do have practice in any new behaviour that has to be acquired as part of a strategy. There is no reason why role-playing should in itself develop any ability to construct new schemes and strategies.

REFERENCES

Brown, W. and Jaques, E. (1965), 'Management Teaching', in *Glacier Project Papers*, Heinemann.

Cooper, J. B. and McGaugh, J. L. (1963), *Integrating Principles of Social Psychology*, Schenkman.

Furlong, V. A. (1969), 'T-Groups for Management Development', unpublished B.A. Business Studies (C.N.A.A.) degree project, Enfield College of Technology.

Gibb, C. A. (1954), 'Leadership', in *Handbook of Social Psychology*, ed. G. Lindzey, vol. 2, Addison-Wesley.

Hacon, R. J. (1961), *Management Training: Aims and Methods*, English Universities Press.

Jaques, E. (1961), *Equitable Payment*, Heinemann.

Jaques, E. (1964), *Time-Span Handbook*, Heinemann.

King, D. (1964), *Training within the Organisation*, Tavistock.

Lewin, K. (1958), 'Group decision and social change', in *Readings in Social Psychology*, ed. E. E. Maccoby, T. M. Newcomb, and E. L. Hartley, Holt, Rinehart & Winston.

Likert, R. (1961), *New Patterns of Management*, McGraw-Hill.

Likert, R. (1967), *The Human Organization*, McGraw-Hill.

Maier, N.R.F. (1952), *Principles of Human Relations*, Wiley.

Meade, J. P. de C. and Greig, F. W. (1966), *Supervisory Training*, Ministry of Labour Central Training Council, H.M.S.O.

Parsons, T. (1954), *Essays in Sociological Theory*, Free Press.

Schein, E. H. and Bennis, W. G. (1965), *Personal and Organizational Change through Group Methods*, Wiley.

Secord, P. F. and Backman, C. W. (1964), *Social Psychology*, McGraw-Hill.

Stogdill, R. M. (1948), 'Personal factors associated with leadership: a survey of the literature', *J. of Psychol.*, 25.

Thurley, K. E. and Hamblin, A. C. (1963), *The Supervisor and his Job*, Department of Scientific and Industrial Research, H.M.S.O.

Tilley, K. (1968), 'A technology of training', in *Industrial Society*, ed. D. Pym, Penguin.

Woodward, J. (1958), *Management and Technology*, Department of Scientific and Industrial Research, H.M.S.O.

CHAPTER 13

Training in Skills

Overview

The chapter divides into three sections, and in the first, the introduction, we consider what skill is, and suggest that for training we can usefully analyse skill in typically connectionist terms. In the second and third sections we introduce the approaches of skills analysis and mathematics.

INTRODUCTION

In industry, as in everyday activities, skill is everywhere. Training in skill is relevant to a wide variety of occupations with some manual content. Though the craftsman's job looks very different from the operator's, both contain tasks that involve some level of skill. The job of the craftsman, however, contains a greater variety of tasks, and these have a higher skill content than those in the operator's job. The craftsman's work also entails far more knowledge.

What is skill? We can recognize skill in its most outstanding forms, as in the play of a brilliant sportsman. But it is present also in the performance of a machinist and an assembler, as becomes obvious if we compare the performance of a trainee with that of an experienced worker. Such a comparison might suggest a view of skill similar to Guthrie's (1952): 'Skill consists in the ability to bring about some end result with maximum certainty, and minimum outlay of energy and time.' Similarly King (1960) characterizes industrial skill as follows: 'Industrial skill is characterized by the ability to perceive fine variations in the requirements of the task, and by the ability to distinguish and provide the responses which are appropriate to these requirements at any given moment.' Examining these definitions we can see that skill might be described in terms of an individual's response to a stimulus.

Skill involves a perceptual sensitivity to a stimulus, and appropriateness, timing, and economy in the response. In other words, a skill could be analysed in terms of the specific stimuli and relevant responses involved, and such a breakdown might provide the basis for training.

Frequently training has not been based on any such analysis. For example, many young people entering factory work have learnt their jobs through the exposure or sitting-by-Nellie method: 'the woman who had been made responsible for teaching her was known as Nellie to her fellow-workers' (Earle, 1931). The girl watched Nellie do the whole job, tried herself, slowly at first, and then speeded up.

In Chapter 8 we suggested that training in the organization can usefully be thought of at three levels. In skill training we are primarily concerned with the acquisition of actions; this is the case regardless of whether the motivation is that of compliance, identification, or internalization. What techniques and methods are there for the acquisition of these actions or perceptual-motor skills? In this chapter we will introduce approaches adopted by two major writers in this field, W. Douglas Seymour and Thomas F. Gilbert. In terms of the headings in Tilley's model (see p. 213 above) we are concerned here with investigating two approaches to job description, task analysis, specification of knowledge and skill requirements, statement of training requirements, and the development of appropriate training methods.

Skill Training and the Connectionist Tradition
If, as suggested, we see a skill in terms of connections between various stimuli and responses, then a different approach to skills training emerges. Such an approach makes the reductionist assumption, that the total skill is no more than a sum of its constituent s–r bonds. This approach characteristically breaks down the skilled performance into sections. The trainee attempts to learn not the whole task, as did the girl who watched Nellie, but sections of it. He learns and practises not wholes but parts in isolation, practising until he reaches some previously determined target time. These parts need to be joined into the total behaviour that is the skill. This is done by having the trainee practise these parts, learnt in isolation, together, first in twos, then in threes, etc.

Such an approach to skill training is in the connectionist

tradition, since learning is seen as an acquisition of habits, responses, s–r bonds. The operator learns discrete habits or s–r connections which become linked in some sort of chain of muscular responses, set off by certain stimuli, and which constitutes the total skill. Such a view does not concern itself with cognitions, cognitive maps, or other central processes, but primarily with the operator's perceptions and responses. This approach to training can be analysed in terms of Thyne's (1966) typically connectionist cue, force, prompt, and reinforcement model outlined in Chapter 9.

The parts-method approach, with its underlying reductionism, has been shown to be highly effective for training in perceptual-motor skills. This possibly suggests that connectionist theory is more relevant than cognitive to the non-symbolic learning involved in skill acquisition. A cognitive explanation may provide a better account of the learning of symbolic content in the acquisition of knowledge.

A similar distinction emerges in hierarchical group factor theory. Referring to the k:m major group factor, Vernon (1961) says: 'It would appear to be not so much a positive practical ability as an aggregate of all non-symbolic capacities. . . .' It is possible that k:m plays an important part in skill acquisition, and this process of non-symbolic learning is usefully described in connectionist terms. Similarly v:ed may have an essential role in the learning of knowledge, and cognitive theory be of more relevance to acquisition of symbolic material such as number and language. Interestingly it was Skinner's attempt to explain the acquisition of language that produced one of the most significantly damning attacks on the connectionist position (Chomsky, 1959). Cognitive explanations abound with concepts such as 'insight', 'understanding', which seem more appropriate to the essentially meaningful content of knowledge, as when we learn English or about gear-ratios. With a skill, such as in assembling a relay, we learn a direct experience and apprehension, not anything that is cognitively meaningful. We learn perceptions and movements.

SKILLS ANALYSIS

Skills analysis has evolved out of the parts method of training. The following brief account is adapted from sections of Seymour's two main texts (1954, 1966). Seymour (1954) outlines four stages in the skills analysis approach, which are:

1. 'An analysis is made to determine the skills used by experienced operators on the job.' The job analyst breaks down the total skilled performance into parts, normally stating for each part how long it takes an experienced operator to complete it.

2. Any parts of the total skilled task which are unusual or particularly difficult are noted. Special training exercises are developed to enable the trainee to master these more difficult sections.

3. A trainee practises these special exercises. He then practises individual parts of the total task, until he can do each at the speed of an experienced operator. He finally starts practising successive sections together, two at a time, three at a time, etc., until he is practising the whole task at speed. The method has become one of progressive parts, as indicated in Table 13.1 from Seymour (1954).

TABLE 13.1 *Arrangement for four-part practice under progressive part method of training* (from Seymour, 1954)

	Singles	Pairs	Threes	Four
A				
B				
C				
D				

4. The trainee now practises the whole task, attempting to achieve an acceptable quality of work at target time once, then twice, then for a whole hour, for two hours, for a morning, a day, etc.

The first stage, the actual analysis of the skill, is particularly difficult. It is necessary to determine what the experienced operator does and how he does it, in terms of the stimuli he perceives and the responses he makes to those stimuli. A process chart would normally be used here, detailing not only, say, the relevant hand movements but also the activity of the senses involved, vision usually being most important.

Seymour (1966) points out it is necessary also to determine what diagnostic skills are involved, as in recognizing something wrong with a machine's performance and taking appropriate action. Information and knowledge are normally involved here.

And so a skills analysis, using a process chart, and adopting the sorts of headings suggested by Seymour, might be as Table 13.2.

Seymour (1966) suggests that the completed analysis of the skill needs to be examined carefully. The examination may reveal unusual or difficult movements and responses involved in some element of the skilled performance. It may reveal unusual or difficult sense discrimination required in some part of the skill. We are here at the second of the four stages Seymour outlines for skills analysis. If any particularly difficult response or sense discrimination is entailed, then special training exercises are developed, which the trainees practise (the third stage). This examination of the analysis also enables the trainer to break down the total task into parts for practice purposes. The breakdown into parts provides the basis for the rest of the practice in the third stage.

Seymour's second stage is related to Flanagan's concept of 'critical incidents' and to Rodger's differentiating characteristics approach in selection, both of which we discussed in Chapter 7. Similarly in describing job analysis generally in Chapter 1 we suggested that contrasting efficient with inefficient workers, and satisfied with dissatisfied ones, frequently proved a fruitful source of information and ideas. Seymour (1954), discussing the actual analysis of skills, says: 'Here again, the sensory component of the skill can be better recognized by comparing the efforts of an experienced worker with those of a moderately experienced, and with those of an inexperienced worker.'

It is useful to introduce here Seymour's concept of 'perceptual stringency' (1966). The demands of a skilled task on an operator's sensory perception may be slight, or alternatively a task might make severe and stringent demands on the operator's visual, kinaesthetic, or tactile sense. Training for such a 'perceptually stringent' task would need to concentrate on this difficult perceptual element, possibly introducing special exercises. This point returns us to the reductionism of skills analysis, its emphasis on the parts method, since Seymour on the basis of his research states: 'On the capstan lathe it was found that part methods offered no advantage over whole methods where the task was principally one of movement, but that where the task was

TABLE 13.2 *Part of a skills analysis for an operation of drilling and cutting tubes*

Item	Left Hand	Right Hand	Vision	Other Senses Comment
1 sites tube	takes tube from hopper	—	Examines tube for obvious faults	
	pushes tube into jig to first stop	grasps drill		
2 drills tube	holds tube steady	engages drill		Right hand feels drill bite into metal
		increases pressure		

perceptually stringent—which is normally the case—parts methods were superior.'

In conclusion we will refer to two other advantages in the parts or progressive part methods of training for skills. First, in Chapter 10 we suggested that the plateau on the learning curve may in part be a product of an approach to training whereby the trainee learns a task correctly but slowly at first, and then speeds up. A progressive part method may reduce the extent of the plateau.

In our earlier discussion of learning theory in Chapter 9 we saw how most connectionist theories emphasized the importance of reinforcement. Thyne lists reinforcement as one of the four requirements for learning. In discussing Skinner we saw that if we wish to reinforce behaviour positively, we must ensure that the correct responses occur. This we can only do by breaking down a complex skill into a number of parts which we can learn up to target times in a reasonably short period. The trainee is reinforced for learning part of a total skill in this way, by praise and his own sense of achievement. We may of course think of this situation in terms of goals, and the parts approach providing short-term and immediate goals. When the emphasis remains on the objective of acquiring the total skill, as in the whole method approach, the goals are remoter—or the reinforcement more delayed and less frequently given.

T. F. GILBERT'S MATHETICS

Gilbert has attempted to develop out of reinforcement theory, and specifically from the generalizations of Skinnerian empiricism, a theory of teaching. He has termed it mathetics (from the Greek μανθανειν, meaning 'to learn'), and its basic statement is given in two articles (Gilbert, 1962a and 1962b), now jointly reprinted under one cover (1969).

In the first of these two articles Gilbert says: 'Mathetics may be defined as the systematic application of reinforcement theory to the analysis and reconstruction of those complex behavior repertories usually known as "subject-matter mastery", "knowledge", and "skill".' Later in the same article he says: 'Mathetics is a specialized animal training system adapted to the human animal.' A basic derivation from work in this area, and one which Gilbert makes much of, is the principle of conditioned reinforcement. A stimulus or response, originally neutral, may itself become reinforcing while associated with some other reinforcement. Reaching the end of the maze is reinforcing for the rat if this is associated with then being given food. Similarly, choosing a correct path earlier now becomes reinforcing through association with the new reward of finishing the maze.

Mathetics then is an approach to training or teaching. The set of generalizations that are its basis derives from Skinner; we cannot say it is theoretically based in Skinner because Skinner has no theory. The sorts of predictions that emerge from mathetics in the areas discussed in Chapter 10, such as knowledge of results and transfer of training, are essentially Skinnerian.

Gilbert's definition of repertory provides a useful introduction to mathetics thinking (1962a):

> Repertory. The collective behaviors existing at strength in an animal at any given time. The initial repertory refers to the available behavior prior to instruction, the mastery (or terminal) repertory to the behaviors constituting skill in the subject-matter.

Mathetics is concerned with terminal behaviour ('the mastery or terminal repertory'). Its starting point is a finishing point. Teaching and training need to start with a prescription of what behaviour the student must end with, as does Skinnerian shaping.

Using the symbols of behaviourism mathetics analyses learning in terms of the appropriate stimuli and responses that have to be connected by reinforcement. Gilbert sees three main categories into which all behaviour may be categorized, and these are chains, multiples (multiple discriminations), and generalizations. They may be represented as follows (Gilbert, 1962a):

$$Chain \quad S \to R \cdot S \to R \cdot S \to R \cdot S — \cdots \cdots \to R$$

$$Multiple \quad \begin{matrix} S \to R \\ S \to R \\ S \to R \end{matrix}$$

$$Generalization \quad \left. \begin{matrix} S — \\ S — \\ S — \end{matrix} \right| R$$

We will give an example of a chain, and use the chain to illustrate the principle of conditioned reinforcement we have referred to. Our example is that of a drilling operation. We will assume that, since the operator is paid by the amount he produces, the final response in the chain, that of producing a completed component in the hopper, is experienced by the operator as rewarded—in his pay packet. The chain is as follows:

S → R	·	S → R	·	S → R	·	S → R
sees grasps		sees engages		feels releases		sees places
left drill		washer drill		drill drill		washer washer
hand handle		in		penetrate		adequately in
place with		jig		washer		drilled hopper
washer right						
hand						

Picking up the pay packet on the Friday may be one real reinforcement, though there are others. Handing a hopperful of finished components to the shop-clerk and receiving a docket, though originally a neutral response which is eventually rewarded, becomes itself through conditioning a reinforcement. It reinforces, say, the response of placing a drilled component in the hopper. Through the reinforcement of this last response the stimulus which occasioned it, seeing the satisfactorily drilled component, becomes itself reinforcing; it reinforces the response of releasing the drill. In other words each stimulus for a further response provides also reinforcement for the previous response, right back through any learning process.

The best way of training in any situation will depend on the nature of the s–r structures involved, chain, multiple or generalization. 'A simple chain of behavior', he states (Gilbert, 1962a), 'is best established by retrogression through the basic exercise model. . . .' Embodied in this statement, which we will return to, is a Skinnerian emphasis on contiguity and immediate reinforcement.

The multiple or multiple discrimination is a learning to discriminate the relevant stimulus, to distinguish a cue from among many stimuli, and so to associate that stimulus and no other with this response. The child learns to call one object on the table a 'fork' and another similar object a 'spoon', eventually learning to discriminate between a teaspoon and a dessertspoon. Multiples are temporally prior to chains, since we cannot acquire a chain unless we can first distinguish the appropriate stimulus. However, much of the discrimination involved in a new task will already have been acquired by the trainee in his everyday experience. In an analysis for training we are only concerned with those multiples unfamiliar to the trainee. But, as we have previously suggested, perceptual discrimination does frequently constitute a large part of what has to be learnt in the acquisition of many skills.

Since training is determined by what types of s–r structures have to be learnt, we need to establish in the prescription (Gilbert's equivalent of a job analysis) what chains, multiples, and generalizations are involved in the job. The sample exercises from Gilbert, given in Figure 13.1, help principally with the learning of multiple discrimination. Training for discrimination learning should emphasize the distinctive features of the cue or relevant stimulus by means of a prompt. The prompt could, for example, be a form of visual aid, such as greatly enlarged examples of faults an inspector must learn to perceive.

In generalization we are concerned with what other writers have referred to as concept formation. The child who has learnt to discriminate between knife, fork, teaspoon, and dessertspoon, must also learn they are all cutlery, especially if he is to cope when his mother asks him to 'put the cutlery on the table ready for breakfast'. He needs to have generalized and know what the term embraces. Many intelligence tests are principally concerned with measuring the capacity for generalization. Such generalization, concerned as it is with concept and symbol, is more part of what we have termed knowledge, than of the non-symbolic processes of skill. Learning generalizations seems a gradual process, and, as the behaviour of Kohler's apes might suggest, requires a period of familiarization with the situations involved. Thyne's requirement of cue applies particularly here, since for generalization to occur training has to provide a variety of situations having in common the relevant concept and symbol.

The Process of Mathetics

Gilbert outlines four stages in the process of mathetics, those of prescription, the development of a domain theory, characterization, and exercise design.

Prescription. A prescription is a specific kind of job description. It is concerned with the mastery or terminal repertory which we have already referred to as 'the behaviors constituting skill in the subject-matter'. It provides a description of this behaviour, using the s–r notations. A prescription states what a trainee actually has to learn to do. As Gilbert points out, it approximates to what is normally meant by 'practice', as opposed to theory. With mathetics we attempt to describe and analyse this mastery behaviour in the three main categories we have outlined, chains, multiples, and generalizations.

Development of a Domain Theory. In order that he can generalize what he has learnt to other situations the individual needs what is usually called understanding and what Gilbert refers to as domain theory. This development of another sort of prescription, concerned with understanding, is the second stage of the mathetics process. What Gilbert says of theory is relevant here (1962a): 'Theory can be thought of as a repertory of selective looking behavior, as a set of words that we use to stimulate ourselves to look at the key and relevant features of an otherwise confusing jumble of detail.' We need a theory of the job, skill, terminal repertory, that have to be learnt, explaining them and indicating the purposes of the various activities.

An example from Gilbert illustrates the point. The prescription of the terminal repertory for a proofreader's job would consist in part of the symbols he must use to indicate errors and the many possible corrections. But in training a proofreader it is necessary to teach him what the job is all about; it is necessary to teach him its domain theory. Here it is simply that there are three sorts of behaviour in a proofreader's job—he indicates an error in the text with a symbol, he indicates the correction with a symbol at the margin, he separates one symbol from another. Only with such an explanation can the trainee generalize and transfer what he learns to other situations.

Characterization. The third stage is a more detailed account of the prescription. Here certain kinds of information are sought, such as what generalizations need to be taught, what interference and confusion is likely to be caused by the trainee's present state of knowledge, etc. On the basis of this more detailed characterization a plan for the training lesson can be developed.

Exercise Design. From the lesson plan the training or teaching exercise is designed. This is the fourth step. The exercise consists essentially of demonstrating the correct response, prompting its occurrence in the individual, and enabling him to make the correct response so that it may be reinforced.

1(a) Some electrical resistors have COLOR BANDS that tell how much they will resist electric current. On small resistors you can see colors better than numbers. Each color stands for a number.

THE
FIRST THREE COLOR BANDS
ARE READ
AS THE NUMBER OF OHMS
RESISTANCE

THE
FOURTH COLOR BAND IS READ
AS THE
PERCENT OF ERROR IN
THE RATING

1(b) Each of the FIRST THREE COLOR BANDS can have one of 10 colors. Read through this list twice. Learn the NUMBER for which each COLOR stands.

a FIVE dollar bill is GREEN
ONE BROWN penny
a WHITE cat has NINE lives
SEVEN PURPLE seas
a BLUE tail fly has SIX legs

ZERO : BLACK nothingness.
a RED heart has TWO parts
THREE ORANGEs
a FOUR legged YELLOW dog
an EIGHTy year old man has GRAY hair

2. List the number for which each COLOR stands:

RED _____   WHITE _____   PURPLE _____   BROWN _____   BLACK _____
(heart)   (cat)   (seas)   (penny)   (nothingness)

GREEN _____   GRAY _____   BLUE _____   ORANGE _____   YELLOW _____
(bill)   (hair)   (tail fly)   (oranges)   (dog)

3. List the NUMBER for which each color stands:

BLACK _____   BROWN _____   YELLOW _____   GRAY _____   GREEN _____

WHITE _____   PURPLE _____   RED _____   ORANGE _____   BLUE _____

Fig. 13.1 Sample exercises. From lesson on colour codes of electrical resistors (Gilbert, 1962a, by permission of TOR Education, Inc. Copyright 1961 by TOR Laboratories, Inc.)

In considering the reinforcement of human learning it seems only partly useful to regard as reinforcing the weekly wage packet or the meals it pays for, since they are remote from the task. Gilbert introduces the concept of mastery. A trainee must know the terminal repertory required of him, and be able to recognize that he has performed a task correctly when he has done so. If he is sufficiently motivated to learn and master this behaviour, then his actually doing so is reinforcing.

Figure 13.1 provides an example from Gilbert (1962a) of an exercise.

Retrogression through the Basic Exercise Model

Particularly stimulating is Gilbert's idea (1962a) that 'A simple chain of behavior is best established by retrogression through the basic exercise model'. In other words the best way of learning a behaviour chain consists in learning the last bit first, then learning the last bit but one, then the last bit before that, etc.

The best approach to teaching a child to tie his shoe-lace is not to begin at the beginning and go through to the end, since inevitably this way most of his early attempts will be experienced as failures. He will probably give up when he gets to the bow since this is as much as he can manage at first. What he has done on these occasions may be correct but is not reinforced by any awareness of achievement or mastery of the task. If the task is broken down and he starts by practising the last part first, completing the bow, then he has tied a shoe-lace, and his actions are reinforced by mastery. When he is proficient on this last part of the task we add the part prior to it, and he practises them together. Every time he does them successfully he has completed the task, and is reinforced. He moves retrogressively right through from the last to the first element of the learning task. Again the principle of conditioned reinforcement is embodied in this approach. The exercise in Table 13.3, from Gilbert (1962a), illustrates this retrogressive movement.

Conclusion

This brief account cannot do justice to the originality of the mathetics approach, as outlined in Gilbert's two main articles (1962a, 1962b). He attempts to apply principles of reinforcement in the teaching and training fields. His categorization of behaviour into three main types, chains, multiples, and generalizations, is probably not sufficiently comprehensive to embrace such forms of learning as problem-solving. Gagné, for example, outlines eight types of learning (1965). But Gilbert's threefold classification may well be adequate for analysing the sort of learning we are interested in here, the acquisition of skill.

TABLE 13.3 *Exercises in long division (simplified) designed on the mathetical exercise model* (Gilbert, 1962a)

1 Divide 45 by 11

    Here is what you do : (a) Since 4 × 11 is 44,   4

                                  the 44 is placed   11)45

                                  under the dividend————————►44

    Now complete the long division :

                                (b) Subtract 44 from 45

                                to get the remainder—

---

2 Divide 28 by 12

    Here is what you do : (a) 12 goes into 28 2 whole times

                                (b) Multiply the divisor   2

                                    by the quotient (12 × 2) 12)28

                                    and put the product

                                    under the dividend

                                (c) Subtract to get the remainder

---

3 Divide 33 by 15

                                (a) 15 goes into 33 2 whole times

                                (b) Put the 2 in place above the line

                                (c) Multiply the divisor

                                    by the quotient and   15)33

                                    put the product in

                                    its place

                                (d) Complete the division

REFERENCES

Chomsky, N. (1959), review of Skinner's *Verbal Behaviour* (1957) in *Language*, 35, No. 1, 26–58.

Earle, F. M. (1931), *Methods of Choosing a Career*, Harrap.

Gagné, R. M. (1965), *The Conditions of Learning*, Holt, Rinehart & Winston.

Gilbert, T. F. (1962a), 'Mathetics: the technology of education', *J. Mathetics*, vol. 1, no. 1, pp. 7–73, Mathetics Foundation, University of Alabama.

Gilbert, T. F. (1962b), 'Mathetics: the design of teaching exercises', *J. Mathetics*, vol. 1, no. 2, pp. 7–56, Mathetics Foundation, University of Alabama.
(These two issues of the *Journal of Mathetics* were the only ones ever to appear. Both articles have been reprinted in the following.)

Gilbert, T. F. (1969), 'Mathetics: an explicit theory for the design of teaching programmes', *Recall: Review of Educational Cybernetics and Applied Linguistics, Supplement 1*, Longmac.

Guthrie, E. R. (1952), *The Psychology of Learning*, Harper.

King, S. D. M. (1960), *Vocational Training in view of Technological Change*, O.E.E.C., Paris.

Seymour, W. D. (1954), *Industrial Training for Manual Operations*, Pitman.

Seymour, W. D. (1966), *Industrial Skills*, Pitman.

Thyne, J. M. (1966), *The Psychology of Learning and Techniques of Teaching*, University of London Press.

Vernon, P. E. (1961), *The Structure of Human Abilities*, Methuen.

Work Problems

Overview

In the final chapter we attempt to place in perspective guidance, selection, and training, mainly by considering them in relation to the organization. We are primarily concerned with selection and training, since much of guidance occurs outside the organization.

We start with a case study where a firm is faced by a number of problems. The problems might be solved by selection and training, or by other approaches, or by a combination of selection, training, and the other approaches. After the case study we state that selection and training have usually analysed a situation in terms of individuals. We suggest four further ways in which we can analyse a problem: in terms of the ergonomist's man-machine system, in terms of informal social relationships, as a problem of employee motivation, or as a problem of appropriate organizational structures.

Armed with various ways of analysing a manpower problem the practitioner must make a decision and propose a solution. Under the heading, 'An integration of approaches', we make three recommendations. First, the practitioner must adopt a broader basis for selection and training. In previous chapters we have attempted to broaden the framework of selection and training by relating them to the organizations in which they occur. Secondly, the practitioner must be aware of alternative approaches, other than guidance, selection, and training, and if need be adopt more than one approach in any attempt to solve a manpower problem. Thirdly, the practitioner must know the repercussions of selection and training, and how they affect and interact with the total organization. We then examine these repercussions in some detail.

The practitioner needs a framework within which to consider these various approaches and their interaction. The final sections suggest such a frame of reference. We first introduce the idea of a socio-technical system. We then relate the organization as a socio-technical system to its environment through the concept of open systems. We briefly consider how we can view the goals of an organization in terms of the system. Finally we present a simple framework within which to consider alternative approaches to the manpower problems of work.

INTRODUCTION

In the following case study we outline a situation where the management of a factory is experiencing certain difficulties. The case study illustrates a typical situation where different 'solutions' are possible; selection and training are merely two of them. What solutions we see depends on how we see the problem. In the situation of the case study, any one approach would probably only provide a partial solution. A combination of solutions seems necessary.

Alloys Ltd, A Case Study

1. Manufacture at Alloys Limited was now mainly of copper strip for sale to other manufacturers, though the company produced also a limited amount of copper wire. Gradual, unspectacular growth had given way over recent years to a period of extensive expansion, which caused a sudden increase in the size of the labour force. Sections of the factory had been rebuilt, and most production was now on semi-automated process control lines, with the labour force consisting largely of maintenance men and production operators.

2. The firm was situated in a good employment area where jobs were plentiful. And at Alloys labour turnover, especially among production workers and other non-skilled grades, was high—too high, according to Mr Price, the Production Manager.

'It's interfering with production,' he told Mr Baker, the Personnel Manager, one morning. 'The order book's full. Plant is working beautifully—no real technical hitches. But operators keep leaving. They don't even have to do much when they're here—we just have to have enough of them to cover the operations that can't be fully automated. Even keeping up all this overtime may not be enough soon. We may have to close down some of the plant. If it weren't for some of the old faithfuls who've been with the firm years, we would soon be in a mess.'

'Look, I'll get Horan to get on to the Employment Exchange,

to see if they've got any more men we can look at for operators,' said Mr Baker.

'If they're warm, we'll take them.'

3. Back in his office Mr Baker called in Horan, the new personnel assistant. 'I want you to get on the phone to the Employment Exchange about those vacancies. Put some pressure on them to send us some more men.'

'What sort of people do we want?' asked Horan.

'I tell you what; rather than my telling you, go and have a word with one of the foremen. It'll be an opportunity to get to know some of them. See Brown; he's a foreman of the old school. Been with the company a long time—some people say too long.'

4. Shortly after, Horan found Mr Brown in a production department.

'Well, first, these operators don't need much skill,' Brown said in reply to Horan's questioning. 'They just have to feed the stuff in occasionally. There are a number of simple operations they have to carry out from time to time. They keep an eye on the dials—and get the foreman if there's any trouble. And play cards. Safety is very important, of course.'

'What sort of men do you think are best for the job?'

'Can't really say. Many of these operators started life as farm workers.'

5. 'Many of them are—there aren't many young people in this department, are there?'

'That's just it,' said Brown. 'None of these young fellows seem to stay nowadays. Take this department; apart from a couple of fellows, I'd say that most of them have been with the firm about ten or fifteen years. The young fellows just don't want to know. But we're not fussy. We'll take almost anyone.'

6. 'You must have been here a long time yourself, Mr Brown.'

'Yes, I have, nearly twenty years. Came as a skilled man, a fitter. I was a chargehand in the Toolroom for some time, then I was made a foreman on the production side.'

'How did you find the job—did you have any training for it?'

'Well, I'd served my time, of course. And the rest I've just picked up. The departmental manager knows all the really technical side; he's been to university.'

7. 'What are the tough things about your job nowadays?' asked Horan.

'Well, what I dislike most is all the arguments.'

'Who with—the men?'

'Oh, no! I get on with the men all right—though they sometimes kick up when I try to keep them busy. There's a lot of spare time for operators on this job, you know, and I don't like them standing round doing nothing. So I find odd jobs for them to do. They don't seem to like it, but I tell them that's what they're paid for. No, most of the foremen don't have much trouble with the men.'

'What are all these arguments then that you mentioned?' asked Horan.

'It's with the other departments, usually Shaping and Alloying —that's where the copper goes after it leaves us in Refining. There are arguments with the Chemical Laboratory as well. They're always about who's responsible for what—it's usually about who's to blame when something goes wrong. Too many bosses around here nowadays.'

8. 'Anyway, thanks for the information. I'm going to phone the Employment Exchange about these vacancies. Do the men have any other duties, like keeping the department clean?'

'Oh, no,' said Brown. 'I'd better explain. What happens is that when they come here—the unskilled men, that is—they join what's called the General Work Pool. All the new, unskilled men start in this, and they work anywhere in the place, labouring, doing heavy lifting; it's them who do the cleaning. Then when a vacancy comes up in one of the departments the fellow that has been longest in the Pool can have it. It's more money. In the Pool you're on the lowest rate; when you're transferred to a department you go on a higher rate.'

'Does it take them long to train for production once they are in a department?'

'Not really. They are just put on the job with the men, and pick it up. Some time during their first day the safety officer and the foreman have a talk to them about safety. Safety is very important here, you know, with molten copper around.'

'Thanks very much, Mr Brown. I think I've got some idea now what we're looking for.'

9. Meanwhile Mr Baker had been looking at his papers for a meeting that morning with some of the shop stewards. There were two main items on the agenda: classification of pipe-work; apprenticeships for welders.

The first was another demarcation dispute; they seemed to be having more of them nowadays, he thought. The Plumbers Union was claiming for the plumbers certain types of pipe-work which the A.E.F. maintained were fitters' work. Most of the fitters were A.E.F. members.

10. The A.E.F. was involved also in the second item. There was no welding apprenticeship scheme for school-leavers in the firm. The present welders had either been recruited as trained men, or they were ex-mates and production operators who had completed the intensive three-month training course in welding which the firm now ran in its own training school. In fact starting this welding course had occasioned a further expansion of the activities of the training school. The personnel department had, with agreement of the stewards, selected six intelligent production operators and started them in the training school on a six-month course in fitting. The intention was to turn them into maintenance fitters. The firm's present fitters had either been recruited locally or came through the company's traditional apprenticeship scheme. But there was still a shortage of them in the firm.

11. The A.E.F. now wanted the firm to set up a proper apprenticeship scheme for welding. Regardless of the faults or merits of such a proposal, Mr Baker was frightened it would lead to conflict between the stewards. The representatives of the unskilled men might argue that such a move could eventually close one of the few channels of promotion open to the mates and production operators they represented.

In short, management at Alloys Limited is faced with a number of problems, particularly of high labour turnover, inter-union hostility, a shortage of skilled men in certain categories, and hostility between production departments. We might attempt to solve some of these problems by means of selection and training, particularly of operators and foremen.

Guidance, Selection, and Training

When we attempt to solve a work problem by guidance, selection, or training, we usually start with a job analysis—in the case of guidance with some form of categorization of jobs. This illustrates a point we made earlier, that these three approaches to work problems have tended to adopt the individual as the relevant unit of analysis (see Schein, 1965). If turnover among production operators at Alloys is too high we attempt to reduce it by selecting other, more suitable individuals, or by training them better.

Selection, for example, has been regarded as a process of acquiring suitable people for the employment positions in an organization, and its basic units are the individual worker and the individual job. Training supplements and completes this process of suitably filling occupational roles, begun by selection. Training provides the conditions in which learning of the employment role can occur, a process of socialization into an organizational position. In the past, training, like selection, has been based on the individual job and the individual learner. We have suggested that with a growing awareness of the extent to which social and structural factors impinge on the learner, formal and informal structures, and their interrelationships, need to become part of the framework for analysing training.

Guidance fits less easily into this final discussion. We can think here of guidance at two levels, that of the micro-social system of the organization, and that of the larger social system of society. In the organization, guidance is akin to selection. In career planning for a manager, an executive or management development officer may be concerned with what suits the particular individual as well as with what the organization needs. This blend of guidance and selection is sometimes known as placement. Similarly guidance at the level of the wider society is never given without regard to the realities of the external situation. A careers officer would hesitate to advise a school-leaver to enter a trade which is declining, even though the boy's abilities and interests ideally suit him for it. At both levels guidance, functioning within a social system, adopts the individual as its appropriate unit of analysis. Like selection and training, it is also at both levels one possible solution to work problems such as poor employee relations, poor output, job dissatisfaction, and high turnover among employees.

ALTERNATIVE UNITS OF ANALYSIS AND OTHER APPROACHES

At Alloys a number of other ways of solving the various problems are possible. The overall organizational structure of the production departments might be altered. The nature of the foreman's role could be clarified. The system of a general work pool might be abolished, and some attempt made both to group together the new, younger workers and to provide opportunities for advancement to the more intelligent operators. None of these possible solutions would be based on an analysis of the situation in terms of the individual worker.

These alternative approaches view the problems in terms of other concepts. We might, for example, see as the relevant concept the worker, his physical environment, and their interrelationship. Thinking in terms of this man-machine relationship, we would primarily be concerned with solving the problems of work by redesigning the job and its environment to accord maximally with the physical and psychological capacities and limitations of employees. This is the approach of ergonomics.

We are now suggesting three other types of analysis of the work situation (see Schein, 1965). The first, of particular interest to the social psychologist, is that of the informal relationships which exist in an organization. The human relations school, referred to in Chapter 1, perceived the work situation primarily in these terms. Within the formal structure of an organization informal social relationships emerge which generate their own values, norms and attitudes, leadership and status patterns, and channels of communication. Here, the basic unit of analysis is naturally the informal social group. We have previously suggested (see p. 14) the types of solutions that emerge from such an analysis of problems at work.

Alternatively we may perceive the problem in terms of the motivation of employees. We are concerned here with an array of incentives, such as size of wage or salary, method of payment, prestige and status, opportunities for promotion, praise, and approval, and the disincentives and punishments the organization may have in its power to implement. This may usefully be conceived in terms of a 'psychological contract', which Schein (1965) speaks of as follows: 'The notion of a psychological contract implies that the individual has a variety of expectations of the organization and that the organization has a variety of expectations of him.' So for such an approach the psychological contract provides a unit of analysis. Studying work problems in such terms will reveal that the nature of the contract may vary from organization to organization, and in fact depends on what view or theory about people the organization has. In Chapter 2 we outlined three such informal views, those of economic, social, and self-actualizing man. A solution based on such an analysis would naturally relate to incentives that motivate employees. Finally we might adopt a view of a work situation that is characteristic of the industrial sociologist. Our relevant concept for analysing the situation would be the organization, viewed as a total system, a structure that exists independently of the individuals that fill its positions. Our solutions here would be of the nature of clarifying organizational goals, adapting structures to achieve those goals, possibly specifying more clearly individual work roles, etc.

AN INTEGRATION OF APPROACHES

Solving Work Problems

In previous chapters we have argued that in implementing a guidance, selection, or training procedure we are adopting, implicitly or explicitly, a theory of personality or of learning. Such a theory makes a number of assumptions and has certain limitations, and we should arrive at practical decisions only with full knowledge of these assumptions and limitations, and whether they apply in the particular circumstance. We are in a similar position when we consider whether or not to examine a problem in terms of guidance, selection, or training. If we decide to do so, we are by and large assuming that in the circumstances the individual is the relevant or at least a useful unit for analysis.

However, the practitioner has to come to a decision. We are suggesting that the dangers inherent in having to adopt one unit or set of concepts for analysing a work problem, and to reject others, may be greatly reduced in three ways.

First, we need to broaden the approaches somewhat, and we have already argued this, particularly with regard to selection and training. We might, for example, be only partly right in attributing the low output in department X to an unsatisfactory level of operators which could be raised by better selection. Unsatisfactory organization of work and poor morale might also be relevant. To recruit and select a higher level of operator might by itself only make a slight improvement, or none at all if the new, better operators are affected by the low morale. In previous chapters we have attempted to relate selection and training to the broader social system of the organization within which they occur.

We might usefully consider broadening the approaches of guidance, selection, and training, in terms of a widening of their base, job analysis. The sort of analysis of an individual's employment role which we examined in Chapter 1 may be too limited by its emphasis on the tasks, duties, and responsibilities of the job. Lake's study (1963) of management selection suggests that a superior evaluates a subordinate's work in terms of his own expectations. The superior judges performance against standards he has himself set. Lake says the senior manager decides whether to retain or dismiss a subordinate, to increase salary, to promote, on the basis of this criterion. The expectations and standards the superior has for a job occupant need to be incorporated into a job analysis.

There are many other factors that impinge powerfully on the individual in his employment position within the organization. Among them are the nature of the technology, the layout of work, the structure of the formal organization, the informal social and work group relationships that exist, the supervisor-subordinate relationship, and the incentives and motivational forces. When such factors impinge on an individual, we must take account of them. Schemes of job analysis might be broadened to incorporate categories which enable us to examine the relevance of these other factors to the job occupant.

There is a second antidote to the dangers of adopting one particular unit to analyse a work problem. This consists in knowing the alternative approaches and considering them all before deciding on which one to implement. We might decide not to adopt just one approach but several. Personnel officers sometimes receive the following sort of request from managers: 'The girls in the key-punch department are always leaving. The turnover is much too high. Do you think in future we could choose more carefully the sort of girl we take on?' The problem has been seen only as a problem of individuals, to be solved by selection, and no alternatives have been considered. We must consider some of the alternative approaches already indicated, before deciding to solve the problems through guidance, selection, or training.

Thirdly, to counter the limitations inherent in implementing a certain type of solution we need to be aware of its possible repercussions throughout the organization. At Alloys the introduction of training in welding for unskilled workers seemed to be having repercussions in industrial relations. Further automation had affected the foreman's job, and possibly necessitated some retraining of foremen. We will now examine these interrelationships in a little more detail, first discussing the relationships between selection and training. We will next discuss the effects of selection, then training, in other areas.

The Repercussions of Selection and Training in the Organization
Selection and training procedures affect each other in a number of ways. A selection scheme may often create certain expectations in the minds of the selected candidates which the training fails to fulfil. 'This is a challenging and stimulating management trainee position', the selection procedure told the candidate, only for him to find it followed by a dreary six months' tour of the administrative departments.

To learn, the trainee has to be motivated. The selection procedure may have been impersonal and slightly demeaning, its basic message to candidates being that 'the firm really counts, not you'. The selected candidates read the message, and enter the organization a little indifferent and with deadened enthusiasm. If they now enter training they do not do so in a highly motivated state.

Selection requires a specification, so selection for training and not for a specific job makes the task more difficult. One can, of course, attempt to determine the individual requirements for success in training as one would have done for successful performance of a job. The criteria of success are part of a specification. In selecting for training does one adopt the criteria of success in training, or subsequent success on the job, since frequently these two will not correlate completely?

We have suggested that a demeaning selection procedure may adversely affect training. But its effects will not end there. Such a selection scheme may affect morale, as where a company recruits for and fills an attractive senior position from outside the firm. If the organization's selection scheme tells the individual the firm cares little for him, he will reciprocate by caring little for the firm, and become an indifferent and uninvolved employee. This one would expect from Schein's concept of the 'psychological contract' since the expectations the organization and the individual have of each other will interact.

Selection procedures relate to employee motivation in a number of other ways. We have already suggested that implicit in the firm's psychological contract is the informal theory of personality it adopts. This will affect its approach to selection. For example, an organization that functions in terms of social man will in selecting a supervisor search for those factors that a human relations approach stresses as important. Among the expectations that constitute the psychological contract are a number that relate to ethical considerations. These will affect selection procedures through their justification or failure to justify such practices as wife-interviewing and depth-probing personality techniques.

There is another danger, arising from traditional selection procedures, which many commentators have pointed out. Selection usually starts with a specification of the job, and attempts to select people who match up to that specification—in the idiom, it gets round pegs for round holes. The danger is that in only selecting individuals who fit into the present organization, we will be excluding the rebels and innovators who might challenge, change, and develop the organization.

Informal social and group factors may impinge heavily on a position within an organization. This seems relevant to selection because such informal relationships and responsibilities, and the atmosphere they produce, determine in part what the job 'really' is. But it remains difficult to incorporate such factors into a formal account of the job.

Selection and the informal structure of an organization relate also in another way. The nature of the informal social groupings is affected by the personalities of their members, and this is determined by selection policies and procedures.

The character of the formal organization structure and of selection also affect each other in a number of ways. An organization may be changing and developing over a period, attempting to adapt to the altering demands of the environment; for example, a commercial concern may be faced with changing patterns of consumer demand. Technological developments may also necessitate the firm's having to change. When an organization is changing and dynamic, the employment roles within it change also and are usually loosely defined. Selection is made particularly difficult by the absence of a clear specification of a job, and by its changing nature. How can we select for a job which entails these duties today, but tomorrow may be different? The answer would seem to relate to our earlier discussion of management development. We suggested that at a senior level one not only trained the manager to enable him to deal with specific tasks, but educated him to cope with change. In similar circumstances the objective of selection might be the same.

If in a changing organization establishing and developing an appropriate selection procedure is difficult, then its validation proves even more so. In the follow-up one finds that men have been selected, and predictions made, on specifications and criteria that, because of changing situations, are no longer relevant.

In a highly bureaucratic organization, change is negligible, and correct behaviour and the appropriate courses of action are clearly stipulated in formal rules and regulations. But in most bureaucratic organizations personality intrudes, and behaviour and action are invariably affected by the nature of the individual personalities that fill the organizational roles. Selection which determines what sort of 'personalities' enter the organization in this way has repercussions on the formal, bureaucratic structure. This applies particularly to selection for supervisory and management positions, since here especially the personality of the occupant can affect the organizational structure.

We will now examine further repercussions of training procedures and the effects of other factors on training. To learn, a trainee has to be motivated. If the nature of the technology is such that the tasks are dull and unsatisfying, then one intrinsic incentive to learn the job is eliminated. Conversely good job design affects training not necessarily by making the tasks interesting, but more probably by making them easier and within the learning capacity of more people.

A bad training scheme which, like impersonal selection, shows little interest in the individual and fails to give him the help he needs, lowers morale in the organization. A good, well-considered training procedure, where an organization invests in the individual trainee, strengthens the psychological contract.

Informal relationships within the organization interrelate in a number of ways. Induction training may affect the socialization of the new employee and his integration within the informal groupings in the organization. Similarly the training of individuals and particularly of supervisors will affect the functioning of social groups. It is significant that the human relations school has always emphasized the importance of training supervisors in inter-personal skills.

Training is not given in a vacuum but in the social system of the organization. Even if the individual is trained for the job at the local technical college or at a management centre, he will return to that organization. We may teach supervisors and managers to act in certain ways on a course at the technical college, and they will probably act that way while at the college. But back at the firm their behaviour is determined more by the social climate of the firm or their department, and by their formal and informal relationships with superiors and colleagues. This is true at many levels. In the training department an operator is trained to produce a certain output, but he moves to the shop floor and is affected by the expectations and influences that operate within that social system. In certain situations these may act as a pressure on him to restrict his output.

Supervisory and management training often operates to make men dissatisfied with the *status quo* in their organization. This can cause them to leave. Alternatively they may stay and attempt to change the organization. In this way training at a senior level should operate as a cogent factor in changing formal and informal structures in an organization. On the other hand the influence may operate in the reverse direction. Behaviour is conditioned by environment. If the formal organizational structure or formal relationships as embodied in the rules and regulations change, or if the nature of the informal social system alters, this will impinge on employees in the organization, and modify their behaviour.

Our final point was discussed originally in the chapter on supervisory and management training. Where the organization is dynamic and changing, to see training in terms of specific goals and objectives, or terminal behaviour, would be too narrow and limited an approach. Training an individual for a task that will be obsolete tomorrow is useful only for today. In situations of change it becomes an essential part of training to educate and prepare managers to cope with change.

A FRAMEWORK FOR CONSIDERING ALTERNATIVE APPROACHES

In considering work problems there are, then, dangers in adopting units of analysis that are too limiting and which provide only partial solutions. Faced with a number of approaches to a work problem, all having different repercussions, we need a framework or model within which to consider the alternative approaches, and criteria against which to evaluate them.

What are the criteria for decisions on placement and training in the organization? Here we are suggesting three. The first criterion is the effectiveness of the individual employee; the second is the satisfaction of the individual employee; the third is the effectiveness of the organization. We will subsequently suggest that within a systems approach, which we will now outline, the first criterion above can be ignored.

The Socio-Technical System

A systems analysis provides a useful framework within which to consider, against the above or other criteria, alternative approaches to work problems. How, then, might we usefully think of the organization in terms of a system? Rice (1958) gives the following account:

> The concept of a socio-technical system arose from the consideration that any productive system requires both a technological organization—equipment and process layout—and a work organization relating to each other those who carry out the necessary tasks. The technological demands place limits on the type of work organization possible, but a work organization has social and psychological properties of its own that are independent of technology.

The application of systems thinking to productive organizations gives rise to the concept of the socio-technical system which stresses the interrelatedness of technology and work organization. The nature of the technology in part determines the nature of the social system of the related workplace, as the studies of Woodward (1958, 1965) have shown.

For our purposes it seems useful to consider productive organizations in broad terms, to include not only industrial manufacturers but also commercial concerns such as retail firms, and schools, even churches, leisure societies, etc. Similarly we might think in terms of a mutual interaction between 'technology', such as a press shop or classroom, and the social, psychological properties that characterize the personnel of the organization, be it engineering firm or school.

In this way we can see the interaction between the organization's work and technology, and its personnel, as a two-way process of influence. A production technology, such as highly automated process control, may partially determine the nature of the work organization, and in this way influence the sort of personnel the company employs, the form of the psychological contract, of informal groupings, etc. But influence may go in the reverse direction, where, for example, the personality of a few individuals may affect the formal structure of the organization, or may change the technology through research and development. Influence in this direction is likely to be greater where the technology is less all-encompassing. Thus the unsatisfactory layout, inadequate equipment and poor lighting of an ill-equipped and old school building places some limits on what happens in the classroom, but the personality of a headmaster and of enthusiastic staff might transform the character of that same school. And the Longwall study suggests that even in a manufacturing organization the pattern of social relationships may become firm enough to resist any pressures for change emanating from a new production technology (Trist and Bamforth, 1951).

Open Systems
The organization functions as a socio-technical system in an environment with which it interacts. The model needs to incorporate the environment, and this is done through the idea of an open system. Katz and Kahn (1966) clearly outline the concept of open systems:

> Our theoretical model for the understanding of organizations is that of an energic input-output system in which the energic return from the output reactivates the system. Social organizations are flagrantly open systems in that the input of energies and the conversion of output into further energic input consist of transactions between the organization and its environment.

The nature of the energy input depends on the kind of organization or socio-technical system. In a factory the chief energy inputs would be the work of employees, material, money, machines, and information. In a retail firm they would be the work of employees, goods, money, and information. The energy input into a school is mainly the work of teachers and students, classroom equipment, and educational aids.

This input of energy from the environment is transformed within the socio-technical system. Products are made; goods are sold; students are taught. In other words, work is done. But some energy is, of course, lost and wasted in the process—strikes, accidents, scrap, student failure. But the energy successfully transformed moves out of the organization and back into the environment, in the form of goods sold and students qualifying. This is the output. In industrial and commercial organizations outputs are normally converted in the environment into money, which feeds back as an energy input into the organization, re-activating it.

Goals of the Organization

Most approaches to the study of organizations are faced with the problem of discovering and then defining their goals and objectives. This is often difficult. Seeing the organization as an open socio-technical system avoids this problem, since it means we can think of its goals not as the objectives of this or that group, founders, directors, employees, shareholders, but rather as outputs which enable the organization to survive. Goals are energy outputs, such as products from a factory, which move into the environment and obtain from it inputs of energy back into the organization, which serve to maintain the organization.

If we ask the founders of a firm or its directors, managers, rank-and-file employees, shareholders, etc., what the goals and purposes of the organization are, we should obtain some useful information (and some different opinions). But it would only tell us half the story; it would only be a statement of a variety of conscious intents, like a list of the manifest functions of an institution which makes no mention of its latent functions. But an analysis in terms of energy outputs which feed back through the environment to maintain the organization provides a full account of goals and purposes that are actually being pursued. Organizations, such as commercial firms, educational institutions, churches, are usually founded for specific purposes, but with time these aims alter, and become complex and confused. To identify an organization's goals at a given time one needs to analyse what actually happens in practice.

In practice there are usually a number of such goals or outputs. There will normally be one or more goals or outputs that must be achieved if the organization is to survive. With commercial concerns one such primary objective is making a profit, since if it fails to do this the organization will not survive at all.

The Framework

In Figure 14.1, adapted from Bass (1965), we represent the commercial organization as an open socio-technical system. In the figure we refer not to the input, transformation, and output of energy, as we have up to present, but adopt the terms of imports, conversion, and exports (Rice, 1963), and of waste.

The commercial organization is seen as an open socio-technical system, importing from the environment men and their labour, money, materials, services, and information. These imports are converted. Instrumental in the conversion process of a commercial organization are its production technology and work layout, its organizational structure, those employee-management relationships and informal social relationships among employees that affect work behaviour, incentives and other motivational pressures that affect performance, its training, selection, and placement. These factors are instrumental in the conversion process, which produces valuable exports that are moved out into the environment. Inevitably in the conversion process some waste occurs. In the environment the exports are converted into different kinds of imports into the organization, maintaining it.

Exports are seen as the goals of the organization. But what is experienced and perceived as relevant goals and objectives by those involved varies according to the individual. A shareholder may see the exporting of products to obtain money from the environment as the real goal. A union official may see the export of employees' wages as the organization's main purpose. A research scientist employed by a firm may view those exports of his own work satisfaction and the extension of scientific knowledge as particularly important goals.

Such a view of the organization provides us with a framework for considering alternative types of solutions to the problems of work. However, in adopting a socio-technical approach we find that one of our three original criteria against which to evaluate solutions is not always relevant, that of the effectiveness of the individual employee. Trist (1963) suggests that optimum efficiency in the total system may necessitate a less than optimum efficiency

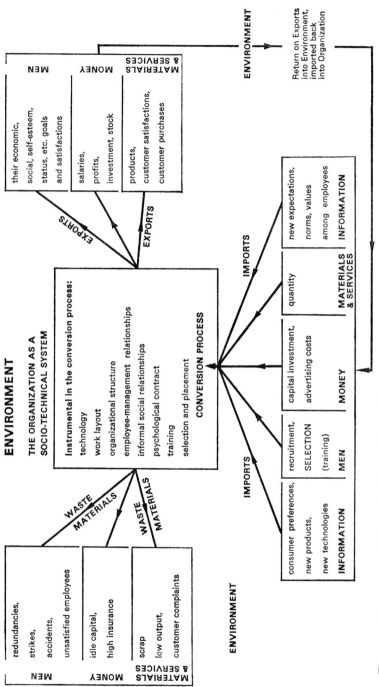

Fig. 14.1 The commercial organization and its environment as an open socio-technical system (adapted from Bass, 1965). Exports are perceived as the goals of the organization

in some parts of the system. For an organization to function at its best in a given circumstance, it is not always essential for every employee to be his most efficient. For example, production departments may need to produce below maximum when sales are falling.

If we view the organization as an open socio-technical system, the question we should first ask of a work problem changes significantly. We no longer begin with a more specific query, such as 'what sort of selection do we need?', 'how should we train our managers?', 'what kind of an organization is appropriate?' We must first consider what total mix or combination of production technology and work layout, industrial relations procedures, organizational structure, informal and group relationships, motivational system, selection, placement and training, would maximize organizational effectiveness and employee satisfaction.

REFERENCES

Bass, B. M. (1965), *Organizational Psychology*, Allyn & Bacon.

Katz, D. and Kahn, R. L. (1966), *The Social Psychology of Organisations*, Wiley.

Lake, J. R. (1963), 'A Follow-Up Study of Managerial Appointments', unpublished Ph.D. thesis, University of London.

Rice, A. K. (1958), *Productivity and Social Organisation: the Ahmedabad Experiment*, Tavistock.

Rice, A. K. (1963), *The Enterprise and its Environment*, Tavistock.

Schein, E. H. (1965), *Organizational Psychology*, Prentice-Hall. A number of specific references have been made to this book; however, many sections of this chapter have been influenced by Schein's book.

Trist, E. L. *et al.* (1963), *Organizational Choice*, Tavistock.

Trist, E. L. and Bamforth, K. W. (1951), 'Some social and psychological consequences of the longwall method of coal-getting', *Human Relations*, 4.

Woodward, J. (1958), *Management and Technology*, H.M.S.O.

Woodward, J. (1965), *Industrial Organization: Theory and Practice*, Oxford University Press.

Further reading on a systems concept of organizations is found in Katz and Kahn (1966), Rice (1963), and Trist *et al.* (1963).

Sources of Tests and Inventories

Different tests and inventories require varying levels of expertise from the user. Accordingly when someone places an order, suppliers usually consider his experience and training before deciding what tests and inventories to send him. Clinically orientated techniques, for example, often need considerable expertise to administer and evaluate, and are normally supplied only to clinical psychologists and psychiatrists. Tests and inventories for occupational purposes usually require a more modest level of expertise. Some are made available to any responsible person. Others are supplied to individuals with various levels of experience, qualification, or training, depending on how much knowledge is involved in giving, scoring, and interpreting the particular test or inventory. Suppliers listed below provide information on the availability of the various tests and inventories they stock.

Among the main suppliers of tests in the United Kingdom is the National Foundation for Educational Research, 2 Jennings Yard, Thames Avenue, Windsor, Berkshire.

The National Institute of Industrial Psychology, 14 Welbeck Street, London W.1, supplies tests developed by the Institute's own staff, and provides training courses in test administration and interpretation.

Three other sources are: George G. Harrap & Co. Ltd., 182 High Holborn, London, W.C.1.; H. K. Lewis & Co. Ltd., 136 Gower Street, London, W.C.1.; and University of London Press Ltd., St. Paul's House, Warwick Lane, London, E.C.4.

The Connolly Occupational Interests Questionnaire, referred to in Chapter 4, is supplied by the Careers Research and Advisory Centre, Bateman Street, Cambridge. The C.R.A.C. run one-day courses to teach the administration and interpretation of Connolly Questionnaires.

The following text, as indicated in Chapter 5, provides information on a wide variety of tests and inventories: O.K. Buros, ed. *The Mental Measurements Yearbook*, Rutgers University Press.

INDEX